SAMIDHA

Sadhana Amte is the wife of the renowned social worker, Baba Amte. Born in Nagpur, in the state of Maharastra in 1926, she hails from an orthodox Hindu brahmin family. She chose to marry Baba Amte, against the wishes of the members of her family and came to stay with outcasts and untouchables. She has stood by Baba in every social venture and likes to make light of her labour by calling it a romance. Though gifted with a fine sense of humour and a talent for writing, she had to be coaxed into writing these memoirs.

Shobha Pawar is a student and a teacher of English literature, and currently a lecturer at S. P. College, Pune. She has been a visiting faculty at the University of Pune and other colleges for some years. Poetry has always been her first love and area of research too.

You can e-mail her at *shobhapawar@gmail.com.*

Samidha

SADHANA AMTE

Translated from the Marathi by
Shobha Pawar

Foreword by
M S Swaminathan

Orient BlackSwan

SAMIDHA

ORIENT BLACKSWAN PRIVATE LIMITED

Registered Office
3-6-752 Himayatnagar, Hyderabad 500 029 (Telangana), INDIA
e-mail: centraloffice@orientblackswan.com

Other Offices
Bengaluru, Bhopal, Chennai, Guwahati, Hyderabad, Jaipur, Kolkata, Lucknow, Mumbai, New Delhi, Noida, Patna, Vijayawada

First published 2008
Reprinted 2015, 2017

The Marathi original of *Samidha* was first published in 2001

Since this work is autobiographical in nature,
the views expressed in this work are entirely the author's

ISBN: 978 81 250 3404 9

Typeset in Adobe Garamond 12/15 *by*
OSDATA, Hyderabad 500 029

Printed at
Rakmo Press Pvt. Ltd.,
New Delhi

Published by
Orient Blackswan Private Limited
3-6-752 Himayatnagar,
Hyderabad 500 029 (Telangana), INDIA
e-mail: info@orientblackswan.com

To the hand that split the rock for Anandwan to blossom:
Sadhana Amte

Foreword

Smt. Sadhana Amte (affectionately referred to by everyone as Sadhanatai) and her husband Muralidhar Devidas Amte (again affectionately called Baba Amte) are the greatest Indians living today. Each one of them is a legend in their own right. It has been an act of love for her countrymen that Sadhanatai wrote *Samidha*, her autobiography. It has been equally our good fortune that Smt. Shobha Pawar has produced an English version of *Samidha* in order to get Sadhanatai's message across to all the young women and men of our country. Both for Sadhanatai and Baba Amte, their life is their message. Shobha has rightly pointed out that Sadhanatai represents a rare combination of confidence and compliance, work and worship, and labour and love. Shobha is right in pointing out, "to say that Sadhanatai is the woman behind the great man, Baba Amte, is to belittle her contribution to the mammoth work Baba has done. She is the woman *beside* him, extending her hand in things great and small, in times dark and bright."

Baba Amte and Sadhanatai have also inspired their children through their personal example. Thus Vikas, his wife and children are continuing the great work at Anandwan, while Prakash and his wife Mandakini are doing remarkable service both to tribal families as well as to wildlife in the dense forest of Bhamragad in the Gadchiroli district of Maharashtra. To Sadhanatai and Baba however all members of the human family are the same. They thus embody the spirit behind the concept, "Vasudeva Kutumbakam" in its totality. Sadhanatai has provided support to all the movements for human wellbeing and environment protection initiated by Baba – whether it is in the field of giving purpose and joy in life to those affected by leprosy or the Bharat Jodo (Knit India) movement or the Narmada Andolan. In every one of the activities of Tai and Baba one can see God leading people on the right path.

This is one of the most moving and inspiring books I have ever read. Had not Shobha Pawar translated it into English, I would have lost the inspiration and guidance one gets when reading the book. I would like to express our deep admiration, respect and affection to Sadhanatai for this labour of love for fellow human beings. Both Baba and she are excellent examples of the spirit behind the following poem by Rainer Maria Rilke:

Again and again in history
Some special people wake up
They have no ground in the crowd
They move to broader laws
They carry strange customs with them
and demand room for bold audacious actions
The future speaks ruthlessly through them
They change the world.

M S Swaminathan

Acknowledgements

The privilege of having been entrusted with the translation of *Samidha* is my greatest good fortune and I prefer not to thank but to remain indebted forever to Baba and Sadhanatai Amte. Their unflinching moral support and confidence added might to my pen. Delight is mine that Baba and Tai found me worthy of such a job. I am grateful to Tai for allowing me to rewrite certain parts of her memoirs. But for the courtesy of Dr Sheetal Amte, the readers of this book would have missed the beautiful images on the celluloid. Being a perfectionist and a diligent worker from the third generation of the Amte family, she shot a few fresh ones for me. The transparent love of the entire Amte family is my safe deposit.

Fortune favoured me once more when Dr M. S. Swaminathan, a scientist with a poetic mind and much more, without a moment's hesitation, agreed to write the foreword to this book and he did it in record time despite his round the clock schedules. It is a moving script which mirrors his innate goodness. This meeting with the mind that is firmly rooted in the soil and dreams of new horizons for humankind was made possible through the solid but silent help from Kaustubh Amte. He pursued it with zeal until he succeeded in contacting Dr Swaminathan. Mr Ramesh Kacholia volunteered to fill the gaps in email-correspondence with Dr Swaminathan in an ardent spirit of a true worker. Dr Pol and Sitakant Prabhu were ever ready to answer my queries. My sincerest thanks are due to all of them.

Memories of my father, my first guru of English, knocked at the gate of my mind throughout this journey. He gave me the first lessons in English at an early age and made the choice of English for me, and it has made all the difference. My mother who whole-heartedly granted me space to work has been my moral support in all odds and evens.

I can never forget the continual encouragement and support from my friends, Swati, Sudha and Philip who spared time for perusal of the first draft during the early stage of writing. Smita, Meena and Manjiri have been my anchor in the most difficult times. Their friendship has been my blank cheque. I am indebted to them in many ways.

The magnanimity of Ujwala Pradhan, who, despite being a stranger to me,volunteered to type a large part of the manuscript free of charge, was a pleasant surprise to me. My computer literacy being limited, she extended help in the nick of the time and made my task easier.

I appreciate the efforts taken by Orient Longman for helping me spread the Amte story worldwide.

On Translating Samidha

A fairy tale romance and a blueprint for anyone who wants to venture into social service, this autobiography of a woman who chose to marry a frenzied man and a dreamer, is also a tale of her willing surrender in love without the slightest loss of identity. It reveals without explicit intent the reverse of the beautiful carpet they wove together with their love and their labour.

The reasons for the urge to translate *Samidha* – the autobiography of Sadhana Amte (Sadhanatai), wife of Baba Amte (known as Murlidhar Devidas Amte) – lie not only in its literary merit but also in its social relevance. It is an autobiography with a difference. Considering its episodic nature, to call it 'memoirs' would be just but the presence of the speaking self involved in every incident is so conspicuous that such a label sounds inadequate. Written without a stance, the distinctive simplicity of this transparent narrative has the power to stir its readers, I must say, with its tang, like the salty sea-air, and the warmth of a fruitful mad pursuit of a goal—at once personal and impersonal. Beyond its literary merit, it is my love and respect for the Amtes and their work that has always inspired me and has been the primary motivating force.

Unlike many other autobiographies by women, there is neither the loud protest against male domination or exploitation, which is common, nor the aggressive self-assertion or justification. In this account, written in a characteristic documentary style, you will meet a woman who was always liberated without ever being a feminist. To say that she is the woman *behind* the great man, Baba Amte, is to belittle her contribution to the mammoth work Baba has done. She is the woman *beside* him, extending her hand in things, great and small, in times, dark and bright. She is a perfect consort who has the ability to tame the living storm Baba Amte. She did not know when she became a part of the storm but it marked the beginning of an endless journey of the hardest toil. If Baba split the rock, she watered the saxifrage, I should say. A silent spring that feeds the bouncing stream!

This autobiography traces the journey of a woman from orthodox faith to rational belief; it presents the portrait of a woman who hails from a 'high-caste' puritan Hindu family with a legacy of learning and comes to identify herself with the lowest of the low, the untouchables. It is the portrait of the man whose life is an adventure in itself. Interestingly enough, there is no attempt to glorify or criticise him; only an honest, effortless portrayal of him in his true colours—as a husband, as a lover and as a social worker. In other words, this book reads like a story of eternal love which is the secret of Sadhanatai's fruitful relationship with the man of many parts, Baba Amte. Their work is only an extension of this love.

The most commendable aspects of this narrative are the absence of ideological biases, its commitment to the truth of experience and the author's sincere desire not to tell (with pride) but to share a few facts of her life with the readers, without any endeavour to sit in judgement upon them. She had to be persuaded into writing this. The long chain of events and encounters with people – great and small – which is presented vividly and in a lucid style, lends to the narrative an authenticity and commands full absorbtion of the readers. A book like this – a saga of suffering, difficulties, hopes and tensions, as well as the thrill and pleasures of work experienced by Sadhanatai and Baba while pursuing their goals – will serve as the beacon of light for posterity, I thought; and as a model for human relationships. In a world racked by violence, it tells us, without any encumbrance, how simple it is to be human. The picture of this woman as it emerged – beside the man and behind the words which come from the depths of truth; a woman who realises herself through her life's work and her personal relationships; a woman who successfully tries to maintain a delicate balance between the rights and duties, the claims of public and private life; and tradition and modernity – haunted me as I read on. What a rare combination of confidence and compliance, work and worship, labour and love! This was sufficient to undertake the translation of this work and the challenge lay in capturing this image of Sadhana Amte in another language. My greatest privilege was to have known both Baba and Sadhanatai at close quarters, for the past twenty years, and my good fortune to be entrusted with the translation of *Samidha*.

To translate is to embark on a creative journey. There are no set rules for the translator to follow. To do so would be to force the translator to commit the sin of an unimaginative act of mimesis. I wonder whether any translator begins with a theory of translation. For anything to achieve the status of theory, as Heidegger puts it, calls for a sound philosophical basis. I believe that there is no poetics of translation that precedes practice. The translator stands for praxis, whereas theoretical intervention is the need of the critic engaged with translation studies.

The most frequently asked question in translation studies is, of course, about authenticity, faithfulness of the target text to its source. The fetish for faithfulness may have had its origin in the prolific translations during the European Renaissance, biblical ones in particular. Hidden behind this unreasonable obsession is the fear of distortion of facts (which is reasonable), though little care or concern is shown while defining the nature, boundaries or contours of facts.

Faithfulness is a slippery proposition and rests on certain assumptions: one, the translator is an agent, a carrier; two, the language is unequivocal; and three, the translator must stick to the word on the page and merely replace it with another. This may be true of scientific and technical writings because the language of such writings is, to a great extent, unequivocal and mostly referential, depending heavily on denotative meanings. It has 'translatability'. The language of literary works need not be referential and in fact, it defies its finitude. It is language that separates a literary piece of writing from a scientific one. If this is true, a literary work becomes the site for language to reveal itself. Consequently, the rhetoricity and the self-reflexivity of language leave scope for multiple interpretations. Any act of writing or reading a literary piece involves understanding and interpretation, which cannot but be subjective to a certain extent. In translation what is transmitted is not the word but the meaning, as fathomed by the translator. The linguistic means by which a translator conveys what he or she understands may vary from person to person; it could be symbolic, a way of representing an idea through an image, like in the case of a metaphor, where literal translation is dispensed with either for aesthetic considerations or for want of its efficacy. Along with subjectivity, cognitive understanding also demands radical changes in the use of language, style and form while translating such a work. 'A perfect double', as Heidegger puts it, is impossible. Had it not been so, a good dictionary (Heidegger uses the word 'wordbook') would have sufficed for the translator.

Only a literalist would depend heavily on the dictionary. This accounts for the multiplicity and variety of translations to which a literary work lends itself. This may infuriate the faithful band of literalists. However, the symbolist, at the same time, would never run the risk of discrediting the strictness of the thought, the denotative meaning, commonly shared by various readers. Conformity and creativity do not generally go together. There is the need to maintain a delicate balance between the two; it is a kind of tightrope walk. It is indeed difficult to draw lines demarcating the literal, symbolic, or free rendering of a work in translation. The relation of the translator to the author is as complex as that between a playwright and a director, perhaps like that between a Chekhov and a Stanislavsky. For practical purposes, a good translator would prefer to be eclectic in his or her approach rather than baldly commit to any one. The translation of *Samidha* endorses this fact.

In my view, the area to be problematised in translation studies is not fidelity but the distinctiveness of each translation along with a comparative study of numerous translations of the same work wherever available. No two translations are alike, a truth to be acknowledged. Both can be authentic or equally inauthentic, and interesting too. You will find an excellent parallel in Indian classical music; the *raaga* is the same, but its manifestations are entirely different. I would even say that if I were to translate the same work again, I would do it differently. Focus can also shift to the study of genre-wise art of translation. It is possible that the exigencies of the various forms may dictate the terms of translation of a particular work.

Autobiography is a complex literary genre which combines in itself a variety of sub-genres such as chronicles, history, saga, confession, narration and memoirs or passive reflection. Even here, the chances of one (co)lapsing into the other are high.

The greatest challenge in translating an autobiography lies not in deciphering facts mechanically but in capturing the image of the author that peeps from behind the words. It is as enigmatic as Mona Lisa's smile, as elusive as good poetry. Just as a good painter busies himself, in equal proportion, with the search for the inner man as he works on the length of the nose or the shape of the lips, the sensible translator of an autobiography must grapple with the figure and the spirit that peeps from behind the words. The translator must hold a lamp and not a mirror to the image of the author as it emerges from the work. Translating the rhythms of a language – not of words but of emotions they convey, no less than the tone and the mood – is not an easy task. The only means most have are the words of the author. However, I had the privilege of getting back to Sadhanatai whenever I felt the need apart from being a silent witness to their work for the last twenty years.

A certain amount of subjectivity is inevitable in translation and more so in the case of autobiographical writing because one has to take the responsibility of translating a life and not just the words of the author. Liberty is also required in matters of language. A translator finds himself in a double-bind. His loyalties lie in two places, the *content* of the original work and the *language* he translates into. The two are not always hostile. However, the target language has its claims on the translator. Words in every language have an aura, a flavour, a behaviour pattern and rhythm. Some words come in pairs, like nouns and adjectives—like 'abiding memories', trite indeed, but when together, they continue to catch on. The translator chooses one and is tempted to include the other. In fact the two, when used together, enrich and enhance each other. As a linguist the translator focuses on achieving naturalness in the target language. There is the need to smoothen out an expression, to shed the look of contrivance. Fluency in thought and language has to be prioritised. A word, a sentence, even a short paragraph slips in to fill up the gaps; without any intention of encroachment on the thought of the author. It may only act as a complement. This is the beginning of the translator's romance with the language into which he or she is translating. While translating *Samidha* such necessary 'transgressions' have occurred. No translator would like to have his or her readers feel that they are reading a translation. Once you accept this premise, limitations of literal translation become clear as there is a probability of creating blockages, both on the level of language and thought, obstructing their free flow. Loyalty to the word on the page has to be sacrificed, at times, at the altar of fluency of language and thought.

During the process of translating *Samidha*, there have been modifications on different levels. Foremost among them is that on the structural plane. The original lacked organisation, I thought. Besides the fact that it was an exercise in memory for Sadhanatai whose failing health deprived her of the necessary leisure to luxuriate in such external matters as form and structure of sentences, this lacunae was the result of another inconvenience—her inability to write this herself. She was coaxed into speaking and Sitakant Prabhu did the writing. Since memory is not chronological, details were scattered in many places. Had discontinuity been a conscious technique for this narrative, I would not have dared to change it. In the absence of the use of any such narrative technique on the part of the author, I proceeded to shift passages from one chapter to another only to maintain the unity and the flow of narration. It was for this same reason that I shifted a large chunk from the author's foreword to the relevant chapter. The foreword had to be only a pointer and brief enough to rouse interest.

There have been additions and very few deletions too. I made a conscious effort to strengthen the reflective part of this narrative because it seemed to me to have remained undeveloped in the original work. That is why Sadhanatai called it a narration and not a reflection, in her foreword. Hers has been a life of action, no doubt. Where was the time for reflection? Baba and Tai were never drawn to abstraction. But both have such beautiful thoughts that I did not want the world to lose this wealth I have often enjoyed, during meals or while accompanying them on their walks, during my yearly visits to their projects. Moreover, she had no special reason to withhold this wisdom from the world. Perhaps this was also due to the fact that she only spoke and Sitakant Prabhu wrote down all her words. He tried his best to put her scattered thoughts together. But for his labour of love, this story would never have reached those thousands who felt enlightened on reading it. However, in this kind of exercise she missed those moments of privacy, required for profound reflections. After the publication of the original, she too had a feeling that something was left out. When she spoke to me about it, I decided to coax her into talking about these things. There were many such half-lit spots in the original work and I got her to talk, during my visits, on various issues—conjugal rights of the lepers; faith and reason, especially with reference to her analysis of Baba's personality; equality; belief and forms of worship; justice, and she graciously allowed me to include the same in the translation. Deletions are marginal, an incident or two, just to avoid repetition.

Translation is an art, perhaps more difficult because the translator is not as autonomous as the creative artist. Moreover, the rate of exchange into a foreign language varies from language to language for the simple reason that the (pur)chasing power of one is decided on the basis of its cultural distance, difference from, or its resemblance to the other. The difficulties encountered while translating *Samidha* are not essentially different from those experienced by others engaged with 'interlingual translation'. Let me put down a few. Mrs Amte's penchant for metaphors, puns and wordplay could not have been overlooked. They are an inseparable part of her personality. When literally translated, these stylistic devices lose their force and their nuances. The alternatives are: One, to use a new metaphor or pun which fits naturally in the target language; two, to opt for a literal translation to safeguard the cultural flavours of the source language (impossible in the case of a pun); three, to paraphrase it; and four, to leave it out. I preferred to use the first but did not make a rule of it. This replacement need not be exactly for the original one with the same meaning or in the same sentence. One may use a metaphor or a pun anywhere. The purpose is to maintain the features of the author's characteristic style. The same is true of humour. I think this is the most difficult part for the translator. If it is humour that arises out of word play (like in P. G. Wodehouse), I wonder whether it could ever be literally translated. If it is situational, there are chances of considerable success. While translating *Samidha*, I had no problem with this type of humour in one or two places. Humour is deeply rooted in culture, gender relations in that culture, social ethos and moral concepts. There is no question of the literal translation of humour. One can only look for parallels in the target language. The greatest unease is generally experienced while translating poetry. The poetry in *Samidha* belongs to the old school of poetry; rhyming lines with straightforward meaning, and I tried to follow the same style in the translation. I would leave it to the readers to judge its success.

The aura that surrounds the title 'Samidha' cannot be fully rendered into English. Literally, the word refers to the dry herbs used as fuel in the holy fire in a *Yadnya.* The twigs are procured from different plants, carefully selected according to their purity. To keep the fire burning, one has to drop them into the fire one after the other. Perhaps, it is an apt reflection of Baba's work as a *Mahayadnya,* a mammoth task and Sadhanatai's continual support. He lit the fire and she kept it burning. 'Samidha' becomes a metaphor for her commitment to their work without any expectation. It speaks of her role in Baba's work and her attitude to life as well. No expression in English would have adequately captured the essence of this word specific to our culture. I would have liked to call it 'Love's Labour' but Sadhanatai insisted on retaining the original title.

The variety of English for translation too is a hotly debated issue. Those who try to keep close to the native speech of that language are charged with cultural infidelity and submission to western imperialism. Others who use Indian varieties may come under scathing criticism for producing substandard stuff. (With globalisation and the rise of English Literatures the world over, there has been a discernible shift in this attitude. Even the Standard English Dictionaries are adding non-native words every year to widen and strengthen their stock.) There is nothing wrong in resorting to any one of them. Use of Indianisms at different levels is useful at times. When it comes to translate a word that is culturally loaded into a non-native language such as English, one has to fall back upon Indianisms. Moreover, it is an opportunity for the translator to introduce his or her culture to the foreign readers through language. Take a word like 'Mahamahopadhaya.' It is closer to the word 'wrangler' but the latter cannot signify all other connotations of the first. My use of Indianisms is restricted to vocabulary only. English itself absorbed Latin words widely once upon a time and continues to absorb words from many other languages even today. But to insist on the use of either of the varieties is to politicise the issue. I think it is better to leave the choice of English to the translator and best to allow the book to dictate the terms of translation. I have neither poetics nor politics. While translating *Samidha*, language was an issue under consideration. It was more a question of the idiom than of the variety of English. The idiom in which, for instance, Arundhati Roy or her contemporaries write, would not have been appropriate, I thought. Nor would I have been able to write in that. Style and idiom carry the stamp of personality. In *Samidha* the author has used formal Marathi and I chose to keep close to it while translating it into English. I could not overlook her fondness for figurative language and wordplay. It speaks for her poetic temparament. The diction of subjectivity in *Samidha* is comparable to that used by English romantic poets. Words are often emotionally charged. They have the power of expressing her life's rhythms—the most difficult thing to translate, whether in poetry or prose. Translators have their fancies too. Preference for one word over the other or the sentence structure they choose reflects their personality. Language thus becomes a creative gesture. It may lead to a tussle between the author and the translator, who comes to dwell in the house that is built by the former. One owns it; the other who dwells in it will do everything to belong to it. If this is true, limitations of a machine translation become clear. Far from being a mechanical reproduction, I think a good translation is like procreation. I leave it to the readers to judge whether the present one bears me out. For me, it was a joy-ride.

AUTHOR'S PREFACE

That I would ever be called upon to recall an eventful past – dotted by many untoward happenings – rearrange it, and make it public property in the form of an autobiography, seemed unlikely just a few days ago. The saga of suffering and hardship that began when we voluntarily made a choice for this way of life, was never the material for the comforts of an autobiography. There were, however, persistent demands from friends and well-wishers that I should write one, and I was finally won over by their love and faith. There were problems on the practical plane too—in maintaining the chronological order, given both, the lapses in memory as well as the myriad experiences of our lives. Standing at the farthest point of the spectrum of our life—one filled with adventure, excitement, agony, and impasse—I realise how difficult it is to travel back in time and recollect vividly these moments for the sake of a record.

The phrase 'easier said than done', may be true for others, but for me, things are easier done than said. Life for us has never been a bed of roses. In fact, most of the time, reality has been stranger than fiction. A chain of misfortunes marked the first half of our life and calamities followed us faithfully wherever we went. The second half is crowded by the unlimited expansion of the various projects we had undertaken, and our involvement in the rehabilitation of the displaced in the Narmada Valley. The list of problems does not end here—there is failing health due to old age now and memory, too, has failed. But I must say that the mind is still very active. It vibrates with the same intensity even today.

Nothing can be as difficult as selecting a few things to write about. If I were to go by the degree of difficulties and hardships encountered, foremost on the list would be our experience with the Hemalkasa project. This place has acquired a new face today. But, what do I do with the hands that worked for it? Did I not change? Where should I really begin? The transformations within, go hand-in-hand with the transformations without—and holding a mirror to one, is like holding a lamp to the other. This book is the story of our work—and of the man and the woman behind it.

It may sound incredible, but I have lived many lives in one. What have I not done? The life that we chose demanded and extracted hard labour at every step. But there are no regrets. Others may call it sacrifice but we crucified that word long ago. What can I say? It was nothing more than love's labour and it had its blossoms. Many close friends and well-wishers tried to coax me into writing about our journey but where was the leisure for that? The rising curve of our work left no room for this luxury. Perhaps it would have been better, if I had written earlier because most of the experiences were fresh in my mind. Today, I have to bribe my memory even for simple things.

Life, for me, has always been a tightrope walk. While living against such odds, I discovered the art of balancing. It has become a daily routine now; only the context has changed. The bullock cart is replaced by the four-wheeler but there is no break in the act of balancing. How the past imposes itself on the present, you can never tell, until you find leisure to sit down and think about it. Memory has its own logic. If it is sharp, it will split the frozen mass of your past without effort. Mine is rather weak. It fails me, scattering all those moments of adventure, excitement, struggle and toil in the deeper recesses of the mind. Nevertheless, this exercise has its rewards; it opens up a space where a dialogue with the self begins. You become a stranger to yourself temporarily—you look within, if you dare. And it need not always be unpleasant, this peeping in. The writing of this autobiography has been punctuated by a continual sliding inwards. Besides, the temptation of self-indulgence was there too. After all I am human, though the world is eager to cast me in another mould. It costs nothing to deify others as you can comfortably escape the responsibilities. But can I not judge myself? I have my own likes and dislikes, my own preferences, obstinacies. However, I honestly feel that I have been true to myself, and have always stood by truth. Hypocrisy and affectation have been my enemies and artificiality – mental or moral – always distanced me from people. Compassion is what draws me to people and helps build a bridge of kinship in no time. I think that is a god-given gift. I did not have to do anything for it. I remember parting with my woollens once for those shivering in the cold, and having sat up in bed for hours worrying about them.

This autobiography has been made possible only because Sitakant Prabhu pursued it sincerely and seriously. It was originally to be written by Shri Balasaheb Urdhwareshe, but I feel guilty that I could not give him the time. My sincere apologies to him! I am grateful to him for the love and respect he has always given me.

This book is neither a reflection on the past nor a historical account of my partnership with Baba, both in pain and pleasure. It is a straightforward narrative, and is not strictly chronological. In other words, I would like to call it an interlacing of emotion and thought recollected in those tranquil moments of repose.

I have always been fond of flowers and have often gone into a frenzy of making wreathes and garlands to adorn the gods. Among the recipients of these floral offerings from my garden, are gods from Amritsar to Kanyakumari. The flowers in the garlands, are of various kinds—wild, as well as ones you would find in any garden, like the rose and the jasmine. In the same spirit, I offered these words dipped in truth to Sitakant Prabhu, and he worked very hard to wreathe them into this book. I leave this offering in the hands of the readers now.

Sadhana Amte

ONE

While rambling in the dark kingdom of oblivion, sometimes the clouds vanish in an instant and things become luminously clear for a moment. The august light of abiding memories tempts one to linger awhile, and bask in its warmth. Memories crowd the mind's landscape, one after another. Tears follow faithfully. It is no wonder then that words become strangers. Try as you might to make them, they refuse to stand in their place or fall in line with the exigencies of a sentient self. The flicker reveals the treasure of lived moments. Willful words slip and slide. The mind cries in desperation. A moment later, the memories fade. Like a flash of lightning in the clouds, they vanish. Stillness returns once again. But the flicker is mine. Whatever I could see in it, I have tried to put together for you. The obliterated rest belonged to god, who promptly claimed it.

Clad in the sweet scent of incense and the soft light of the oil lamp lit in front of god's idol in the puja-ghar of an old-fashioned ancestral house, are my memories of childhood. The resonance of the bass notes, in which the holy mantras were chanted, keeps them permanent company and the floral offerings that adorned these idols provide the backdrop. These reminiscences smack of a legacy of sacred rites and rituals. They were devoutly performed by the members of the conservative Ghule family, generation after generation. My grandfather, my father's uncle, Shri Krishnashastri Ghule, was known in the Nagpur region for his learning and profound understanding of the vedas as well as for his skill in bringing this knowledge within the ken of the common man.

The Ghules were previously known as the Bhattas. Their family lineage can be traced back to the well-known Gagabhatta, who participated in King Shivaji's coronation ceremony. Our ancestor, Gangaram Bhatta, preceding my grandfather by eleven generations, worked in the court of the Peshvas at Pune. He left for Kashi along with the Peshvas, and settled down there as a priest in the Shiva temple. His son was Bhairam Bhatta. His grandson, Anand Bhatta, was known for his extensive writings. There was a legend that Ved Vyasa himself blessed Anand Bhatta, telling him that his legacy of learning would be carried forward for generations.

Bhaushashtri Ghule was a descendent of the sixth generation of the Ghule family and the honourable mahamahopadhyaya Krishnashashtri Ghule was his son. Krishnashastri Ghule studied at Neelcity High School in Mahal, and passed his intermediate examination from Morris College. While at college, he set up an institution called Manimanjusha. He had a good command over French, Marathi, Hindi, Bengali, Gujarati, Urdu, including Sanskrit. His book *Patitoddhar Mimansa* (A Critique on the Upliftment of the Downtrodden) is a very incisive dialectic on how those who change their religion from Hinduism could be converted back. Inspired by Lokmanya Tilak, in 1904, he started a magazine in which he published verses from the Rig Veda, translated into lucid Marathi. He worked as the editor of *Wageshawari*, a magazine published from Nagpur, for many years. He was made president of the reception committee of Vidarbha Sahitya Sammelan. He gave religious discourses at the Dakshinamurthy temple in Nagpur and many of his sermons and articles on Vedanta have been published by Balshastri Hardas. Among those influenced by his philosophical thinking are Dr Shivdas Barlinge and Dr Bhanji Daftari. The tradition of the mahamahopadhyaya in our family ends with Krishnashastri Ghule. It was also the end of the vedic tradition of learning and scholarship in the Ghule family.

The special characteristics of our family can be listed in the three words—puritan, religious and traditional. Obviously, I could not help being influenced by and trained in the same tradition. Being apprehensive of sins, I have always been overconscious of observing customs, conventions and religious practices in the house. If I have abhorred and protested against anything in my life, it is injustice. I would never forgive myself and would not rest until I atoned for injustice even if done inadvertently.

I was only ten when I lost my father. I have very few and vague memories of him because we rarely interacted with him closely. In those days girls hardly talked to their fathers. A mixed feeling of fear and respect always kept us at a distance from him. He worked in the secretariat. After an argument with his boss about arriving late at the office on one occasion, he resigned his job and took up another in the directorate of accountant general, post and telegraph. He also opened a cloth shop Ghule Silk House, dealing exclusively in silks. The unexpected death of my father not only left my mother inconsolable, but also upset the entire household in many ways. My time was often divided between housework and school. Reading was obviously a marginalised activity and was confined to the reading of religious books. I also had to take on the responsibility of my youngest sister, Suma, who was only two months old. In a sense, motherhood was thrust on me at a very tender age. When little Suma looked at me with her big expressive eyes, my heart skipped a beat and the spring of motherly love in me was released.

My uncle, Laxmanshastri Ghule, gave discourses on the puranas at the Jagruteshwar temple in Nagpur. He wrote poetry and made beautiful clay sculptures. He was a charming and endearing man. Recognising his talent the shankaracharya had conferred the title of kavi vinod on him. As children, we would walk five kilometres to the temple to listen to his tales from the puranas. It was our good fortune to be introduced to religious books such as *Kathakalpataru*, Mahabharata, Ramayana, and *Jemini Ashwamedha* through him. He showered boundless love on us. He had a son and a daughter who stayed and played with us in the same house.

My uncle excelled in the art of making idols, especially of lord Ganesha and goddess Saraswati. He used a special mix of clay, ash and camphor which was his own formula. My younger brother inherited this talent for sculpting from him. I tried too, but did not succeed—often starting with one thing, and ending up with something else! My uncle celebrated Ganesh Chaturthi with great devotion and fervour. Having trained in music, he would set the bhajans to a new tune for each day of the festival. He was accompanied by a percussion artist, Balirampant Pande. The celebrations went on for ten days. The immersion ceremony on the tenth day was attended by a special guest—His Highness, Raja Raghuji Bhosale. We used to linger on to see the women from the royal family, all dressed gorgeously. A ceremonial parade of elephants, horses, palkhis and specially decorated sedan chairs could also be seen in the royal procession. This festival pageant was much awaited. The pearl and diamond jewellery, and the richly brocaded costumes the royal women wore would be the topic of discussion among the women of the town for months. Immediately after Ganesh Chaturthi my uncle would proceed to his music concerts. His devotion to music took him to far off places such as Aundh, Indore, Bhopal and Washim.

One day, my uncle suddenly lost his sweet voice. It was said that the cause was some sindoor that he consumed. Sindoor is harmful for one's voice. It was mixed in some paan and offered to him; it was an act of wilful damage on the part of someone who was jealous of him.

I had my primary education in the National Girls' High School. I could hardly find time for studies; in spite of this, I always stood first in school. Later, I joined another school which was headed by Mr Appasaheb Jamdar. He was a righteous, charming person with a gentle smile! It was he who insisted that I appear for the scholarship examination when I was in class nine. It was the time when the whole country reverberated with the slogan 'Quit India'. Nagpur was tense during that time and we had our end of the year examinations. There were British soldiers patrolling the streets and it was quite frightening for us. But, Appasaheb was very encouraging and supportive. He even accompanied us to the examination centre where we took our examinations under terrible stress. I not only passed the examination but also won the scholarship—back then an amount of five rupees a month, for the next three years. Apart from studying, I participated actively in the rallies and marches which had become regular features of India's freedom struggle. I remember the meeting held after Barrister Abhyankar's release from prison very clearly. It was a meeting that was attended by thousands of people. I went with my brothers and sisters. I still remember the song that my sister sang at that meeting.

The wedding hour is come;
With her forehead

Adorned with kumkum,
Sits the goddess of freedom.
Play on, you pipers,
Guns be your drums;
Like lightning and the thunder,
Democracy will sing louder.

We children loved such activities. How overwhelming a thought it was, even at that age, that we were doing something for our country! Houses hummed with stories about revolutionaries. Mahatma Gandhi and Jawaharlal Nehru became household heroes. Indians worshipped them as they did their family gods. I remember a few lines from a song that was sung during marches and rallies:

The day breaks,
Awake my brother;
With the garland of freedom,
The day breaks.

Around this time a memorable incident took place. Veer Savarkar was released from prison. The citizens of Nagpur had arranged a grand felicitation at Kasturchand Park, to welcome him. We were witness to it. It is a matter of pride for me that I was a part of the chorus performance on that day. I remember the song faintly:

We Hindus are all brothers,
Lord Shiva, our father.
Bramhin, kshyatriya, vaishya or shudra,
This holy land is our mother.

I got a pat on my back and blessings from none less than Savarkar. This has left a lasting impression on my mind. He did not forget to recognise me as the granddaughter of Ghule Shastri and showered lavish praise on me. Even a glimpse of such a man who sacrificed everything for the love of his country, was a great reward for me.

I was extremely shy and did not have many friends. I was so shy of talking even to women; conversation with men was next to impossible. I remember my father's friend's words, 'A word from Indu cannot be had for love or money. It is as expensive as a jewel.' I was comfortable only in the company of children, and I always avoided contact with elders. My obstinate refusal to speak, often invited the wrath of my mother and I did pay the price for it. They thought me unfit for outdoor jobs. Would you believe if I told you that I was shy to even collect my prize during the annual school ceremony? Going up to the stage was an ordeal for me. How I wished at that moment that I had not stood first in the examination!

While most people complain of the price that is to be paid for speaking the truth, I have had strange experiences of benefitting from it. This happened when we were actively involved in the Narmada Bachao Andolan. A satyagraha was arranged at Manibeli and Medha Patkar was already there. Around two thousand policemen were deployed at the site. Baba had already left for Manibeli. I was to leave with Vikas who had come to Kasrawad for some other work. It was Thursday. I suggested to Vikas that we visit the temple of Lord Dattatraya on our way. At Badwani, we were held up by a sub-inspector of police who had been instructed not to allow any associates of Medha Patkar to take the route between Badwani and Manibeli. He naturally enquired about our destination. I thought for a minute, and said to him 'Look, we want to go to Manibeli and stop on the way to pray at the temple at Rajghat. If you do not allow us, we will go back to Kasrawad.' To my surprise, he let us go with no further questions. Baba was waiting for us at the Gujarat border. Everyone was shocked to hear how the inspector allowed us to pass after coming to know the truth. After two days, when we returned to Badwani, the same inspector respectfully offered us cold drinks.

Waking up to the truth is often accompanied by a feeling of restlessness and disgust. It does not happen overnight. Slow and steady was the process of my growing out of customs and conventions ingrained by tradition, and there was the consequent irritation and repulsion. Reason, bound in the shackles of age-old practices, could not be easily freed. My mind was often torn between the opposite poles of reason's demand for rational truth and the moral obligation of respecting tradition. However, it was Baba who removed all the cobwebs obstructing the light of reason in one stroke.

Compassion is second nature to me. This spontaneous overflow of compassion, however, has often deprived me of my power of judgement. I cannot bear the sight of tears. They move me instantaneously. On such occasions I do not bother to find out whether they are true or false. It often takes me a while to discern pretensions. But the fact remains that tears disturb me a great deal even today.

Of course, my generosity had its limitations too. It could not transcend the boundaries of contemporary social mores. And rebellion was a far cry. There was a public water-place in front of our house. Women from the harijan community, branded as the untouchables, would come to fetch water but they never dared to touch the tap. They used to sit and wait, sometimes for hours, for somebody to come and open it for them. I gladly volunteered to do this. Whenever there was no water supply,

I would draw water from the well for them. I did, however, take care that I did not touch them while filling their earthen pots. I would often distribute food grains to the beggars. There would be a reserved quota for them in our house. No one ever went away from our house empty handed. The natural spring of mercy in me could find a hundred such outlets. There was a cow, that was particularly notorious for kicking everyone who came near it, but the same cow allowed me to touch her and scratch her back with a comb. It was my privilege to be the only one who could milk her.

I passed my matriculation examinations in 1944, with a second class. My elder sisters were married by then. I wanted to pursue higher studies. I joined college, but domestic responsibilities, and the work in our shop, were overwhelming. Consequently, I was unable to attend classes, and finally had to drop out. It was extremely frustrating to have to give up college due to these circumstances. But going to college was not in my fate and I accepted it gracefully and without complaint. This temperament – to adjust and accommodate – helped me later when I was called upon to withstand Baba's creative frenzies.

My brother lived only for five years. He was a handsome and lovely child, the apple of our eyes. This death was intensely traumatic for me. Even time could not heal the wound. He died of smallpox. In those days it was customary to use herbal medicines. People also had faith in spiritual remedies such as the worship of the mother goddess. I clearly remember my visits to the temple, carrying neem leaves and a pitcher of water. The pain he went through was more than a child his age could bear. Finally, he vomited blood. A day after the propitiation ceremony in the temple, he passed away. Our dear little mischievous brother was no more. He left me, weeping for how many days, I do not know.

I have experienced quite a few moments of such overwhelming grief in my life. My father's untimely death brought chaos into our world. I think he had an intimation of his approaching death. Diabetes and appendicitis had already taken a toll on him. Long before he died, he kept talking of his end. We were too young then, but my mother could see the pain in his eyes. In spite of the pain and anxiety, my father felt the need to absolve my mother from following certain cruel customs that widows had to follow. A widow's head was shaved and she was forced to lead a spartan life. My mother was able to escape this ordeal because this radical proposal came from my father. It must have given her the strength to face her loss. My mother was only thirty when she had to shoulder the responsibilities of the family.

Women, in those days, were strictly confined to the domestic sphere. The gosha system prevented them from participating in any activities pertaining to the public domain. Respectability and prestige of a family in society, depended on confining women in their homes. My mother was anxious that there was no man to support the family. Without our father we had no choice but to succumb to the social pressures. We were not allowed to attend public meetings, and we could attend school or college only if some male elder escorted us. If there was no one to accompany us, we had to miss our classes. No one was really concerned about our studies. Reading novels, short stories and plays was strictly prohibited. Our achievements and accomplishments were restricted to the domestic sphere—skill in all kinds of housework and hospitality towards guests. Nothing more was required or expected of a girl. What happened in the world beyond the threshold of the house was not supposed to be our concern. Only when we found some leisure after the housework, did we turn to our books.

I cannot say that we were unhappy. We loved and enjoyed what we did. I was known as my mother's right-hand and she gladly relied on me to help with the housework. I always did the work even before I was told and felt happy with my reward—a pat on the back. I do it this way even today. But Baba is not so generous with his praise. I always felt the absence of my father. But, my mother's strict discipline in bringing us up has its mark on everything that we did, the people we are and the things we do. I have come to abhor artificiality and vanity. I find it stifling to be with pretentious people. I never try to hide my feelings, be they of anger or love; nor do I try to disguise them. I still remember how tears rolled down my cheeks while reciting a poem from a textbook when I was in the fifth standard:

Twisting in his bed,
The poor child waited for his death,
Far away from the mother,
Only the nurse by his side,
The little one groaned in pain.

I was fascinated by stories of courage and chivalry. The exciting history of the Marathas would thrill me. Luxuriating in such emotions, I was completely unaware of the imminent entry of a man into my life—a man with Madan's passion, camouflaged by the austerity of a yogi. The moment that would turn my life around was drawing nearer. An eagle that only soars high and abhors the banality below was to come to roost in my nest. Absorbed as I was in my secure little world, I could hardly foresee the impending storm.

The unexpected arrival of Baba in our house in the summer of 1946, created a ripple in my otherwise silent and steady flow of the stream of life. It happened like this. My great-uncle (my mother's uncle), Govindrao Pol, was a lawyer in Bemetara in Madhya Pradesh. Baba's elder sister Sundarabai was his wife. Govindkaka would visit us occasionally. That summer, Baba came along with him. Everything changed for me since that moment. He not only changed the course of my life but also became the cause of my estrangement from my family.

Two of my sisters were already married. The third sister and I were of marriageable age. It was unthinkable, and against the custom, to marry off the younger one first. So there was no question of my marriage taking place before my sister's. The elders at home began eagerly to look for a match for my sister. Govindkaka once visited us in this connection. He was Baba's brother-in-law. He had purposely brought Baba with him as his caretaker because he knew that Baba was very close to the gentleman my sister was to marry.

I hardly knew anything about the Amte family at that juncture. As a child, I had visited Baba's house a couple of times with my mother's aunt—Baba's sister. But I had never seen or met Baba although I knew his sisters. In a strange coincidence, a match had been proposed twice between Baba and my elder sister but had been promptly turned down on either instance by Baba's father because their horoscopes did not match.

When Baba first visited our house he was certainly not the handsome young man in search of a bride. He was dressed like a sage—with a long black beard down to his belly, long hair down his back, a staff in one hand and a cloth bag hanging from his shoulder. In his bag were clothes and a kambal. He was clad in a white hand-woven dhoti, and a saffron-coloured long shirt, enough to inspire faith in onlookers. All of us peeped from behind the door to catch a glimpse of him.

I reported to my mother that a sanyasi had come to our house. She laughed and said, 'Oh, he is Murli, Murli Amte.' I had once heard my mother mention about one of the Amtes joining a revolutionary group. At the time, I had neither reason, nor will to know more about him. On seeing Baba in that outfit, my mother, trying to suppress her laughter, mumbled, 'Why has he dressed up so strangely?' It was beyond the pale of her imagination to accept what she saw—the son of a rich zamindar with a large estate, a motor-car and a bungalow clad in saffron and choosing such an austere way of life. She had no idea about his aims and activities, except that he was involved in some nationalist cause.

Baba respectfully bowed to my mother despite his impertinence—Baba always bows down before elderly people. Now it was our turn to be introduced to Baba. After having introduced two of my sisters, my grandfather turned to me. He praised me liberally, attributing to me all those qualities and accomplishments that a marriageable girl was expected to have—good housekeeping skills, cleverness and studiousness.

Baba looked at me. Our eyes met, and the next minute, as befitting my natural modesty, my eyes turned downward. Baba only smiled while my grandfather waxed eloquent in my praise. To tell you the truth, I was won over by Baba in that strange outfit. His face glowed with an unusual radiance. I cannot tell whether it was the radiance that drew me to him. But I must confess, that it was the beginning of a strange, hitherto unfamiliar disquietude. Somewhere in my heart of hearts, there was a ripple. The day of Baba's arrival was marked by strange coincidences. Just a few hours before he came, I was introduced (with explicit intent of marriage) to a boy who had completed his Ph.D. My refusal to accept that proposal not only shocked my grandfather but invited his fury as well. He tried his best to persuade me to reconsider the proposal, but to no avail. All this was promptly reported to Baba, whose social status commanded such confidence. My mother and grandfather did not forget to mention their disapproval of my outright rejection of a such a worthy proposal. Baba consoled them by saying that he would find a good match for me. I wonder if he had any feelings for me at that time.

During that visit Baba stayed with us for a week. He had come for my sister's wedding. I was assigned some special duties, such as receiving and looking after the guests, and making provisions for their comforts. Baba was certainly a special guest in our house since he hailed from a respectable and renowned family. I felt a strange delight in entertaining him.

The wedding had turned our house into a store room. I had no idea that Baba needed a secluded corner for his daily prayers. On the first day, he somehow managed to find enough room to sit in padmasana and recite his prayers. For the next day, I cleaned up a corner of a room on the previous night and kept it ready with a carpet making it a comfortable seat. It became my daily duty from that day for as long as he stayed with us. When his prayers started I would stand on to the staircase and secretly listen to him. I remember a few of the lines he uttered:

Weary eyed I stand and wait
Pining for you day and night

Those lines acquired a new meaning. During that week our communication was limited to a word or two a day, and that too on formal grounds. But both of us were aware of the change within. We could feel the galloping speed at which our feelings raced on our mindscapes. My services were conveniently interpreted by Baba as an expression of my fondness and I was no less intelligent in understanding the meaning of his furtive glances. Before long, things advanced to a stage when people teased me about Baba. There were speculations that Baba would readily marry me. But when the time came, they were all flabbergasted.

A week after my sister's wedding, Baba visited us again. This time he was perfectly at ease and did not hesitate to order me to run errands for him. He gave the whole family a long discourse on the importance of khadi. He had not yet revealed his feelings about me openly. I had experienced an emptiness on Baba's departure the first time itself. I did perceive all this but was unable to resolve the conflicting impressions: an ascetic in a sadhu's apparel and that of a romantic lover. But there was a great longing in the heart for him. In fact, Baba was miles away from the image of a life partner that I had cherished for so long. But the magnetic force that pulled me towards him was real. For me this chemistry was incomprehensible. By then Baba had started taking a keen interest in our domestic matters. He talked freely with my mother and sister, whereas, contact with me was minimal and only restricted to the contexts of the odd jobs I did for him. His presence always charged up the whole house, but his departure made me pine. There was a blank, a yearning, to be filled.

Baba went back to Warora and a big, fat letter arrived, addressed to me. It was the most unexpected thing and created a hubbub in the house. A letter from a young man to a young unmarried woman was too much for them to take. My feelings, however, were mixed—euphoria on the one hand and fear on the other. The letter was opened by whoever got hold of it first. It was a panegyric—a series of compliments to me for my capacity for diligent work, my penchant for serving the needy and an appreciation of my beauty. With trepidation, I proceeded to record the reactions of my family members who were vehement in their anger and sarcasm. Some were amused; others remarked mockingly, 'Fancy that! A self-proclaimed bachelor bowled over by feminine beauty!' It was not their fault. How could they have reconciled themselves to the contradiction of Baba's ascetic appearance and the romantic contents of his letter! Of course, there was no direct proposal made in the letter. So, feigning incomprehension of the implied meaning of the letter, I wrote back a simple letter which was scrutinised by all the elders in the house before it was posted. But before I sealed it, I did not forget to add the complimentary close 'Yours' instead of 'Ours' (the honorific plural, quite common in India, implies a distance maintained from the addressee and is generally used out of courtesy for older people).

Baba did not have to look for excuses now. Letters poured in, written in high-flown language. I could not respond in the same style because every letter of mine had to pass the acid test of approval from my family—the domestic censor board! I could not defy, at any cost, the age-old customs and lifestyle of our family. Once, I left two of his letters unanswered because I was afraid. Baba's irritation surfaced in the next letter he sent. It had the appearance of a condolence letter. He wrote, 'Dear Indu', and left the paper blank, but signed off with 'Yours only'.

I was not free to write as I liked, until the marriage was formally settled, and had I ventured to do so, I am sure it would have caused quite a furore in our house. Suppression and suffocation in such matters – commonly experienced by Indian women – was my lot. In the circumstances, I had no alternative but to content myself with several re-readings of Baba's letters with devotion. He paid another visit to Nagpur in this connection. He cleverly declared that his letters were being misunderstood. Baba has always been an expert in driving his point home and my mother even felt guilty, on hearing his explanation, for having done injustice to a gentleman like him.

She asked me to bow to him and the next minute I was lying prostrate before Baba. Only I knew that he dropped his shawl intentionally as I bent; for everyone else it was an accident.

It took me some time to realise that his vehement defence of his letters was a pretence. No sooner did he go back to Warora, than the letters started pouring in again. He then directly asked for my hand in marriage. There was a high-level meeting held in our house. My immediate acceptance of the proposal shocked my family. I met with their stubborn resistance to and repugnance for such a marriage. They tried their best to dissuade me, telling me that I deserved a better husband and that they would definitely find me one. They had their reservations, especially about Baba's age, appearance and lifestyle. They continuously brainwashed me until I gave up. I wrote to Baba, 'What will be, will be. You are free to choose another partner.' He was shocked, but I was helpless. The thought of rebellion could never have crossed my mind. So strong was the hold of the conventions and customs that I was brought up in.

On the other hand, the mystery behind Baba's decision to marry after taking the vow of celibacy, was totally incomprehensible to many. It was even more incomprehensible to them that I had decided to marry Baba against the wishes of all. May be, somewhere, deep down in my heart, there lurked a desire to take the untrodden road. When the time came, it surfaced promptly. Otherwise, such a decision for a shy girl like me would not have been even a distant dream. I told you how my hands had trembled with fear while accepting the prize during that school ceremony.

What a strange coincidence that a gregarious man like Baba should be attracted towards a loner, unlike other girls of her age! When Baba spoke, words came in a torrent, and when I opened my mouth, it was just a trickle. Baba is a traveller in the dream world; I am deeply rooted in the real. But when the weft and the warp cross, a beautiful fabric is woven. People look at this fabric in wonder, even today. Neither of us could have imagined that our union would produce such beauty. The inner urge to tear down the artificial barriers of convention coupled with love at first sight worked a miracle.

In the meantime, Baba did not sit quietly. He collected, very astutely, a lot of information about me from my mother and the other members of my family. He knew about my involvement in the domestic chores, my concern for the poor, my charity towards the untouchables (even though it was restricted to providing water to them only), and the way I looked after our cattle, especially the cows, at home. It was my habit to help, secretly though, the maidservant in the house with the cleaning and the washing. She stayed in our house. I would even make her bed. During winter, I would see to it that she had a blanket or some woollens to keep her warm. When the untouchable women came for water, I promptly filled their pitchers, usually at the back of the house. When I looked at their beaming faces, I felt happy. Similarly, I found great joy in simple acts like feeding the cow. I never made a duty of these things. But it was these little things that impressed Baba. Before he made up his mind to marry me, he knew everything about me. I had no idea of what was happening on his side and I never bothered to 'know' him in the same way. I was won over by the lover in him and the eternal lover in him still holds sway.

The help that I extended fetched me a lot of blessings from old women. They blessed me from the bottom of their hearts and wished a good husband for me. Whether Baba is the man of those blessings, I will let the readers decide.

Two

Finally, on the 9th of August, our marriage was settled. Baba was impatient to get married. My family, on the other hand, needed at least four months time, and they had their reasons. First, the marriage season would begin only after four months when chaturmas would be over; and second, they did not want to arrange the wedding so hastily and needed the time for elaborate preparations. Conservative as they were, they wanted to follow the customs and conventions strictly. Besides, they were sure that Baba's aggressive self-assertion would stand no chance in this matter. They knew when to be firm with him and when to submit.

This interval of four months turned out to be a blessing in disguise for the two of us. We got the time to know and understand each other. Now that the wedding was fixed, I felt a little bolder. During this time, I experienced myriad feelings. Uninhibited yearning and longing strengthened by absence, yet, tempered by the fear of public disapprobation filled my heart. It was a persistent struggle between forced restraint and the need to listen to the true voice of heart-felt emotions. Emotions knocked against reason's wall, but my mind was custom's slave. All those days were marked by the contradictory impulses within me. And this was also the period of heavy traffic of letters since there was no need for concealed communication or secret correspondence. No one now dared to open Baba's letters to me. But this profusion of letters before marriage only added to their disapproval of Baba. I turned a deaf ear to what they said or thought. Baba's romanticism soared higher and higher still. His letters were drenched in carefully selected lines of well-known poets such as Yashwant, Anil and Borkar. The letters were the inhabitants of love's dream kingdom.

I remember the lines he wrote in the very first letter:

I wandered far and wide,
My eyes always set on thine.
A game of passion unbounded
Hardly responded.
Many a note did my heart sing,
Those of love only could last long,
Note to note added,
Murli's song was made;
Dear Radha, when time did your heart unlock,
Hari entered into wedlock.

It was just a fleeting glimpse of the treasure of Marathi poetry that was to be unravelled soon. Often, the hour of rest at the end of the day, as I sat watching the evening sky, would bring back these lines that Baba wrote:

In the sky the evening star,
A gentle breeze or puff of air,
From my beloved a call clear.
Come and sit by my side,
A wreath of your hands
Round my neck weave.

And everything changed in a minute. Now it was not the sky I saw, but Baba's image right before my eyes.

A weekly visit now became an unwritten rule for Baba. When he was around, distraction from housework was inevitable and it happened precisely when my mother expected me to help her more, because my sister was pregnant and had come for her delivery. Baba would generally stay for a day or two. We never knew how time passed. Baba had a special skill in elaborately describing something and when he found a listener like me, he went on and on. Once, when we were completely engrossed in our converstaion, my mother asked me to cook rice. It was late evening, she had put the curry to cook on the stove. Mistaking it for boiling water, I put rice in it, and it created a pandemonium in the house. The fury of my mother knew no bounds. In fact, Baba was the real culprit in this case. What a price to pay for losing myself in his talk! I lost my hard-earned reputation of being a good cook in no time. My mother had to cook the rice again. When we sat together for dinner, she served the rice I had cooked and asked Baba to describe it. He never needed encouragement in such matters. He found another reason to tease me. The pleasure of teasing was his and he lost no opportunity to publicly draw attention to my cooking.

My decision to marry Baba invited scathing criticism from my relatives. To prevent further speculation, Baba was promptly introduced to them as my prospective husband. According to them, Baba fell short of many accomplishments required of a bridegroom. It is easier to detect from a girl's face whether she is of a marriageable age or not. With boys, it is difficult. In Baba's case, it was next to impossible for them to accept him as an eligible bachelor. Of course, he had shaved his beard now and hair had just started growing on his shining scalp. In his unusual apparel—a rough khadi dhoti, a long shirt, a staff in hand (which he carries even today) and a kambal hanging from the shoulder he looked like a man in his fifties. He was, in fact, only thirty-two at that time. People raised their eyebrows quizzically when he was introduced as my prospective husband. The expression on their face was proof enough of their disapproval.

The ascending order of their reactions—shock followed by silence, few words uttered with reluctance, open contempt, and vehement disagreement with my mother—mirrored their displeasure and opposition in every possible way. Soon it became a routine matter and we got used to the slandering. Habit took away the edge of anger.

On the other side of the fence, many fans of Baba were extremely happy with Baba's decision to marry and they even made special efforts to see me and congratulate me on my choice. Among them were barrister R. K. Patil (the then food minister of Central Provinces) advocate Barlinge, Kamaltai Hospet, Mohini Bandhu and H. V. Kamat. Perhaps, they must have wondered as well. It would not have been unreasonable on their part to have wondered how a girl like me – small, clad in a nine-yard sari – would get along with Baba, a spartan sage-like person clad in Khadi. Nevertheless, they were amused and welcomed the idea of Baba's entry into matrimony.

For six long years Baba had strictly committed himself to an austere way of life, allowing his beard to grow since 1940. He would wake up at 3 a.m., walk bare-foot to the river for a bath, in rain or shine, on a path marked by undergrowth of thorny bushes and ferns. He would have only one meal a day, which consisted of only three chapattis and vegetables cooked without chilli. Sugar, jaggery, buffalo milk and ghee were strictly prohibited. Complete silence was observed during the meal. He would wash his own plate, bowl and glass.

But every thing changed with my entry into his life. All his vratas were gladly sacrificed at the altar of my cooking. It was the day on which my elaborate cooking matched Baba's taste. That day he was accompanied by Haribhau Mohni. Baba relished each of the items. He especially liked the saaram made from tamarind. I said jokingly 'Like the saaram, life should never lose its sara'. Baba's intention to end his vratas at my hands was a part of his essentially romantic temperament, which he has been able to maintain even today. It has lost neither its flavour nor fervour.

The period preceding the wedding had an unforgettable charm. No other emotion except longing and impatience to meet each other occupied our minds. Responsibilities were far away. Life gravitated only in one direction. Love could make the sun stand still. The result was that I had to face my mother's fury off and on for neglecting my domestic duties. Soon I got used to it and, in fact, it ceased to matter. Baba too became progressively bolder. Snatching things from my hands became a regular trick. He needed no excuse to linger on till late evening. Consequently, our evening meals were delayed because he neither shared the evening meal nor did he leave early. He wanted to keep his promise that he would be back at his home for dinner. Because of Baba's pranks, my reputation in the house was on the wane. But Baba was cool as ever. He is the sort of person who never worries about what people think of him. He has the poise of a sage! Perseverance is another characteristic of his. Once his goal is fixed, nothing will deter him from achieving it. He will not lose a single opportunity, when inspired by his goal. I would call him an opportunist, in jest.

The period of courtship was marked by quite a few moments of adventure and chivalry too. I remember Baba's visit to our place ten days before our wedding. By this time, we were sufficiently acquainted with each other. It was only a question of publicly and formally putting a seal on this relationship in the presence of people and through a ritual performed by the priest. All the shopping was done. My wedding sari was kept in the room in which Baba used to sleep during his visits. That night all of us stayed late until midnight, chatting. I casually said to Baba, 'It is not right for you to sleep with your feet towards the photo of our family goddess.' In those days, Baba was too obedient to defy any request or order given by me. He promptly moved his feet away from the picture. I was happy to tell him, 'Now the goddess is near your head and she will always bless you.' Baba retorted, 'It is enough if my goddess (my wife) is pleased with me.'

In those days, we were often worried about thefts and robberies. In the absence of a responsible elderly male figure in the house, it would be difficult to deal with such situations. During the visit I was talking about, it was Baba's turn to confront the thieves. A day before Baba arrived, someone had already put up a ladder behind the house, into the gallery of the room upstairs, but it had escaped our notice. The next morning, we tried to trace the person who had put it there, but could not, and finally returned the ladder to the police. The same evening, while casually chatting, I asked Baba, 'What will you do if thieves come? You are a follower of Gandhiji and believe in non-violence.' Baba promptly retorted, 'I will tell them, 'Here are the keys to treasury. You can gladly take away whatever you want and next day if you feel guilty, fast for a day for the purification of your soul'. We were amused by his answer.

We slept in the rooms on the ground floor. It was the month of December and it was cold. We had closed the doors and windows of our rooms tightly. Baba slept in the room upstairs with the door and the windows open. It was Baba's habit from childhood to get up at 3 a.m., so that night when he opened his eyes around that time, he saw two human figures with knives in their hands entering the room from the terrace. The most surprising thing was that he could see the thieves, only because he had changed the direction of his feet while sleeping, that very night on my instructions! The thieves were completely unaware of Baba's presence; they could not see him. They entered the room and turned towards the staircase, which directly led to the rooms downstairs. Baba knew that we were in our rooms downstairs. In order to keep the thieves away from us, he yawned loudly and diverted their attention. The next minute one of the two thieves was beside Baba's bed, the knife pointed at Baba's head. Baba waited for a minute, and then, all of a sudden, he pulled the thief down into his bed by tightly closing his legs round the thief's waist. Baba was a good wrestler and knew all the techniques of wrestling very well. The thief's efforts to free himself were unsuccessful, and in desperation, he bit Baba's toe with such strength that Baba's hold loosened immediately. This toe had been causing him pain since the previous night. Now, it was an open fight. Baba's prowess in evading the thief's knife and kicking him at the same time was commendable. He held the thief's hand (with the knife) tight. The other thief tried to stab Baba with his knife. Baba fought them off fearlessly. He kicked one of them in the stomach so hard that he sent the man rolling back in pain. But the thief had his revenge before he absconded. His knife made a deep gash on Baba's head. Baba almost fainted, but kept on fighting the other thief in that condition. Since he held the thief's hand (the one with the knife) tightly, his fingers were bleeding as well.

Baba was not so familiar with our house but the thieves seemed to have known every corner of it. He pushed Baba into the gallery and jumped over it. He had jumped from the height of fifteen to twenty feet and was injured when he fell to the ground, moaning in pain. We were fast asleep on the ground floor only to be awakened by Baba's loud call. We immediately rushed to his room. What a terrible sight it was! A blood bath from top to toe! His clothes and the bed cover were fully drenched in blood. There was a splatter of blood on the wall too. All of us were shocked. I fainted.

Baba received seven to eight injuries two of which – one on the head and the other on the shoulder – were serious. His eye had a narrow escape. Even in that condition Baba's penchant for humour and wit surfaced. He asked, 'If I become blind, will you still marry me?' I promptly replied, 'By all means. Your blindness will be an emblem of pride for me. I love you a hundred times more for your heroism.' In the morning, Baba was admitted to the Mayo hospital. They stitched and dressed his wounds. People thronged to the hospital to see Baba. It was now my privilege to nurse him. Many of Baba's friends, especially the wrestlers and their sort openly appreciated Baba's fortitude. His sister too was with us in the hospital.

Baba's honesty and simplicity often surfaced in casual conversations. He once shared a few things close to his heart with my elder sister Shanta Mankikar. Baba did not hesitate to tell her that when he came to our home for the first time, he was decided on remaining a bachelor for the rest of his life. But he changed his mind after meeting me. His confidence became apparent when he confessed to my sister that he was then convinced that he would be doing a good thing by marrying me and that I was the first and the last woman in his life. For him all other women were either sisters or mothers. He also went on to tell my sister that, if his proposal was turned down by my family, his life would change its direction. While Baba talked to my sister I was eavesdropping because I had never talked to Baba till then. When he was about to leave, he told my sister, 'I have lost my heart to Indu and I have to drag my feet to go home.'

Baba's words kept ringing in my ears throughout the night. Such an open confession of love at first sight! Ecstacy was mine. Sleep was miles away. How I wished he had stayed on. To know that someone is longing and pining for you! The next day my sister sent a note to him saying that his proposal had been accepted. I need not tell you that he was excited too. One thing that has always fascinated me is Baba's capacity for joy, and his unrestrained expression of it. And this has not withered with time. I have derived much pleasure from such cherished moments in our life.

However, this joy did not last long. The arrival of a very close relative the very next day created a commotion. He vehemently opposed this marriage and took everyone to task for accepting the proposal. It did not take much time for the others to change their mind. My sister was the first to do this. The next day when Baba came, the scene had completely changed. It was Baba's wish that the wedding be arranged during the rainy season. My sister however refused to give him her word and said that there was still enough time to think about it. She was very much against there being a long interval between the engagement and the actual wedding. She did not hesitate to tell Baba that he should rethink his decision to marry me.

Baba was shocked. Tears welled up in his eyes. What could he have done? Being a thorough gentleman, he did not even ask for the reason for breaking up the informal engagement. My feelings were not very different from his. I could not bring myself to accept this decision. But I was not strong enough to assert myself either. I wept and wept. I wanted to tell my family that I did not want to break off the engagement, but my courage failed me. Later, I regretted this timidness. But I was so shy!

Baba left for Dharampeth and sent a note with his brother saying, 'I am returning all of Indu's letters. My principles do not allow me to keep a young girl's letters with me. It is not good for either of us. I am sending them back lest I should be tempted to misuse them some day.' The note contained one line for me, 'May you live happily for ever my love; my heart be with you though.' My heart melted away as I read that and I was won over. I do not know how I got the strength to fight them all, but I had changed completely. I told them not to think about my life and declared to them that I wanted to marry only Baba. They must have thought me audacious to do so. But nothing could have changed my decision. I left no alternative for them but to accept my wish. We immediately left for Dharampeth in a tonga. Everything was explained to Baba and he too was happy about my firm stand.

Now all the impediments were cleared. The marriage was now formally settled. Both of us now longed for each other's company. Being a girl and belonging to an orthodox family I could not visit his house before the wedding, but he came to mine quite often. This did not meet with the approval of our elders. His visits became a matter of ridicule for them. I told you that Baba never cared for others' opinions. Like all legendary lovers, he turned a deaf ear to what they said. All lovers think alike; they speak the same language and perhaps act in the same manner. He never allowed custom to rule his conduct. As the saying goes, everything is fair in love and war. And isn't love a kind of war too? When his conscience echoes his feelings, he does not wait for others' endorsement and proceeds rapidly towards his goal with unparalleled energy. His progress is never hampered by customs and propriety. I am exactly the opposite. I never had the courage to violate norms, written or unwritten. The question, 'What will people say?' is always uppermost in my mind. I cannot endure the tongue of mockery, whereas Baba easily makes a sport of it. However, Baba's company worked a miracle. It was like coming out of a cocoon. I found my voice now. Baba's skill in making even the dumb speak is unparalled. Whenever he came to see me, children would spy on us. It hardly made any difference to him. He became aggressive in his courtship now, because he thought it was his right, but the iron curtain of custom and convention divided us. His moods were continually changing. Sometimes in utter desperation he used to say, 'Oh, you are so near and yet so far'. Nevertheless he has a way of getting things done as he wills. Instead of waiting for opportunities, he would create them or snatch them. He was far from being a bashful lover.

The longing grew stronger day by day. He wanted to be with me for as much time as possible. When it was time for him to leave, he would have to drag his feet with a lot of effort. Once, he was so reluctant to leave (in those days he never stayed overnight as none would have liked it) that he went to the other room and sat in a meditative pose. He pretended to meditate while he shot furtive glances at me. I was fasting that day. So I had a bowl of kheer in my hands when I stepped in to the room in which Baba was striking a pose. I took a bowl of kheer made of sago and came out. It was my turn to be surprised—Baba had closed his eyes and joined his hands in prayer. This was unlike him. Moreover, what he did on that day went against the rules he had made for himself. He refrained from eating sugar or jaggery as a rule, but on that day he asked for a bowl of kheer. On my refusing to give it, he snatched it from my hands and tasted a bit of it. During the four months of courtship such moments of romance were not far and few between. It cost me my well-earned name in our house.

There was no electricity in the house then. Lanterns were what we used. I liked cleaning the glass shade, and then lighting the oil lamp before the idol of our family god. These lamps consumed up to 250 kgs of edible oil at a time, but oil was quite cheap in those days. My brother once said to Baba jokingly, 'You will get Indu if you can set up electric lamps in your house.' It was a coincidence that it was Baba who first brought the electric lights to our house.

Many things in our life happened through chance and coincidence. After Baba's first visit to our house, he shared information about me and my family with the members of his family. But no one suspected that he had marriage on his mind. During the first year after my sister's marriage, she was supposed to perform the mangal-gauri pooja (a ritual commonly performed by newly-wed women in Maharashtra). Around that time, my sister and I were in Dharampeth. Both of us were searching for her sister-in-law's house in Dharampeth. We had no idea that Baba's house was in the same area. Baba was in Warora at that time. While walking by, we came across a nameplate on which flashed the name 'Amte'. We hurriedly tried to walk past the house but Baba's younger sister saw us from the terrace and caught up with us. I wondered how she recognised me, but she invited us to come in. We bowed to Baba's father and after exchanging pleasantries, left for our destination. Baba's father had already heard from Baba about us. When I saw Baba's photograph in the house, something clicked in my mind.

After my marriage to Baba, his sister told me about their father's first reaction on seeing me on that day, 'How good will it be if this girl honours us by being the daughter-in-law of this house! But Baba will not marry.'

THREE

The sun rose a little early on the 18th of December 1946. Baba, a bridegroom in bandages, came straight from the hospital looking like a prisoner released on parole. He did not want to postpone the wedding. More people attended it than we expected. Some came for love; others out of curiosity; and quite a few with raised eyebrows. The wedding was performed in the traditional vedic style despite Baba's displeasure. But what could he do? He had neither the choice nor the right to force me into a rebellion against custom until I got married. Ever since, he has never allowed the priest to enter our house on any occasion, whether auspicious or ominous.

Baba's discomfort was evident during the wedding ceremony. It was not because he was being forced to do something that he disliked (taking part in a ceremony). It was not a question of mere violation of his likes and dislikes but something more than that. Something more serious was at stake. It was for him, an act of disrespecting reason. I have already told you that Baba does not believe in ritual or idol-worship. He has more faith in reason. Consequently, I lost my ease throughout the ceremony and was relieved when it was over.

Ceremonies and rituals punctuated the happiest day of our life—the day of our union. But neither of us could escape them. Moreover, they are a form of social sanction too. For a little while, the lover in Baba receded into the background. The sight of the priest awakened his fury. He fretted and fumed the whole time. In the holy fire, he sacrificed his obedience and since then it has become my property. I have kept it to this day. I have seen the duel between the husband and the lover in him. The two lie side by side—whether the dominating husband is victorious over the lover or the tenderhearted lover asserts himself, the passionate intensity of his emotions is striking.

The respectable Kamaltai Hospet took charge of all the arrangements for the wedding on Baba's side. Baba's guests lodged in her maternity home. A lot of people related to Baba in one way or the other came from Warora. Our wedding had created a ripple amongst many of Baba's friends and 'foes'. Of the latter, many of them did not lose the opportunity to openly criticise Baba for his ways. According to them, it was a serious lapse, an immoral act on Baba's part to stay overnight in our house before the wedding. It was against the social conventions. They were under the impression that Baba would have no courage to show up in Warora because of all this. The thought that they had removed an obstacle from their path pleased them a great deal, because Baba enjoyed an enviable position in social circles at that time. He was either the president or the secretary in no less than sixteen organisations. Whereas, amongst friends, it was curiosity mingled with joy.

A typical Indian wedding is an elaborate affair. Of the myriad rituals and ceremonies, the special lunch is the most popular. It is customary for the bride and groom to take a bite of the sweets offered by each to the other. They offer it along with a piece of rhyming verse in which is interwoven the name of the partner (calling your partner by his or her first name publicly is allowed on this occasion). Baba excelled in this too. When my turn came, I gave him a befitting answer in verse and received compliments from the people. In fact, I had started taking lessons to prove myself as a perfect match for Baba in every sense.

We spent the first month of our married life in the house in Dharampeth. Baba was seriously wounded in the fight with the thieves and the wounds were still fresh. He was on medication.

I was often torn between my duties towards Baba and those towards my in-laws. Moreover, Baba had demanded that I personally answer all his calls as he lay in bed. This was again, against the custom. I failed to win over my in-laws because both of us were too modern in our ways and fell short of their expectations.

I would have happily changed my ways for them, but Baba would have none of it. Very rarely did I stand before Bapuji (my father-in-law). Talking to him was next to impossible. He was reticent and in fact, was worried about Baba's adventure with the thieves. My in-laws strongly disapproved of Baba for staying overnight in our house before the wedding. Consequently, I stepped into house with a feeling that I was not in their good books.

Bapuji was a strict disciplinarian. He believed in the ideal of self-help. He never allowed anyone to wash his clothes or even make his bed. I used to feel bad about this as I was so eager to do all these things for him. All my efforts were rendered futile because he refused to change his routine. To tell you the truth, it pained me to see him doing things himself. Another disadvantage for me was that I was not a very good cook. And I was so shy that I never took any initiative to improve this relationship. I could see how Baba struggled to try and put me in their favour. But his own position in the house was no better than mine. He was an unconventional husband in many ways. He helped me make chapattis, shared the housework. It was uncommon in those days. Moreover, Baba's illness forced me to spend more time with him in the house even in the presence of elderly people. This too was not socially acceptable. In a joint family, this was considered audacity and modernity of an undesirable kind. Had we gone to Warora immediately after the wedding, there would never have been any misconceptions about me (we realised the mistake rather late). I was misunderstood by my in-laws, especially Bapuji, for a long time.

The thought that we were deprived of the blessings of our own parents even though we received them from thousands of others, haunted me for years. But god was kind enough to hear my prayers. During the last days of Bapuji's life, the misunderstandings and misconceptions between us were cleared. Bapuji showered love on me. He started calling me Indudevi. I felt happy that I could serve him at least for a few days. He was far from being fastidious or fussy. I blamed my fate for not giving me the opportunity to serve this mahatma earlier. However, I consoled myself with the thought that finally we were reconciled. During this final phase, even his relationship with Baba improved considerably. On the other hand, there was nothing that Baba would not have done for him. He would sleep by his side, gathering his frail frame in his arms just as he would have done with a child. Bapuji suffered from throat cancer and despite the pain, kept telling everyone how proud he was of having a son like Baba and how happy he was to have found a perfect match for him in me. I consider it the greatest fortune in our life that both Baba and I could look after him at least in his last days.

We spent about two months in the joint family at Nagpur. Living with an extended family calls for a different code of conduct and we disqualified ourselves with our behaviour; our ways were too modern for others. Baba used to say his prayer in the morning. It was usually very long. In course of time, I learnt it by heart by just listening to him.

I was the eldest daughter-in-law in the house. Naturally, I was expected to do all the housework. In the first few days of our married life, as with anybody else, romance had top priority. Baba was inventive in this art and created plenty of opportunities. He expected me to be by his side when the prayer ended (the husband and the lover were active at the same time). I would usually be in the kitchen and on hearing the last verse of his prayer, would rush to his room. Failing to do so demanded a heavy price from me; tempers would rise in no time. I could not make him understand that in a joint family, even such simple acts of romance were next to impossible. And even if I tried, no explanation would have done for him. He always wanted things his way. His expression of anger too was like that of a child; neither controlling nor hiding anything. In some personal matters he cared only for the result and never bothered about the means; by which he would get it; never worried about breaking customs. In public life though, the means were as important as the end.

It is the greatest misfortune of my life that I could not meet Baba's mother before she sank into insanity. Years before I stepped into Baba's house, she had bid farewell to our world. She was free from all bondage. Her insanity was the greatest tragedy that struck Baba's family and had obliterated all their aspirations and hopes. By the time I got married, they had accepted this agonising reality. Only time could have given them the equanimity to accept this. It grieved me to think about our loss; she could have been our greatest source of strength, our anchor. Baba was in fact, the apple of her eye. Being the first son in the family, he was pampered by her and before she degenerated into this state, would dream of her prospective daughter-in-law. She was full of life and took interest in everything. She excelled at knitting, embroidery and cooking. She was obviously very upset when Baba took the vow of celibacy. But later on, when Baba changed his mind and decided to marry, she was ecstatic. She was eager to see me. I remember vividly, even today, how her face glowed with joy. I had a strong yearning to see her too, because I had heard a lot about her from Baba. The incident of Baba's fight with the thieves, however, created a barrier in our relationship.

The attack was linked up with Baba's passion for me, and that, they thought, was the cause of this accident. I was so daunted by such misunderstandings, that it was difficult for me to improve things. Baba tried his best to improve my relationship with his mother but the fear in my mind led me to make more mistakes. Besides, I was new to everything. Many a time, in desperation, Baba used to sneak out of the house under the pretence of some important work, because he thought I was being an obstinate and disobedient wife. I was both embarrassed and pained on such occasions. I used to wait for him to return. But I must tell you one thing; no matter what happened, we always ate our dinner together. No matter how late he arrived, I never ate before he came. Baba made another rule—that we were not to spend the night brooding over the little bickerings of the day. Tears, from both the sides, wiped away all traces of the day's skirmishes. Strangely enough, Baba's anger evaporated with the entry of love. When his anger crossed a certain limit, love, which was never far behind and perhaps stronger than his fury, always intervened. The key to our fruitful relationship and successful partnership lies in this dual nature. Of course, I felt hurt whenever I was the victim of these little misunderstandings and surprisingly enough, even before they were cleared my anger and agony melted away in tears, which always came in torrents. I often wonder 'What a strange man and what a queer combination of qualities! Here is a man who plants love everyday but never bothers to remove the weeds of misunderstanding. Had he taken a little more trouble to transform these weeds, harmless though, into a fertilizer, the tree of our love would have grown bigger and the image of Baba, far more attractive than it is.' However, I did not love him the less for it. And he has many other endearing qualities. To forgive and forget is his greatest virtue; a rare thing. I suppose, it is god-given. How many of us forget anger, hatred or enmity as easily as he does? How many of us can normalise relations as if nothing had happened? Baba has this rare capacity, this resilience. He would almost lay down his life if you go to him in full faith and a chaste heart. Just as bitter medicine is conducive to health, the readiness to accept failure and frustration is essential for success in life. It is a matter of sadhana (systematic training). Unconditional love, which is just another name for it, can work this miracle. It just happens, you do not have to do anything.

Baba's overwhelming and continuous flow of love made me forget everything, even my maternal home. I remember visiting my mother's house only once during my one and half months' stay in Nagpur after marriage. It is quite common for newly married girls to talk about their in-laws to their parents and get some parental sympathy. I made an exception to this rule. First of all, I did not have any serious problems with anyone in Baba's family and even if somebody hurt me, I always spoke highly of my in-laws before my parents. It will not be an exaggeration to say that our marriage proved to be a deviation from norms, from age-old, time respected customs and conventions.

Let me tell you about my first visit to my parents' home after the wedding. In a typical middle-class family, gold ornaments play a crucial role in deciding the status and the happiness of the newly wedded girl. My parents were shocked to see me without a single piece of jewellery. Women in the neighbourhood taunted me. The piquant flavour of their remarks was unbearable. And I was not audacious enough to answer back. They left nothing unsaid, 'Look at the nun. Do you believe she is newly married?', someone jeered.

Time passed. It flew, I should say. It was the month of February; Baba was eager to shift to Warora. Many of his friends eagerly awaited our arrival. I was busy picturing myself and our life at Warora. My thoughts travelled faster than the bus. All the 'dream pictures' of our future were painted in the colours of the rainbow.

Baba's friends had planned to escort us from the station to our house in a procession, with a local band playing music. But knowing fully well that Baba would not like it, they gave up the idea. My first step into our house in Warora lifted my spirit, despite its unshapely appearance and the littered rooms. After all it was our home. A feeling of peace, a sense of freedom and security in being in my own house filled my mind. It was also clear within minutes, from the things littered all over, that it was until now the house of a bachelor. The rooms had not been cleaned in months perhaps. It was as if the house was waiting for me, for a woman's touch, all these years.

There was a large gathering of people there. They were surprised. Baba's entry into matrimony was a pleasant shock for them. We were given a very warm welcome. Some others, especially Baba's opponents, who had thought that Baba would not have the courage to return to Warora, were suitably answered by our arrival. Their disappointment did not escape our eyes. But we had no time to waste over such trifling matters. As soon as the people left we got down to work. There was a lot of cleaning and sweeping to be done. In the evening, Baba helped me clean up the house. Little acts of love, these spontaneous responses from Baba, have always been the foundations of our partnership, in both pain and pleasure. There was never any conscious division of rights and duties and, so we never fought over them. Nothing stemmed from (there were none) premeditated intellectual positions, about the equality of men and women, women's liberation or eternal male domination. We did fight a lot and we do even today, but never over the rights and duties of men and women. That is why I call ours the labour of love. Nothing could obstruct this free flow of love. I am not only talking about our personal life. Our work together and my share in it too is purely out of love. Baba's philosophy of 'care and share' began at home and extended to a large section of society where it was needed—to lepers, the destitute, the physically handicapped, orphans, the tribal and the displaced.

Baba was good at tasks which were considered feminine in those days: cooking, for example. He never thought it below his dignity to do the cooking and mind you, the food used to have a special taste when we cooked together. This was our world, with its simple little joys which might stand in complete contrast with the expensive pleasures of today's fast life. Every corner of our life, private or public, was lit up by this mutual love. We also received immense love and support from the people we lived and worked with. As Baba always says, we are affluent in love.

On the third day of our arrival in Warora, we were given a warm welcome by the harijans in their colony—a humble hutment with public sanitation and common water supply. Baba was their leader at that time. Very few people of the higher castes attended that function. The speeches these humble people made were full of praises, blessings and good wishes. Baba also expressed his heartfelt gratitude in return. The stage on which we sat was carefully decorated. They gave us silver images of Gandhiji and Netaji as wedding gifts. Accepting gifts was against our discipline, but we could not disrespect their sentiments. Finally, when we bowed down to the elderly, they were overwhelmed.

I was brought up in a house in which being a brahmin meant a strict adherence to the practice of untouchability. Brahmins never drank the water touched by the harijans and if ever touched by a harijan even by mistake, one had to purify oneself by taking a bath. In my mother's house, before my marriage, I had observed these conventions faithfully and religiously. Most of the fruit sellers used to be harijans and I also remember having changed my clothes after buying fruit from one. And here I was, among them, on the third day of our arrival in Warora. I left the stage and sat among the women. It was their custom to wave their hands round the body and from head to toe, to ward off evil drawn towards the newly wed. While warding off the evil, they did not forget to keep a good distance from me. Many of them came from the caste of the scavengers. It was their habit, forced by the curse of untouchability, to distance themselves from the higher castes. This was the result of the continuous humiliation they had to suffer in society. They dared not touch me and were even scared and they cringed when I put kumkum on their forehead. Some were a little bolder and asked me if I would take a bath after going home. I assured them that I would not. They were astonished. This incident helped reduce the distance between us. Now they did not hesitate to visit our house regularly. I also started teaching some of their women and children. Baba's sister sometimes joined me in this. But the joy did not last long.

The news, that the harijans visited our house, reached our landlord and we were asked to vacate the house immediately. Having lost our roof, we went to stay with Shri R. K. Patil (Dada), Baba's bosom friend. He also offered us his old deserted bungalow on the outskirts of the village along with seven and half acres of his land for our experiment in community living. This bungalow was situated right in the middle of a jungle, the natural habitat of vipers and scorpions. The land was barren. I can never forget Dada's contribution to our experiment. Not only did he give us land, but also shared the work. He would clean the rice regularly as if it was his duty.

Nightly visits to the harijan colonies became a part of our routine now. Baba knew a number of patriotic songs composed in praise of Mother India. Both of us taught them these songs and got them to learn these by heart. We did it religiously. For a few others, it was a subject of ridicule. Baba struggled to create an awareness among the harijans about their basic rights. Baba's speeches were generally on topics such as the injustice meted out by the higher classes and castes, and the atrocities perpetrated by some of the rich on the poor. They had a magical effect on the listeners. They were inspired.

They began to realise the importance of cleanliness. Baba's efforts soon bore fruit. They were motivated to take up the cleaning of their area. They even cleared out and prepared a ground for wrestling. Such little acts by both sides built the bridge between us. Baba commanded tremendous respect. This had its seamy side too. It was interpreted as a deliberate attempt to pit the untouchables against the higher castes. Some labelled Baba as a communist.

Severe criticism poured in from every corner. For us, it was merely a matter of getting used to it and Baba did not care about all this. Instead, he went a step further. He now made efforts to seek free entry for the harijans in a hotel. The harijan community consisted mostly of the lower castes such as the scavengers, the cobblers, the mahars and those who made bamboo baskets, ropes and brooms. One day Baba entered the hotel with the representatives of each one of these communities.

The owner of the hotel was flabbergasted when he saw Baba with these people. Against his wishes he had to offer tea to all. But later on, he separated the cups used by them. Eventually Baba received many threats, not directly but indirectly. They even started pelting stones at our house at night, though no one was ever caught. Baba's fearlessness surpassed these dark deeds. Nothing could unnerve him or stop him from doing what he believed in. His indestructible faith in himself, coupled with his all-embracing concern, manifested itself in creative acts such as the ones described above. This was a period of political turmoil too, the late forties, when the freedom movement was at its peak. Baba was fighting for the liberation of the social outcasts on Gandhian lines. He saw no difference between the suffering of the untouchables and that of the political prisoners who were condemned to live in the notorious prison houses of the Andaman and Nicobar Islands.

Baba had stopped practicing law a month before our wedding. He was the vice president of the municipality at Warora then. He was also an honorary member and office bearer in many institutions. Naturally, many people came to our house for something or the other. Our privacy and freedom, gained after some struggle and, indeed, much needed during those early days of marriage, was continually threatened by thronging visitors. And neither of us knew the art of avoiding people. Sometimes we had to invent excuses to keep out people who had little work but would hang around anyway. At other times hours would pass before we could sit down for a meal. A meal at the appointed hour became a luxury for us.

When these things got on our nerves, Baba resigned all his memberships except for his vice-presidency of the municipality. It was during this period that I saw Baba's selflessness and many other qualities. I have vivid memories of that day. Baba had gone out on some work. I was alone at home, busy with the housework. Two men entered the courtyard, perhaps with trepidation in their heart. They carried a sack filled to its capacity. They looked like fishermen. I told them that Baba was not at home. They said, 'All right. We will come later. We have brought this for you.' And without waiting for my reply they dumped the sack in the passage and went away. Curiously I looked into the sack; it was full of rice. I got back to my work. I forgot the men and the sack they brought. Baba returned home in the evening. As soon as he entered the house, the sack caught his attention. 'What is this?', he enquired; and before I could complete my report, up went the sack with all its contents scattered all over the courtyard. As if this was not enough, the two men turned up at the same moment. Fire emanated from Baba's mouth leaving the two half-dead. They were completely baffled by Baba's reaction to their gift because it was a common practice, almost an unwritten law, to offer such gifts in return for getting the contract allowing them to fish in the lake. They were shocked by Baba's fury at what they thought was courtesy. Finally, expressing regret, they went away. After some time Baba cooled down. It was a lesson for me; an example of the purity of thought and action especially required of those involved in social service. I felt enriched.

Baba's creative eccentricities showed up not only in his public life but in our private life as well. His obsessions and obstinacies, like his passion, are incurable. His capacity to completely involve himself in everything he does is amazing. In the early days of our marriage, a late marriage at that, his world revolved around me. There were no constraints of a regular job. We made the most of our time then. At that time he was the trustee of the Korgaonkar Trust and received Rs 150 as an honorarium. In fact, we did not need much. Our needs were minimum. Being nomadic in spirit and lifestyle, we never wasted time and energy worrying about the future. Nor did pleasure mean rest from work. We never made any distinction between work and leisure. You may think I am being proud in telling these things to you. But in all humbleness, I am only trying to present the facts before you. I do not know whether our horoscopes matched perfectly. But to tell you the truth, love was the driving force behind everything. I was talking to you about our early days. The cup of life was filled to the brim, the world was colourful and the ardour invincible. Those were the days when our spirits were carefree but our minds forever contemplating. Except for a pain in the back and a cough, which was perhaps the result of Baba's fight with the thieves, Baba never had problems with his health in those days. But giving the report to the Trust every month was a problem because there was not much work going on.

My memories of those early days are made up of elements of excitement, adventure, panic and ecstasy. People and places continue to haunt me even today. Details of apparently trifling incidents compel me to luxuriate in the emotions, moods and waves they elicit. Our village lay five miles from Warora. It was a feudal country estate then (it is history now). We decided to go there. A bullock cart was ordered. After all, it was the word of the zamindar (Baba is the son of the zamindar). A pair of strong and sturdy white oxen, arrived next morning. Baba loved to drive a bullock cart. The oxen were handsome, but rather wild. No one except Baba could control them. A slight push and off they went speeding past trees until they reached the destination. The path was enchanting, flanked by trees on both the sides, the shallow furrows made by the wheels, the jingle of the bells round their neck and the continual bumps. No other elixir would have done for newly weds like us. On our way, the river Wardha opened its waterway. We could not have passed it unless Baba had his swim, and a long one, until butterflies in his stomach drove him out of the stream. He never liked me to carry tiffin with us wherever we went. He preferred freshly prepared food. Making an oven by putting stones together and cooking rice was a pleasure he would have never missed even for sweets and such kind. A simple but freshly cooked meal, even rice and curry, would do for him. Today, we travel on wheels but the rules for food are still the same. In those days he used to help me with the cooking. It was paradise. Our journeys together have been marked by such laborious little acts but we have always relished simple, natural things. It involved a heart-to-heart dialogue with nature. Sometimes I would ask questions, especially related to agriculture. I could not identify the crops unless they were fully grown. I could never tell what the saplings were. When my ignorance was exposed, I used to feel ashamed.

The news that the zamindar was coming to the village with his bride had spread from village to village. People thronged to see us. Their curiosity to see me was not misplaced because someone like Baba had broken the vow of celibacy for me. They were looking at me as if I was an object in a museum. I felt awkward. It was our custom to bow down to elderly people, not just join hands in namaste but also lie prostrate before them as a sign of respect. Baba bowed to them irrespective of their social status, their caste or religion. Many of them belonged to the harijan community. I was being educated in the school of life by Baba. Ever since, I have never hesitated in bowing to elders, whatever their social status. In fact, according to the custom, it was the zamindar and his wife that had people bowing to them. We made a departure from these conventions of our caste and class. Why, we gladly bowed down to the elderly servants in the house too. Some people take pride and pleasure in money, others in the talent they are gifted with, but for us the heartfelt blessings of these humble folk have always been more valuable than anything else and they have lasted us our lifetime. Without them, we would not have been able to steer clear of the snags in life's journey. As for myself, the conviction that I can safely follow Baba's footsteps everywhere and my complete faith in his righteousness gave me the courage to take this untrodden path. In fact, nothing is unusual when you choose it at your will. The only natural thing is to follow your own nature. It did not take long for the mind-forged manacles of conventions to drop. Nothing like the sense of liberation of the spirit that one enjoys then! You cannot call it adjustment because adjustment involves an awareness of going against your inclinations or a deal, a contract where there are considerations of profit and loss. Between Baba and me, the only bond was the bond of love. Nothing could ever shake it or break it. That is why we could hold our hearts together through turbulent storms. It also made us tolerant of each other's failings, shortcomings and eccentricities.

If I were to record each and every incident in our life, this story would be too long. And as I have said earlier, selection is difficult. More difficult is omission. Besides, when you start walking down memory lane, one path leads on to another, and you do not know where you started from. Details pop up, pressing for inclusion in this omnibus and if you are not aware, you are likely to lose your way.

So the journey to our village, which was marked more by breaks than by continuous stretches, was more than a simple trip from one place to another. We often met interesting people on the way. People always interested us as much as anything else. At one of the places, kunabi Patil's family arranged dinner for us. Baba never had a problem as he could eat in any house. Mine was a different case. Till then I had never eaten a meal in any house other than a brahmin's. Our host looked very worried. He thought it a sin to make me eat in his house. He immediately sent for a brahmin to cook for me. When I came to know about it, I felt uneasy and insisted on sharing the same food that was prepared for all. I will not say that I had to make special efforts to change myself or grow out of the time-honoured beliefs imposed by my upbringing. My faith in Baba made everything easy. I never lost my ease over such matters. The menu for dinner was interesting—the special dishes were puranpoli (sweet chapatti) and pakodas (very spicy as would suit the taste of the people of the village). I would have gladly had both but for Baba. At that time Baba was very strict about what he ate. Like the other vows, he had made a rule for himself not to consume sugar, chilli, milk (except cow's milk) and spices. He observed this strictly at all times. So Baba ate some plain rice and dal. I wanted to eat the puranpoli, and although Baba would have never stopped me from doing it, there was something in me that held me back. To tell you the truth, our tastes in food did not match at all. But I accepted his indirect domination willingly. Later, I tried to change his taste by changing his heart, and succeeded considerably. I thought it was indeed an injustice to the people not to taste the food. However, at that time, Baba's rules were more important for him than people's feelings.

We left immediately after dinner. After one and a half hours ride we reached our ancestral estate. The servants in the house joined us before we entered the village. They ran before the cart, as was the custom, in spite of our loud protests. When we got out of the cart, we could see thousands of pairs of eyes lit up in admiration. Warm water was offered to wash our feet. They rushed in to pay us their respect—there was a lot of pushing and jostling for it. There was something special about it. They held their toes as they bowed down. Baba was helpless. Somehow he managed to gently push back the older members and then both of us bowed to them. Their joy knew no bounds.

This was all new to me as I was born and brought up in an urban setting. I had never been to a village until I married Baba. The simple village folk, their ways of life, their love, their problems, their aspirations and their miseries had become a part of my life now. Everything changed. Baba changed too. Who would have believed that a sanyasi like Baba would become a romantic lover? I do not know whether there is anything common between the two. Before marriage Baba in his peculiar outfit of a sanyasi, long hair, beard and loose cassock, carrying a staff in the hand, held a sway over the people in the village. They were familiar with Baba's morning bhajans, marches, sweeping and cleaning but everything changed after I arrived. They might have thought of me as a woman who had seduced their leader. But this had its bright side too. Women now made bold to come and talk to him freely. Earlier his celibacy had forced them to brand him as a misanthrope and naturally, they were scared of him. On the other hand, it had boosted his ego. But now there was a sea change in his image. They were no longer overawed by him. Instead, they became quite friendly. They started sending us vegetables, as a gesture of neighbourly love. We received invitations to dinner. For them, I was the daughter-in-law from a renowned family. But my conduct broke this image quite often. I did things, which were least expected from a newly wedded bride from a renowned family, like going out for a walk with Baba every morning and evening. We would have our lunch and dinner together. Our parley voo also shocked people. What could I do? It was not my fault. I only obeyed Baba's wish. I was obedience incarnate. Our favourite haunts took us away from the village. The older people of the village were worried by this. They believed that these places were haunted or that evil spirits dwelt among the tamarind trees. They also felt that as a new bride, I was more vulnerable to the evil spirits. I could understand their anxiety for us. But there was no question of giving in to their superstitions, even though it was a gesture of selfless love.

Most of our early days together were spent in our ancestral village. We had some property there and we lived like free birds without any compulsions or constraints. It felt like eternal spring. Being our own masters, we used to set out for long rides, in our petrol-free four wheeler, the bullock cart. Disregarding all the social norms we went sporting anywhere, anytime, with minimum cooking equipments. There were many enchanting spots around. I remember our first excursion to a place not far from the village. There was an old devi temple surrounded by nature's bounty; a murmuring brook, shady bowers, the temple beside the stream; its ancient architecture speaking of the old times to which it belonged; it was perhaps built in the well-known Hemadpanthi style. Baba is not an atheist, but as I told you, he hates idol-worship. He would not pray even as a formality. Baba and formalities have never gone hand-in-hand. He firmly holds his ground in matters of reason and strongly opposes rituals. Belief and faith in an unseen power he certainly has. But his ways of acknowledging it are rational. There was never any confusion in his mind. I have often wondered at his clarity of vision, his unflinching confidence in himself and his conviction about the truth. However, he would not impose anything on me. He never entered the temple, but respecting my faith in god, he took me there. And once convinced about his antagonism towards idol worship, I never insisted on his visiting the temple. As far as I understand, he hates ritual worship as he does communal antagonism, especially that between the untouchables and the higher castes.

We mostly wandered through rural areas. The spots by the riverside were our favourites. Baba is innately fascinated by water and caves. Nothing would stop him from venturing into a cave. Once, on finding one beside a stream, he proceeded to take a bath and then entered the cave. He cleared a patch of ground and sat down, hands joined in his favourite prayer. His beard had been growing for at least five to six months. I looked on. His beard reminded me of Vishwamitra. There is something common to both of them, I thought. Both of them are made of the same stuff perhaps. He started muttering his favourite lines, 'Weary eyed I waited . . . .' I was laughing to myself, wondering why he was singing this line when I was so close to him and I asked him. He only smiled.

Our next halt was at the farmhouse of a small Marwari businessman from Hinganghat, just next to a small place called Shindi. Here too people poured in to see us, as they would do to see circus animals perhaps. The host was a perfect gentleman and his hospitality, par excellence. He brought fresh milk for us in a pitcher, took out his handkerchief and filtered it. Can you fancy somebody filtering milk with a used hanky? This was the best that he could do for us. If you had been in our place what would you have done? Perhaps you would have avoided drinking it by giving some excuse. Imagine our plight. We could not say no. The hanky flashing before our eyes and the man had a cold! My god! We emptied the glass in one gulp. Our ethics did not allow us to disrespect his love—you need all kinds of tolerance in life. It is needed everywhere, even in matters of love. Perhaps our civility demanded it. Where love becomes the primary focus, everything else disappears; out goes fear, disgust, and nausea. Had they not become irrelevant feelings? Baba would have never ventured to associate with the lepers had he not cast those feelings away. Our host too watched us in wonder. It did not take long for us to read his thoughts. He looked at us one by one; what an odd couple, he must have thought. A bearded man and a perfectly urban lady! His silence betrayed everything that his heart wanted to say. We too were amused by his musings.

As the sun set in the west on that day, we arrived at Appaji's house. Appaji Manglikar is simply unforgettable. I had heard about him from Baba. He was known, in that region, as a very enterprising zamindar who had done many experiments in agriculture. He was Baba's close friend. He was undoubtedly delighted to see us and made our fortnight-long stay enjoyable. He was in his forties then, and a romantic by temperament. He was liberal in his views. The reforms he introduced in his small place were proof enough of his liberalism. He owned quite a few orange orchards. There was a small stream that ran through the village. Though it had dried up, it still had dense thickets on both the sides. His wife had gone out of station at that time. In this situation, Appaji conveniently handed over the charge of the kitchen to me. He said to me, 'Now you are the host and I am the guest in this house.' I did not like cooking then, and was far from being a good cook. Here was the challenge for me. I was to cook for Appaji who, unlike Baba, was known for his sharp and crazy culinary instincts. To make the matters worse for me, Appaji's wife was known to be an excellent cook. The thought that I would make a fool of myself gnawed at my mind continually.

But the oven has never betrayed me and I did manage with considerable success. I felt proud that no one starved. I think the absence of Appaji's wife helped me in many ways.

I escaped the criticism I might have been subject to for not being a proficient cook and obviously enjoyed more freedom and privacy. Everything was in our favour; the absence of Appaji's wife (the chief keeper of the house), the verdure of the landscape and the magnanimity of the host. We did not have to follow the sun's diurnal course. Long hours in leafy bowers, among the whispers of birds, the caressing rays of dusk, vibrant spirits, ardent hearts and what else? Nothing more was required. Appaji had everything ready before we returned home, even the food. I used to feel guilty. But what else could I have done? Our age played the mischief. The days had a magical charm. It makes one blind and deaf to everything else, even public censure. Ours was a self-sufficient world and there was immense pleasure in letting ourselves go and drift along with the current without resistance. Nothing else mattered, not even ordinary comforts. Within the world that surrounded us, we carved our own. It was paradise. Only the fortunate can experience this. There is something common to those lucky few; a recklessness of a kind, a passion, a yearning, an intoxication, a longing and and the most prominent of all, an urgency not to waste a single minute. I thought Appaji also must have gone through this experience. That is probably why he was so understanding. He made us feel perfectly at home. People like Appaji are rare in this world.

It was time for us to return to Warora. Promising Appaji that we would come again, we left his house. All these excursions had a rejuvenating effect on us. Nature's beauty and bounty transformed us. But that is not all. We might have closed our eyes but our hearts were open. Self-sufficient, we certainly were; but not complacent. Even a passing thought about our society bound by the chains of custom, tradition and casteism filled our minds with overwhelming gloom. Baba's innate love for the underprivileged would have definitely made him the leader of the dalits in Maharashtra, if he had not come across that leper. Society would have found him on the same pedestal as Ambedkar and Phule. I have been talking more about Baba as a romantic lover and you might be wondering what happened to the social worker. And indeed, you might ask, aren't the two incompatible? My answer is, 'No.' The strain of uninhibited sympathies was there right from the beginning, before we met, from his childhood. Perhaps the streak of romantic madness was an accident. It was a sudden discovery to him and to others as well. But the two have never contended with each other. One quality has been the support for the other. Portraying him as a lover was easier perhaps. Holding a mirror up to his greater love, calls for a mightier pen.

Until Vikas was born we used to regularly visit the territories of the harijans separated from the residential areas of the high castes. For me, it was a metamorphosis, because, before that I never used to drink water even in the house of a saraswat brahmin (because they eat fish). I remember having said this to Madhubhai Pandit once. But once, Baba gave a long lecture to the members of my family, on equality and the futility of the caste system and religion. I was convinced about the truth in his argument and only then gave consent to this marriage.

Our daily contact with the harijans, among whom were members of all lower castes including the untouchables, had its price too. We became outcasts in our own families. No one came to our house, neither from Baba's family nor from mine. According to them, we had indulged in a gruesome act of corruption. It almost amounted to sin. And we were sinners in their eyes. Six months before our marriage, Baba had rented a place. The landlord was a brahmin. When the daily interaction between the harijans and us began, he asked us to leave immediately. People became aggressive in the expression of their hostilities; we had nowhere to go, because there was hardly any place where this problem would not have arisen. In the existing social structure, the taboo against untouchability was so firmly rooted in people's psyche, that no place would have been safe. The mind of the majority was numb to reason. Perhaps they found more security in the prison-house of tradition and blind belief and why not? Tradition makes life easy as there is no burden of thinking for oneself.

We went through some tough times; fighting even for daily necessities, searching for shelter. In the midst of this insane majority, we came across a few beautiful minds. R. K. Patil was Minister for Food at that time. He owned a bungalow near the Muslim cemetery. It was completely deserted except for the rats and such. A thought crossed Baba's mind. He said to me, 'Let us perform an experiment—an experiment in community living. The scavengers, cobblers and all those, who are socially ostracised, will live together with the socially privileged, in that house.' And some twenty or twenty-two of us moved into the house. It wasn't easy though. There was strong opposition from the self-proclaimed custodians of culture and morality, the so-called high-born. They forced us to leave. We then made for R. K. Patil's farm . . . .

FOUR

It was not easy to persuade people to accept our radical views and our novel experiment of equality. Slaves of habit as they were, it was beyond the pale of their imagination to even think of living with the untouchables. Around this time Baba was thinking of another experiment. The idea was that people belonging to all castes – such as the mahars, the cobblers, scavengers, cane workers, and pardhans – should live together, work according to their own capacity and choice, and bring all the earnings together to a community pool. It was called Shramashram (a name given by Shri Yadunath Thatte) and it was an experiment in communism. Baba called us all to come together to live as a community. He wished that the people live together, share their earnings and likewise, share each other's joys and sorrows too. This share-and-care philosophy held a long sway in our private and public life later. I won't even call it a philosophy. It was the simple art of living based on love. Baba never luxuriates in empty speculations. A principle, if not practicable, is discarded; and practicability is not the only test of validity. It has to have the sanction of the conscience.

The experiment began with Shramasharam. At dawn the people went in all directions, looking for work. In the evening, when they returned, they would put their earnings together. The money that was collected was spent on the daily necessities such as food grains, groceries etc. Every evening prayers would be held. Baba also taught them to read and write. Baba strongly believed in the dignity of labour and so he used the small piece of land we owned for growing vegetables. He looked for other means of income too. He would buy goods from the market and sell them at a marginal profit—things of daily use, anything, brooms for example (made from the spine of the cononut leaf), chappals, cutlery, even food grains. Among these things of daily use, there were books on Vinobaji. Books by Gandhiji and Vinobaji were available at Sasta Sahitya Mandal. If Baba failed to find any buyers for the books on any day, he would fast. The railway station was near by, and the passenger train that arrived late at night sometimes fetched buyers for such stuff. Not that it was a profitable source of income, but every pai was important in those days. When the men went away for work, many odd jobs consumed my time. You would not believe perhaps, but picking lice from the girls' hair, giving them a bath and doing their hair became a part of my daily routine and gladly did I do it, for the simple reason that both Baba and I worshipped cleanliness and had a sincere desire to impart to others, everything that we found to be good. I even learnt to make those brooms. It was not easy of course. Often my palms would get scratched and the delicate skin peeled off. I found it quite laborious initially, but soon got used to it. To tell you the truth, difficulties never stopped me from doing anything. When you master the art of making something, the pleasure is the joy of creativity. I became a master artist, excellent brooms I made! The other reason, I told you, was that money was always wanting. Nevertheless, we enjoyed a rare sense of serenity and peace of mind. In the midst of these novel experiences, an interesting thing happened.

Mr R. K. Patil (Dada) was then the food minister of Central Provinces. He was a Gandhian and a very progressive thinker. But he came from a very orthodox family. On one occasion, when his brother's wedding was fixed, he invited Baba. Baba formally received the invitation, but did not forget to tell Dada that he would attend the wedding with his entire family which consisted of all the members of the community including the untouchables. Dada said that he had no objection and insisted that all of them attend the wedding. But on the day of the wedding, when Baba went with his family, all of Dada's relatives were shocked. In fact, Dada had made separate arrangements for their lunch. Baba could not accept this. This kind of discrimination was an insult to his family and he insisted on having lunch with all of them. The host was helpless and there was a bit of a mess during that round of lunch. After this incident, Baba received very few invitations. The orthodox found Baba's revolutionary practices revolting. They ridiculed Baba for his uninhibited participation in the public sanitary services and even I could not escape their scathing criticism. Dada of course apologised to Baba.

It is common knowledge that your first choice restricts the choices available to you in future. You have the freedom to choose only the first thing. The rest follows automatically. If you make your choice consciously, you will never have to regret it. We had made our choice long back. So our struggle continued. On the 27th of October, 1947, Vikas was born. He was born in Warora. There was no question of my going to any other place for the delivery as we ourselves had become outcasts by then. He was the heir of the well-known zamindars, the Amtes, but what he saw on his birth was dire poverty. Nevertheless, the naming ceremony was arranged in the town hall and was attended by the people in Warora. Kamaltai Hospet ordered three cans of ladoos. People brought presents but we returned everything. This earned us their displeasure. This was a rule we had made for ourselves and there was no reason for us to violate it.

The arrival of Vikas in the family was a great relief from a sense of isolation for me. Hours would pass watching his pranks and listening to his babble! Baba was busy and used to be out of the house most of the time. He had many friends too. There was no fixed hour for his return. Sometimes, I got tired of waiting for him. But Vikas distracted my attention and provided the necessary relief. Gradually, Baba also started spending more time in the house.

Baba's elder sister lived in Chindwada. Once we planned a visit to her. We were to travel by train and trains moved at a snail's pace in those days. The railway compartment was overcrowded. Suddenly a voice came from the midst of the crowd 'Aashak mast phakir huei'. Someone was singing Brahmanand's Bhajan, Baba's favourite, in a sweet voice. It was a boy of sixteen or seventeen, with bright sparkling eyes, and a golden voice. Baba was impressed by the waif and asked him to join us. The boy was obviously travelling without a ticket. He came with us to Baba's sister's house. Baba introduced him as his friend. Baba's relatives were not surprised, because by now they were used to such unexpected 'friends'. Therefore, this new friend was given a warm welcome. If Baba took a fancy to someone, it took him no time to form close ties with them and it was never without a reason. Baba possesses a commendable virtue of detecting and appreciating talent in any one. He is almost crazy in his yearning for the good and the beautiful.

When we returned from Chindwada, this boy came with us to Warora and became a member of our family. His name was Gopal Bhatnagar. With tremendous enthusiasm and full absorption, he participated in Baba's novel experiment. Whether it was joining the morning prayers or eating neem leaves, he was with us in everything and everywhere. He joined Baba in his activity of cleaning the public toilets; never behind in selling the books Baba brought. He had an impressive personality and proved himself to be a good salesman. At night Baba used to teach him to read and write. Gopal also helped me in my housework; in everything from cleaning, sweeping and washing to babysitting. One day, all of a sudden, he disappeared. The story behind his disappearance is shocking.

He was on his way home after a day's work. That evening he lost his moneybag while he was on the train between Wardha and Warora. He did not have the courage to come back empty handed even though it was not his fault. So he boarded another train and went away. However, ill luck followed him there too. That was the time when the Razakars, militant muslims, who had strong anti-India feelings, were engaged in anti-national activities. They were especially active in Hyderabad. In order to curb them, a Sikh battalion of the Indian army was deployed at Ballarsha. Gopal was mistaken for a Razakar and was beaten by the army-men travelling in the train. Fortunately, the station master, who knew him, intervened and rang Baba. We were anxious over his disappearance, so Baba immediately left for Ballarsha, but before he reached there, Gopal had already run away. One year after this incident, he came back singing the same song and joined us on our new premises near the cemetery. Vikas was seven months old and Gopal used to take him to the cemetery every day. He sang, sitting on a tombstone, while Vikas played about. He did not stay long this time either. He disappeared once again. We missed him for a long time. It was difficult to forget him. He had endeared himself to all of us within a short time. Only time could heal these wounds.

This autobiography may look like a long chain of events and incidents, material enough for a voluminous novel. But how can I avoid them? Our life is like that, something was always happening or perhaps we invited things; and neither remembering nor forgetting is a voluntary action of the mind. Memory may either fail you or take you along the lanes and by-lanes with an unseen force. Sometimes it is hard to come by, whereas at other times it comes in swiftly, just like the fish in the aquarium, that moves back and forth, up and down, at the slightest stimulation. Moreover, remembering is not something mechanical. On the contrary, memories are complex and variegated. Sometimes you watch your past from a distance, in a state of detachment or at other times you become so engaged with it that you re-enact and relive your past.

Now let me tell you about a most unforgettable incident, a fatal one indeed. It was the rainy season – a quiet evening and an overcast sky accompanied by a continuous drizzle – the last traces of light had already disappeared from the sky. It was time for the lamps to be lit. That evening Baba came home as usual but he was limping. People gathered round him in no time. It was clear that the pain was caused by a snake bite—a deadly viper. The signs were visible on the leg. Baba started sweating. I did not know what to do. I was scared. Baba could not tell what kind of snake it was because he had not seen it. The fiend had attacked in the darkness. What could I do? You know what it is like with simple uneducated folk. Suggestions poured in, someone said, 'Give him green chillies to eat'. It was believed that a person with a snakebite must not sleep. Throughout the night, people held on to Baba's shoulder, trying to keep him awake by singing the well-known bhajan, 'Raghupati Raghav Rajaram'. He was forced to eat green chillies. I could only pray to god, and took a number of vows. At midnight Mr Mangalikar arrived unexpectedly. He knew of some herbal medicine. Finally, that worked, and Baba got relief from the pain. That day I saw god in Mr Mangalikar. If you believe in god, he reveals himself in some form or the other. For me, it was more than a simple coincidence. My faith is strengthened by many such experiences.

During our stay in the house of Dadasaheb Patil, I was to witness many strange incidents that revealed to me the complexities of human nature. Mr and Mrs Patil used to live in Nagpur. They had employed some people to look after their property in and around Warora. Among them was his accountant, who used to watch me every day at the well, washing clothes and cleaning utensils. In those days, women from high caste families never did this work, so he conveniently took me for a maidservant. One day he quarrelled with me over a trifle and spoke rather rudely to me. I told Baba everything. On hearing this, Baba lost his temper and took him to task. When he came to know that I was the wife of Amte, the zamindar, he started trembling in his shoes. He apologised to me so many times and fell prostrate before Baba in shame.

We went to Kolhapur to attend the first gathering of the Korgaonkar Trust. Mr Korgaonkar had a golden heart. He was known for his unbounded charity and magnanimity. He donated liberally to many institutions and also helped young social workers. Baba had given up his legal practice then and had also turned his back on his ancestral property. We were offered the membership of the Trust and we received a small amount by way of honorarium which was the only source of income for us at the time. In the beginning we used to get Rs 150 per month. After 1960, it was raised to Rs 200. Today we get Rs 400 every month regularly from the trust. Later, when Maharogi Sewa Samiti was founded, conditions improved considerably. But Baba insisted on meeting all our personal expenses from this honorarium only. The gathering at Kolhapur was attended by stalwarts like Bhau Dharmadhikari, Acharya Bhagwat, Madhavrao Bagal, Atre Guruji, V. M. Bedekar, Acharya Jawadekar, S. M. Joshi, Mama Kshirsagar, Anna Sahasrabudhe, Appasaheb Patwardhan, Baba Redikar and many others. On this occasion, Appasaheb Dabholkar, the political agent of Kolhapur and Bhaskarrao Jadhav felicitated Baba as an expert in co-operative activity.

Baba had faith in co-existence and equitable distribution of resources, hence we were automatically drawn to co-operative work. We always identified ourselves with the have-nots and faithfully observed the well-known Gandhian principle of simple living. The natural spring of love for the poor and the downtrodden shaped our lifestyle. We made ourselves comfortable on railway platforms and in public charity houses. Once, Dr Shresthi invited us to Miraj. On our way, we halted at the house of a Muslim family. I still remember their hospitality. Our next stay was in a small room in the printing press of Dr Shresthi. There was a gentleman called Mr Kore who lived with his wife and daughter in the room next door. He was suffering from some chronic abdominal disorder and was almost on his death-bed. But they were so nice to us in spite of their difficulties, that for many days after we left, I kept remembering them.

Consider life a journey and yourself a pathfinder—wonders await you at every step, adventures beckon you, sights and sounds entice you. During our stay in Miraj, we went to see the waterfall at Gokak. After the sight-seeing, we stopped at a spot for lunch. We had just opened our tiffin box when a man appeared. He made a strange request. He invited Baba to the special lunch in his house—it was the day of his mother's death anniversary. Baba usually never eats with strangers but on that day it was difficult for him to say 'no'. The man lived in a small hut with a thatched roof. That day we had our bath and ate lunch in his humble cottage.

Like people, places also have their own aura and you are sometimes drawn to them as if you have known them for long. Goa always fascinated Baba. The silent beaches, the surging waves of the sea, and the long lines of coconut trees that flanked the beaches were irresistible to him; I was attracted to the temples there. We would wander around for days on end. The red tiled roofs peeping through the coconut orchards, the clean surroundings—all seemed sublime. The serenity of the temples and the buoyancy and the youthful enthusiasm of the typical Saraswat community in Goa made us forget everything else. I also remember having met a Parsee gentleman called Taraporwala who gave us all the information about Goa and guided us in our tour. We walked barefoot in those days. Our use of footwear dates back to 1951 when we started their production in Anandwan. Discarded tyres were used to make chappals.

Besides the mystique of its seascapes, Goa had its specialties too. Places, like people, carry their identification marks. And the ignorance about them sometimes leads to funny situations. While roaming around, once we came across a board which said 'Brahmin's Inn'. Since it was time for lunch we entered the inn. When the plates were brought, I was shocked to see the variety of fish on the plate. The owner of the inn was a thorough gentleman. He could guess from our expressions that something was wrong. He came to us and asked what the matter was. We explained our predicament and he started laughing. In Goa all the sub-castes of brahmins—Konkanastha, Deshastha, Karhade and the Saraswatas—are all known as Bhattas and I did not know that. Then this gentleman took us to another inn where vegetarian food was served. He also joined us for lunch. This gentleman is unforgettable; his hospitality had no limits. Whenever I think of God, I am always reminded of such men and women we have met.

During the return journey we went to Narsobachi Wadi, a holy place, known to be the abode of Lord Dattatraya. Baba had no particular interest but he always came for my sake. In my opinion, Lord Dattatraya is a socialist God because he lived by begging for his daily food. In the Indian tradition, this act of begging implies a certain discipline; that you are to take only what is strictly necessary and are not to hoard anything. Many saints in India have strictly observed this principle. So I thought Baba would not mind visiting this place. It was the rainy season and the river Krishna was almost flooded. The water had already reached inside the temple where the sacred pair of padukas of Shri Narisinha was kept. I went round the temple in knee-deep water. It is always a humbling experience to visit the temple of any god belonging to the Gurusampradaya. There is no room for pride here (which is generally associated with the idol-worship of other gods). When you serve the guru, you surrender yourself totally.

From there we made for Pandharpur. During the journey we got acquainted with a gentleman called Mr Shinde. He helped us find lodgings in the house of a stone-breaker. The housewife was courteous and she cooked different vegetables for us. She made liberal use of chillies in all the recipes but we did not complain because we were overwhelmed by her courtesy and hospitality. We were, in fact, not used to eating this kind of food but whenever and wherever it was a question of people's love, I told you, we surrendered ungrudgingly.

We were back in Warora after this detour and found ourselves in a state of indecision, thinking of what we should do next. The Shramashram was not enough, we realised. Baba was growing increasingly restless about the conditions of the poor and the outcastes. There was no dearth of sights to fuel this concern. One day, as we went for a walk, we came across a blind muslim woman who lived in a hut-cum-tent made of worn-out pieces of jute. Baba was moved and asked her to come and stay with us. We even promised her free food. But she said she preferred to live this way, or even starve, rather than live with kafirs (non-Muslims) like us. Baba would often take food for her. He washed her clothes took hot water for her bath from our house.

She lived in a cemetery, and it was known to be haunted. We had seen the burials quite often from our kitchen window. But Baba being a rationalist would never be taken in by ghost stories. He never lost his equanimity over such blind beliefs. I would stand at the opposite end. The thought of ghosts frightened me. I was brought up from childhood in such an atmosphere, where most people believed in these things. Today when I look back, I feel like laughing because in Baba's company I grew out of this fear gradually.

I also remember Baba having once brought home a boy of twelve – Niranjan Kamble to stay with us – he was studying in the eighth standard. Our neighbour was a couple—Shiva Parchake and his wife Zingubai. Shiva was rather idle but his wife was hard-working and there was something graceful about her. She was a labourer who worked for a daily wage, leaving her little child at home. I did everything that was possible to help her. I even looked after their baby. Children are a weakness. I cannot see them suffer. The spring of motherhood has been flowing since when, I do not know. I have been a mother to Narayan, Renuka, Bijli, Chinni, Maya, and many such children. Gokul, our home for the orphaned and the destitute was set up in course of time, giving me an opportunity to shower my love on several little ones. I told you about Niranjan Kamble. His father used to pick the berries in Patil's farms. One day he came, and told Baba that Niranjan had lost his scholarship to some Marwari boy. Baba helped Niranjan to get that scholarship back. Naturally, the father felt obliged and was drawn to Baba. Niranjan too, came to our house regularly. Baba also became more involved with him. Our team of workers consisted of Hrishi Gopal Bhatia, Kantha and Raghunath, their wives, and Sukrya. When Sukrya died, Baba carried his dead body to the cemetery. Niranjan Kamble, was witness to all these hardships. He later became an engineer on his own merit.

In July 1948, I was down with typhoid and was bedridden for almost a month. Baba took charge of everything; cooking, washing, drawing water from the well and what not! Baba was ever ready to do anything when the occasion demanded it, and even otherwise. The distinction between 'masculine' and 'feminine duties', strictly observed in many homes then, did not exist for Baba. The word 'feminism' was not in currency in those days, otherwise people would have called him a feminist for sharing the housework with me. Baba found a faithful co-worker in Mahadev Ambekar, who worked as a peon in the bank in Warora. He helped Baba a lot. I had a high fever, some 104–05 degrees. He would sit by my side and change cold water strips on my forehead. A nurse came from the Matru Sewa Sangh regularly. Sponging and doing my hair were her responsibilities. Poor Vikas was neglected, so Indirabai Mahabal took him to Matru Sewa Sangh but it was a horrifying experience for little Vikas; the nurse used to shut him up in a room and go away to work. No one bothered to change his diapers or wash him. He used to play or cry in those dirty nappies, so we brought him back within a week. From that time on, I never left him in anybody else's care. I never sent him away. Around this time Baba sent for another worker from Warora. He used to grow vegetables in that small piece of land. The worker too depended on Baba for his meals. Surprisingly, Baba proved to be an excellent cook.

Our greatest solace in all these months of hardship and anguish was the selfless love of Dada Patil. He was a remarkable person. And even otherwise a loving, caring fellow being! Another gentleman—Mahadev Ambekar is simply unforgettable. He was ready to do anything; bathing Vikas was his duty. Ever since I got married, I do not remember a time when there was no illness in the house. Recurrent health problems plagued our family. At such trying times, Mahadev extended a hand of help. He was like an angel. He was just like a brother to Baba; there was not a single instance when he did not answer our call. Our life was certainly enriched by people like him who had a golden heart. They could read Baba's mind well and once convinced about his sincerity and honesty, became his devout supporters in no time. They never even complained about Baba's occasional fits of anger.

Meanwhile, it was election time with all its hurry and bustle. R. K. Patil was contesting the elections. His supporters would keep dropping at home. They came in at all hours. We kept an open house and it is like that even today. In those days, there were no cooks; I was called upon to cook for the visitors at any time of the day or night. I remember having cooked even at midnight. In the morning there were heaps of plates and utensils to be washed. Of course, Baba was my partner in everything. And gladly did he share the housework with me. In fact, he excelled in that too.

Baba is a man of many parts. If I am to mention one quality that has lent charm to his personality, it is his quick perception of others' difficulties and the spontaneous help he extends. I remember the Independence Day celebrations in 1947. We were in Mumbai. Whenever we travelled to big towns, we generally stayed in public charity houses. There were reasons for this. We knew very few people, and those who knew us were not so eager to welcome us; besides, staying in hotels was out of the question because we could not afford it and even if we could, we would have never spent on such things. Obviously, we welcomed the public charity house whenever we went touring. But you will be surprised to know how happy the members of the charity house were to see us. The first thing that Baba did on arrival was to sweep the house clean. He would do that once again before we left. Ours was the 'broom culture' wherever we went. This free service endeared Baba to the inmates of the charity house.

But on that Independence Day in 1947, we went not to the charity house but to the humble abode of Shri Madhavrao Pophali, a tailor by profession, who used to stitch Baba's clothes. He had invited us to come and stay in his house, a small room in a congested chawl in Dadar. We slept in the veranda of his room, a common passage which opened out into all the rooms. There was hardly any space to stretch our legs. On the second day of our arrival Madhavrao's wife said to me, 'Sadhanatai, it was the biggest surprise of my life today. I got up at five in the morning as usual, but somebody had already cleaned and washed all the plates and utensils. Is it not a miracle?' I laughed to myself because I knew who the worker of this miracle was. When Baba came back from his morning walk I demanded an explanation. He smiled and said, 'Indu, I think it is better to live like a member of the house rather than as a guest. I got up at three in the morning and washed all the utensils. I do not want to add to their domestic duties. On the contrary, it is my pleasure to share their work.' From that day I joined Baba in this daily routine for as long as we were in Mumbai. And the pleasure was mine too. The thought that we should not be a burden to anybody was always uppermost in our minds whenever we went to stay, though temporarily, with someone. I must say that we have received a tremendous amount of love from the ordinary and the 'low caste' people more than from our social peers.

It was a memorable day and a thrilling experience to see our country breathing it's first, as it were. The wide sea at the

Gateway of India, the fading skyline suddenly illuminated by electric lights! It was an exciting moment for all Indians. Our eyes filled with tears of joy. A moment of surrender and elation! And inspiration too! We prayed in silence, 'May we be inspired by the light of liberty to break all the man-made shackles of caste, colour and creed.'

Memory is like a bud, its petals are tightly curled; open one, and the others loosen slowly. One detail leads to another, until you get completely lost. Each memory clamours for inclusion. In fact, I was telling you about my illness. I had high fever. It turned out to be typhoid. I could not eat any solid food. I was unable to digest it. I lived only on sweet lemon juice. One day the doctor gave me an injection of quinine. The temperature dropped so fast that it went below normal. I felt giddy, my eyelids, heavy. It was an effort to keep my eyes open. I called Baba and said, 'I do not think I will survive this fever. You will have to take care of Vikas, I am leaving him to you.' And of weariness, I closed my eyes. I opened them the next morning to the caressing touch of the early sunbeams. I moved my hand twice to make sure that I was alive. I could not believe it. Within a few days the temperature became normal.

I was carrying for the second time and I was eight months pregnant. I was worried about the baby to be born. The doctors feared a miscarriage. But I had faith in God, and I believed in his power. There was no one else to turn to because we were not in touch with either of our families. They had distanced themselves from us, or you may say that our choice of life had created the rift between us. It was the price of our violation of the so-called social norms. Baba's secularism and rebellion against custom passed for licentious behaviour, for reckless fanaticism. It was impossible to expect them to have so much understanding and maturity as they were bound by conventions and dead habits. They did not mind spending money on ritualistic worship of their lord, lifeless idols of their favourite gods. They refused to be moved by skeleton-like figures of their fellow beings dying of hunger. The apparition-like faces could not arouse their sympathies. They refused to respond to the dried up tears of the poor who had no energy left even to weep. Any attempt on Baba's part to penetrate their complacency and indifference would have been rendered futile.

I was towards the end of the ninth month of my pregnancy and was expecting to deliver the baby anytime when another mishap occurred. That day, Baba came home complaining of terrible headache. He asked for some medicine. There was no medicine in the house. I looked into the tins and jars hopelessly. There was a big jar on the upper rung of the shelf. It contained lemon pickle which Baba's mother had sent months before. Since there was no medicine I thought of washing a slice of lemon and giving it to Baba. I stood on a wooden box and stretched my hands and almost held the jar in my hand, when all of a sudden I fell down. The jar broke, the pieces scattered all over the room. The lantern too broke as I fell on it. I received a serious head injury. There was heavy bleeding from the wound. Poor Baba, forgetting his own pain, had to run around. In that darkness of the night, Mahadev went with the lantern to call the doctor. He had to cross the jungle to reach the doctor but nothing would have stopped Mahadev. He would do everything, gladly and willingly, never waiting to be asked. An hour passed before the doctor could do anything. The wound was deep and I needed four stitches. Baba unnecessarily blamed himself when it was my fault.

All the arrangements for my second delivery were made in the Mayo Hospital in Nagpur by R. K. Patil. The minor accidents that preceded the delivery had blotted out all hopes of the survival of the baby. One day, Mr R. K. Patil brought home Dr Rangilal, the dean of the hospital. He advised me to shift to Nagpur in order to avoid all risks. I said to him, 'If such a thing had happened to a poor woman, what would she have done? No civil surgeon would have taken her to the hospital. No minister would have taken interest in her and offered her any help. What will be, will be. I am not going to leave Warora.' Both Baba and I had decided to face it, so we preferred to stay in Warora.

The day finally dawned—the 26th of December 1948. Since the morning I had an uneasy feeling. The labour-pains had started. I knew that the time was drawing nearer and nearer. Baba sent for the bullock cart. I was admitted at the Matru Sewa Sangh. The nurse made me comfortable in bed and went away for further preparations. Before she came back, Prakash was born.

On the eleventh day I returned home with the baby. The house was in disarray. There was dirt everywhere. I put the little one in bed and got down to work. I took the broom and cleaned the whole house and then lay down in bed lest Baba would take me to task for bothering myself with all this work when I was supposed to take rest. After a fortnight, Baba's elder sister, Mrs Tai Nipani came and I got some relief from the work.

I resumed my daily domestic duties even before Prakash was one and half months old. Whether drawing water from the well or washing clothes or cooking, there was no end to the work in the house. There was hardly any time for rest. Baba was occupied with his work. However, whenever he was around, he used to do everything—milking the cows, the cleaning, the cooking. I could not bear to see him fighting on both fronts, so

I resumed my share of domestic duties even before I was strong enough to carry this burden.

Baba's next venture was to sell the vegetables that we grew. He would carry a basketful to the market himself. The rates were never fixed. They kept on varying because it was not Baba who fixed them, but the customers who quoted their price. Baba gave the customers freedom to pick up vegetables and pay him whatever they liked. This experiment was intended more as a test of human nature than as a profit-making endeavour. Importantly enough, no poor man ever tried to cheat. They paid according to their own calculations but it was never far below the market rate. There were, of course, a few exceptions. Some of the people would pick up vegetables worth five rupees and pay only eight annas, one-tenth of the amount for it; they mostly came from the affluent class. Baba did not get angry with them because he had decided to just observe people. Baba had his own ways of judging people. He did not waste his energy in criticising them even when the occasion demanded. His faith in and commitment to constructive work remained unshaken. Likewise, when others criticised him, he never tried to answer back or attack them. He never felt the need to explain or justify himself. The serenity of his mind could not be disturbed by anything. It is the serenity of a sage who lives by his own inner strength. No doubt, he is a self-made man and judges himself most strictly of all. Equally strange are his ways of getting the best out of a man. Hence, the appropriateness of this experiment. I think it is his faith in the essential goodness of man that led to such experiments, which were dismissed as madness or sheer imprudence by others. They laughed at him, but quietly he laughed away such ridicule. Some of the other sellers in the market were infuriated when they found a rich man taking advantage of Baba's magnanimity. They voluntarily took such customers to task for Baba's sake. It was a pleasant surprise for Baba. No one would have expected such a deed from one's rivals.

Plunging into social service in reckless youth is one thing. Seeing it through is the real ordeal, especially when money is always short. Unless you are mentally prepared to sacrifice comforts, and an easy way of life, you cannot root yourself firmly in such a sphere. Your endurance is tried again and again. We had voluntarily opted for this way of life. We had the fever and the fervour to live up to this life but sometimes the sight of our own children suffering used to disturb us. It is not easy to put up with the pangs of poverty without losing your self-respect. Neither did we beg nor borrow from others. It was not a question of our suffering because it was a conscious choice for me. But why should our children suffer? Sometimes I felt guilty that we could not give them even the minimum. What we could do for them was less than what the poorest of the poor could have done for their children. I gave birth to them. But I could not even give them sufficient time. The duties of a mother and those of a servant of the society often clashed and the mother was always defeated. There is a world of difference between what you see today in our institution and what it was at first. We could never give our children even simple things such as biscuits. The food they consumed was nothing more than what was required to keep the body and soul together. We could not take them to any other place, not even to the relatives or friends. Think of it! A pack of biscuits cost eight annas (half a rupee) in those days and we could not afford even that. Their childhood passed without any excitement, without the joys that every child has a right to. Mind you, they did not even have any woollens; winters in our region are very severe. When it got terribly cold, Vikas and Prakash used to put on my blouse and curl up in bed. They had to eat moong dal every day because we could not afford toor dal. They suffered from nausea and sometimes complained also, but their complaints were never entertained.

Once a rich guest came to Dadasaheb. His name was Shankar Thakare. He suffered from leprosy. His wife accompanied him and they lived in the next room. He was the first leprosy patient that Baba treated. One day, Vikas and Prakash saw a thick paste of toor dal in a bowl in their house. On seeing that no one was around, they first tasted it and then ate it all. When the lady of the house came back and saw that the dal had disappeared she asked about it. Vikas and Prakash immediately confessed their crime. Their faces turned pale with guilt. I was so overwhelmed with grief that I could not bring myself to chide them for what they had done. Childhood is supposed to be the most blissful period in life. I wonder whether my children can make that claim. For them it was a period of denials and refusals, a time of deprivation. Imagine, if you can, the agony of the mother who was only a silent witness to all that.

This experiment in community living and dignity of labour did not last long; no more than a year. Continual ill health and the financial constraints forced us to leave it. But it had its rewards too; I learnt to make brooms—what do you say? I am not being sarcastic. And you will not believe it, but I excelled in the art. I also remember having presented a pair of them to Dr Bhansali during his visit. Do you know what he said? He said, 'I will sweep all the cobwebs of dead customs and convention, blind beliefs and superstitions with these.' He said this in jest, but his earnestness was well taken. These pleasant little ironies of life were enlightening for us. The great truths of life are sometimes revealed to us in small things. You need not consult great works for that, nor do you need to be highly educated to discover it. As Baba says, what you need is a sensitive heart and the courage to listen to the promptings of your conscience and you will feel it on your pulse without effort.

Honesty of purpose is infectious too; and when the purpose is pleasure and not profit, it will also bring peace with it. Little acts of goodness will suffice, but honesty of purpose is most important. We have experienced this on a number of occasions.

Satishchandra Dasgupta and J. C. Kumarappa along with many others, once visited our commune. There would be prayers every morning and evening. One day, Mr Kumarappa left the morning prayer and sat in a corner of the kitchen brooding over something. Later, when asked about his absence, he said, 'I joined Mrs Amte in her prayer in the kitchen'. The thought of my hard labour – I had to cook for twenty-five people at a time – had disturbed him.

There comes a moment in life when you find yourself standing at the crossroads and your choice turns your life around. Those who arrest this moment, rise up to greatness; others who foolishly let it go live their lives as if it is a burden. Such a moment came in Baba's life too and he seized it. What a difference it made! It was a bold departure from all the trodden paths of life and a beginning of a new life as it were. It was the beginning of a life-long adventure, a prologue to the saga of the joint creative effort of the social 'outcastes', such as the lepers and the physically handicapped.

Baba had stopped practising law, I told you. He was in a state of indecision as to what to do next. Shankarrao Deo, the then general secretary of the All India Congress was also the president of the Korgaonkar Trust. Baba's association with him resulted in us getting an honorarium of Rs 150 from the trust, enough for our daily bread. There was another proposal. Baba was offered the post of personal secretary to Vijayalaxmi Pandit who was the Indian Ambassador to Russia at that time. Baba's father was the first one to put his foot down against this and I made no secret of my disapproval of this job. Also, at the time, the idea of working with and among the tribals was taking root in our minds. We were planning to go to Nagpur in this connection when a sudden encounter with Tulshiram, a destitute leper changed our life completely. How shall I describe that chance encounter? I can only say that it was an encounter with what you would call the 'ugly', the 'repulsive', the 'ghastly' and the 'piteous'. Leprosy was the name for it. Here was a real challenge. Fear gripped Baba's mind for the first time. He felt a momentary but strong impulse to run away. He felt at once—fear, disgust and repulsion. Then a patter was heard; someone was calling from within, from some unknown region of his mind, a voice, a sigh perhaps; he had heard it now and it soon became Baba's calling. That was the beginning and the end!

It was just another day. Baba set out in the morning for his voluntary service of cleaning public toilets. He completed his daily round and was on his way back home. As he walked along the road he saw a human figure – just bone and flesh – lying by the side of the road. A human body without any vital signs of life. It was merely a form. There were maggots wriggling in the wounds all over the body. The ghastly sight sent a wave of fear down Baba's spine. He hurriedly turned back. At that moment, the only thought was to run away as fast as he could. But as he recovered from the shock, he threw a piece of sackcloth over his body to cover him and walked home. He was quiet the whole day, but his face betrayed the inner turmoil. I guessed that something was wrong. After the evening meal, he told me everything. Every word he uttered reflected his anguish and his self-hatred for being a coward. 'Shame on me' he said, 'of all the things, a helpless leper frightened me! Think of it!' He went on to describe what he saw and finally asked me in earnest, 'Shall I nurse that leper?' The thought that he was afraid even if only for a moment, was gnawing at the back of his mind. It was natural, because his image of himself as a fearless man had received a blow for the first time. Nothing had ever frightened him. However on that day, the man lying helplessly by the roadside had worked a miracle. Baba was frightened for the first time. The iron gates of his mind were completely shaken. That a frail human form could create such fear in him was unbelievable. Gandhiji himself had called him the fearless man once. 'Do I deserve it?', he now thought. The thought haunted him and put the soul on trial. It was a moment of rigorous self-assessment in which he stood face to face with his soul. It was a decisive battle with the self. Once stripped of all fear, it shone brightly. That night – the darkest night indeed – Baba pledged in my presence, to serve the lepers, the most 'untouchable' of the 'untouchables'. The mist of confusion glided past. The port was clear now. With an ardent desire to provide a healing touch to them, he proceeded, knowing fully well that the path was arduous.

Helping lepers was our goal now. Baba was, however, ill-equipped for that. He was not a doctor. He was completely ignorant of the scientific aspects of this most dreaded disease. He had no idea about the causes, and cures available, though he was a well-read man otherwise. The first thing he did was to start collecting information. The resources were scanty. There was neither the internet nor the electronic media then. I am talking about the early nineteen fifties. The only accessible media was the print media. Like a man possessed, he read everything that was available. He also gathered information from those who were engaged in the treatment of leprosy. On the advice of Vinobaji, he started working at the leprosy home run by Manohar Diwan at Dattapur. He would go there thrice a week. It became a passion with him. Nothing that he does, is without passion. Passion is the hallmark of our life and work. Nothing precedes it. There is no intellectual commitment or a sense of magnanimity, and if there was any it was only felt within. We were guided on this odyssey by nothing but our inborn faith in love. That is all. May be, it was our need to pour it out or shower it on somebody. We allowed our creative energies to flow freely to those sections where it was most needed just as the water flows from the higher regions to the lower planes. On the suggestion of Shri Chandraprakashji, Baba also completed a two months' training course in leprosy at Sewagram.

Baba's services were required on the home front too at that time. I told you about my ill health. This time it turned out to be tuberculosis. As if that was not enough, I had to undergo an operation for an abscess caused by the injections. All of us shifted to Wardha. We made ourselves comfortable in a tent. I was mostly bed-ridden. Baba had to shoulder all the responsibilities at home too. It was here that Baba came in contact with Dr Wardekar, the internationally renowned specialist in leprosy. Baba received valuable guidance from him. The days we spent in that tent at Wardha were full of hardships. Even small things created problems. Once, our blanket was stolen in the middle of winter and my children, Prakash and Vikas had to sleep in the cold. I could do nothing but watch them shivering like slender blades of grass. However, there were some bright moments too. They may be tiny specks but they provided warmth. I can never forget the help extended by Manohar Kannamwar, a friend of Mahadev Ambekar. I think, in our life, private as well as public, loss and gain walked hand in hand. After two months we went back to Warora. Baba had gathered a lot of information about leprosy by now. He felt confident.

The following months were full of activity. Something or the other was always happening. Chance meetings with strangers, sometimes with people from remote corners of the country or even from abroad was the least we could expect. One day, a gentleman called Hrishi Gopal Bhatia, a refugee from Pakistan, came to us. He was nineteen or twenty then and a graduate, well versed in Hindi. He had heard about Baba from Gopal Bhatnagar and came searching for us to our ancestral estate. By chance, we happened to be there at that time. It was the most opportune moment for both of us because the idea of establishing Maharogi Sewa Samiti was taking concrete shape and we thought of giving this lad some important position in the Samiti. Unfortunately, he fell ill and one day, even vomited blood. There were hardly any medicines available in Warora at that time, so he had to leave. But I remember with gratitude, the contribution he made to our work. He was ready to do anything, absolutely anything, from washing dishes to changing children's nappies. He was from a noble family but worked hard like an ordinary man, doing all types of menial jobs. People like him are rare. You meet them if you are lucky. He has left a permanent imprint on my mind.

With the experience and training at Dattapur Baba could start his own centre for the treatment of leprosy. It was set up next to the government hospital. In 1949 Maharogi Sewa Samiti was founded, with the help of a few friends. Free medical aid to leprosy patients, and their subsequent rehabilitation were the main objectives of the institution.

The recurrence of my tuberculosis forced us to shift to Kolhapur at Panhala for two months. During this time Baba was fighting single-handedly on all the fronts. Fortunately, here too, Annasaheb Sahasrabuddhe helped us a great deal. He even washed my clothes. Like us, he was a man who believed in the dignity of labour. Panhala proved to be a rendezvous point for us—Haribhau Joshi, the editor of *Lokshakti* had come here with his wife. Dr Krishnabai Kelavkar whose bungalow was close to our residence, was very hospitable. She used to send us something or the other in a tiffin-box. Many people came to see Anna here. You will be surprised to know that Baba cooked for many people at a time, without grumbling or fussing. My children were young and it was their first visit to a crowded city. They were so used to living in the jungle, I had a tough time controlling them. They must have appeared rather uncouth to others. Being ignorant about the urban ways, they were often at a loss to know what was appropriate for them.

The weather of Panhala suited me very well. The fresh, pure air had a magical effect on my health and I do not know whether it was Baba's cooking or something else, but my appetite improved considerably as days passed. I put on some weight too. Two months later we returned to Warora.

The proverb, 'A sound mind in a sound body' sounds very well, but we could never live these words. For us, it was always a sound mind in a diseased body. And we have also come across diseased minds in sound bodies. We were far from being healthy and perennial financial difficulties only aggravated the problems. Besides, our ruling principle, never a borrower be, made matters worse. Quite often, we were forced either to neglect illness or use our will to put up with it. Only when it was absolutely necessary did we turn to medicine, and that too when Baba's friends insisted or initiated medical aid.

As far as I remember, it was in 1950 that I stayed at Urali Kanchan, the well-known centre for natural cure, near Pune. Prakash was hardly a year old and he too was ill at that time. I took him with me to Urali Kanchan and left Vikas with Baba. Since I was under treatment, I could not look after Prakash. He was neglected and I felt guilty about it. It entailed additional stress for me. However, here too, Annasaheb Sahasrabuddhe came to my help. He came to Urali Kanchan and it was a great relief for me because he looked after Prakash with such motherly affection. He used to wash our clothes too and even gave me a head massage regularly. Not a single day passed without the thought of Vikas. How little he was! I was reluctant to leave him and come to Urali. I was torn between two necessities; the motherly instinct to take care of my little ones and the need to to get well soon for which my going to Urali was a must. Consequently, there was no choice but to leave Vikas with Baba. During those two months, how often I longed to see Vikas and pined for just a glimpse of him! It was impossible. The distance was too long; the mother's pangs were unbearable. Letters came regularly from Baba telling me about life on their side. The contents were hardly encouraging. Baba had severe pain in the arm, that made writing also difficult. But he kept writing to me. Vikas was only two and half years old, the age when children become very mischievous. Baba's letters were full of description of his pranks. Going through the letters provided a temporary relief. In a minute I could transport myself to Warora and be with Vikas and fondly watch him sporting or crying or hear him babbling. In a letter to me on 16 March 1950, from Warora, Baba wrote:

> Dear Indu,
>
> My love to you! Received two of your letters—could not find time to write back. Vikas clings to me for twenty-four hours. When I show him

your photograph he asks, 'Where is Indu?' and then points out to the nose and ear. I have a tough time making him eat. I have to force him to eat or feed him myself. But do not worry. He will be all right soon. Do not lose heart. You have to face everything boldly, especially the illness of Prakash. And do not waste energy weeping. If god wills it, he will always be with us. I have a lot of pain in the arm. Writing is very painful.

Yours only,
Murli.

On the receipt of this letter from Baba, I wrote back asking him to send Vikas to me. In reply to this Baba wrote:

Dear Indu,

My blessings and love to you.

Received your letter; however, I am not ready to send Vikas to you. I told you not to worry about him. He is getting used to your absence and is quite comfortable with me; and without him what will I do? If he comes to you, there will be vacuum in my life.

Your letters constantly harp on one point; that I should eat fruits, drink milk and have ghee. Indu, do you not know that these things cost a lot? You do not get them free like air and water. I have to pay twenty-one and half rupees to buy milk for Vikas and with that money I can buy only one quarter of a litre of milk. In the given circumstances, where will the money come from to buy milk and fruit for me? But you must take all these things because you are ill. When you are all right, I will change my diet. I owe Rs 500 to the Korgaonkar Trust and some more to others including Bapuji. It is difficult to keep body and soul together. And do not you feel depressed on reading this.

Tomorrow is Sunday. I do not know with whom I can leave Vikas. There is a lot of work to be done. An impulse brought me here to serve the lepers, but I do not know how I am going to manage all this. I have invited Kantha to lunch tomorrow and will be leaving Vikas and the house to him and get back to work in the clinic for the whole day. I need Mahadev in the clinic; otherwise he would have looked after Vikas. It is sweltering hot here. I cannot let him go out of the house. What to do? Moreover the increasing pain in the arm worries me. I wonder if I will be able to give injections to patients or not. I am done.

Take care of yourself. Write to me about Prakash.

Yours only,
Murli.

Baba's letters reflected his urgent longing and persistent yearning for my company; but it never stood in the way of his work. On the contrary, each of his letters was proof enough of his sense of duty towards others. His next letter will show you how deeply involved he was in his work. In fact, our work and our life can never be separated. They are inextricably bound to each other. You cannot tell one from the other. The personal leaps over to the public and whatever is public or social affects us personally. Take a look at the following letter:

> Dear Indu,
>
> I have worked in different spheres till now. But the pleasure I have experienced while working for the lepers is incomparable. I have never experienced this joy before. I am not bothered about success or failure. Nor do I feel worried about the future of the institution; I do not think of it. It may or may not take a concrete shape. Nevertheless, they have an unshakable faith in me and even if I just stand under a tree with a sprinkler in hand, I am sure, they will throng to me. I wish you were here to see all that in the clinic last Sunday. You would have never asked me to come home early. Sixty-five patients waiting for their turn in a long queue! Can you imagine? What does it all foretell? What a joy to see their eyes sparkling with hope! And Indu, they have nothing else but love to give in return, and blessings too. However, their blessings come from the bottom of their hearts. Isn't that enough for you, me and the children? It will definitely see us through. Indu, they pray to God for our health and happiness. I know I should have been with you at such a difficult hour at Urali Kanchan but you would not have liked me to leave them uncared for. I would have had my pleasure of your company only at the cost of hopes and aspirations of these poor, helpless, disabled lepers. In fact, the sense of guilt for having forsaken them would have spoilt

> our joy too. Tell me, do you really think it right to have me by your side in these circumstances?

This was the frenzy in which Baba worked. He would put his whole self – body, mind and soul – into the work. Baba used to write about every little thing in minute detail.

These letters banished my loneliness for a while, and my sense of guilt too, for having left Vikas behind. Nevertheless, I met him in those letters. Baba once wrote to me, in a letter dated 5 April 1950:

> Just as you think of us, we also think of you with no less intensity of yearning. Vikas is getting more and more mischievous by the day. He is the one who keeps watch on me. He feeds me with his tiny fingers. He wants to serve every one at lunch. When I sit down to chop vegetables, he wants to do it. He wants to do everything that I do, even make chapattis. You won't believe but when the morning paper comes, he rushes for it and says 'Hey, give it to me. Now Vikas will read the paper!' He wants to rule over the world, it seems. When asked 'Whose son are you?' he answers, 'I am the son of Vikas.' Sometimes when I scold him, he goes out of the room, fretting and fuming, goes to the cupboard. The photograph of Leela Chitnis flashes from inside. He looks at it and says, 'Shall I tell Indu that Baba spanks me? I have told Indu, I have told her now . . . .'
>
> We are fine. You do not have to worry.

Now that both Prakash and I were feeling better, I decided to return. The next letter from Baba brought good news that the government was ready to donate fifty acres of land for our project, for the colony of lepers. It was near Chimur road. He also informed me that he was thinking of going to Calcutta to study further. Prakash had recovered considerably and was getting naughty now. Dhirendrabhai, who was our immediate neighbour showed a lot of affection for Prakash. Prakash had a free passage anywhere in his house and his explorations often resulted in something breaking, almost every day. I felt embarrassed. I now wanted to return to Warora as early as possible.

When I think of the days spent at Urali Kanchan I remember with gratitude the support and assistance I received from Sharanprasadji, Hoshiyari ben, Appa Bhagwat who was the chief naturopath and Balkaji Bhave, the director of the centre. He came to see me twice a day. But for the love and care of these people, I do not know what I would have done. To think of them is to feel grateful for everything they did.

Within a few days I returned to Warora. It was a part of my good fortune that I came into contact with so many good souls because of Baba's unbounded involvement in the service of the society, his sociability. There is no end to the list of great and good men who visited us voluntarily. They were all gracious and we were lucky to have met them. I remember the visit of Shri Manoharji Diwan. On that day, I had sore eyes and I was chopping vegetables when he arrived. He came straight to me and sat down in front of me. Silence was my natural response to the presence of any great man, at least in those days. He asked a number of questions and I only said, 'Hmm.' After sometime he said, 'I know, you have sore eyes and not a sore throat. Why are you not speaking?' It took quite some time for me to shed my shyness and these interactions with good people were nourishing and enriching.

Baba deeply revered Dr Dharmendra, who was his guru. It was under his guidance, that Baba completed his scientific study of leprosy in the school of Tropical Medicine at Calcutta. This training was meant exclusively for medical graduates. Baba was a lawyer. But Vinobaji and barrister Barlinge put in a word for him and Baba got admission into that school. Dr Dharmendra once told Baba that not much of research had been done in this field because this disease occurs only among human beings and no animal has ever contracted it. So experiments on animals are completely ruled out. Then Baba came forward and offered himself for experiments. However, Dr Dharmendra was not keen and tried to dissuade Baba from such a venture. Baba himself was not well at the time. He had pain in the chest and spat blood. The doctor examined him. On his return from Calcutta, Baba was admitted to Nagpur Medical College, because the doctor suspected tuberculosis. I shifted to Nagpur with the children and stayed at home. It was an ordeal for both of us. Baba was fully exhausted due to continual ill health. Now tuberculosis made matters worse. He lost weight rapidly. The pain in his arm did not allow him to write, but Baba is not a person to be defeated or to be unnerved by adverse circumstances. Despite the pain, he kept on writing to me and his letters held a mirror to what was going on in his mind. He wrote from the hospital to me:

> Dear Indu,
>
> The festival mood surrounds the hospital today. People are busy celebrating Vijayadashmi. There

is a lot of noise on all sides. The Maruti Mandir of Rajbaksha is close to the hospital. The citizens of Nagpur come here for the ritual of crossing the border. Madhu, Baban and Jayant were here a little while ago. They brought me the customary golden leaves. Inside the hospital, it is silent; no movements of any kind. Two of the inmates of the hospital have just 'crossed the border' here—they have gone to their heavenly abode, so to say. The profound contrast is heart-rending; wailing and groaning inside the hospital and a noisy jubilation outside! Long held prisoners of the hospital, the tuberculosis patients did not take the two deaths well. I tried to console them, but in vain! Never before was the longing for you felt so urgently as today. There you are by the side of the cemetery in Warora and here I am among those who are dangling between heaven and earth.

All the doctors unanimously agree on one point; that I must lie down in bed at least for a year because I vomited so much blood. They have also advised me not to strain myself mentally. Manoharji Diwan was here yesterday. He spent more than two hours with me. Indu, you have to look after my institution. You must take care of your health. When it comes to taking care of children, women are far too superior to men and they are equally capable of realising the goals they set for themselves.

Give my love and blessings to Vikas, Prakash, Mahadev and Niranjan. What can I give you? I prefer to think of the Vijayadashmi we celebrated before our wedding, than of the one today.

Yours only,
Murli

Almost after a month's compulsory bed-rest, Baba returned to Warora. We were about to take possession of the land promised by the government for our leprosy home. Baba was now busy collecting funds for the free medical aid to the patients. But the response was very poor. He would feel very dejected on such occasions. His desperation over people's indifference and complacency is reflected in a letter he wrote from Calcutta:

Dear Indu,

Received your letter. It is Sunday today. It's ten at night. I am disturbed, so I decided to write to you.

I feel more worried about the lepers than before. New medicines, in fact, are more effective. They are showing better results. But how insensitive people are! It is surprising that they cannot bring themselves to think rationally and scientifically. The fog of misconceptions about leprosy continues to haunt their minds. They still cling to their irrational beliefs and refuse to take the blinkers off their eyes. Even their love and affection for their own people seems to have dried up completely. It is quite disheartening.

Our institution is yet to take shape. We will have to work hard to raise funds too. Our greatest disadvantage is our failing health, and difficulties

> always come in battalions for us. I am working hard to gather funds. Recently, I was called by the traders from the Marwari community. It was a very humiliating experience. I was turned out for no reason and they asked me to come some other time and that time never comes. They promised tomorrow, and that tomorrow is continually postponed. I have stopped going to them now.
>
> There were a hundred and two patients at the centre yesterday and ninety-five, the day before. We are doing an excellent job here. I received a letter from Dr Wardekar, advising me to take care of myself. He has also recommended a regular check up.
>
> Take care of yourself. How are Vikas and Prakash? Do write to me about them.
>
> Yours only,
> Murli

While in Calcutta, Baba once received a beautiful letter from Vinobaji, excerpts from which he sent to me in his letters. Vinobaji wrote,

> In tuberculosis, the weakness of the mind is far more dangerous than the physical degeneration, because physical decay is an ongoing process and whether or not you are a tuberculosis patient, it will take place. He who is mentally strong, will never succumb to the disease, but will surmount it. Maintaining mental strength is of enormous significance in such a condition. That of course,

> does not mean that the health of the body can be neglected, especially when you know the facts about the disease. Such negligence amounts to crime. And I am sure that god wants you to do a lot of work before you take your leave . . .

Finally, in 1951, Maharogi Sewa Samiti was registered as a society. Four kilometers from the village Warora, and close to the Nagpur–Chandrapur road where a road diverges to Chimur, these fifty acres land, uncultivated and barren, were given to us by the Madhya Pradesh Government. This was the fruit of the incessant labour of R. K. Patil and barrister Barlinge. The Board of Trustees of Maharogi Sewa Samiti consisted of R. K. Patil, Laxmichand Bora, Gulabchand Gothi, Mithmal Bora, Phulchand Baid, Dr Vaze, Ramkrishna Milmilwar, advocate Mahadev Pawade, Mahmadbhai, Milapchand Sipani, Jaganjeet Sarda and the respected Kannamwar.

Under the neem tree, the work of providing medical aid to the lepers began. Sundays were reserved for this work. Baba would personally look for patients in nearby villages and persuade them to go for a medical examination at the government hospital. Dr Dharmadhikari, the government medical officer, had given special permission to Baba to run this centre. It is worth noting that officers in those days, at the dawn of Indian freedom, were quite efficient and honest too. They had a sincere desire to do something good. There was no large-scale corruption, reckless enjoyment or abuse of freedom. The air smacked of a zest for good work. There was no dearth of selfless workers. How things have changed today! It pains me to say but I can't help saying it—a terrible change has occurred. Today, self-interest is the only interest; corruption is almost a rule, and abuse of freedom goes hand in hand with abuse of power. Everything has changed completely. When Baba set up his institution, the antagonistic forces were limited to blind belief, superstition, absurd faith in one's own illusions, and the banter about Baba breaking his oath of celibacy. However, there were role models too in people like Gandhiji, Vinobaji, Sane Guruji and many others. Inspiration came from many sources. Mind you, I am not just talking about the golden past. Nor am I talking about the customary gap between your generation and mine. It is not as simple as juxtaposing the past and the present. The descent and the decay I am referring to is the moral one.

FIVE

If you are prepared to drift along the current of time with me, there will be many discoveries awaiting you. It is almost like entering into another time, because the buzz of activity that marks Anandwan today, was a mirage in a desert then. Imagine yourself standing at the edge of a piece of land – barren, deserted, half hidden by the undergrowth, a blank space, without a face – gaping at you. It was just three kilometres from our house, but in the absence of any means of transport, it seemed a great distance! Only silence and solitude, breathed here. A dirt road connected our house to this place—flanked by thick plantations on both the sides. It crossed the Nagpur–Chandrapur road. There never was much of traffic on this road. When it got dark in the evening, no one dared travel alone. We set up our medical centre here. For the first six months, we would travel up and down every day from the village where we stayed. We could acquire fifty acres of land without much difficulty through

R. K. Patil who was the food minister then and barrister Barlinge, the health minister. Both of them knew us, and the type of work we wanted to do. However, there were other problems. Getting funds and patients was not as easy as getting the land. Our purse was empty, so each member of Maharogi Sewa Samiti donated fifty rupees to set up our cottage. Today you see well-constructed buildings in Anandwan—in fact, a complex of buildings.

Manoharji Diwan had sent five patients to us. The first among the five, was our Shankardada. We shared our house with all of them until arrangements for their stay had been made. I used to cook for all of them. Later, when the well was dug, they shifted to their own hut. They had come empty-handed for obvious reasons; they were disowned by their own families first, and society afterwards. What could they have owned? I gave them a set of utensils—a part of our ancestral property.

There was no vehicle then except the bicycle. Everyday we would travel from the village Warora to this place on the outskirts with our children hanging on to the bicycle, with a lunch box and a water bottle. It was an eight kilometre walk everyday. It used to get dark in the evening, as there was no electricity even in Warora. The road went through the jungle. Our ventures with the wild – the fox, the bear – became a part of our routine. Clearing a spot under the banyan tree, we used to eat together. Months passed like this. Once we brought Baba's father here in a bullock cart. I was the last one to get in. The cart was overloaded, and when it went over a pothole, I fell out but was unscathed. It was, indeed, a narrow escape.

Bapuji's heart sank to see our labour. He could not help saying to Baba, 'It is time for me to enter into vanprastashram, leave for the forest at the evening of my life. But you have made for it with the little ones before I could think of it.' Baba gave a characteristic answer, 'Isn't it better to enjoy the romance in youth rather than in old age?' That is the attitude and the spirit with which Baba looked at life and work. To be one with whatever you do and whoever you work for—what else is romance? That is why I call it love's labour. Whether it is the labour of love or the love of labour, it comes to the same thing. I believe, no father would have said anything in response to such a comment from his son.

In the early phase of this work, the first thing we would have to do was to dig up a well and clear a part of the forest. Bodhulal and Appanna Wadar had volunteered to do this work. Baba always ate with the patients. They now cooked for themselves; sometimes he exchanged his tiffin with them. Now it was necessary to set up a few more cottages. There was a strong protest from the inmates of the forest – serpents and deadly scorpions – against our encroachment on their territory. They popped out of holes every now and then, sometimes giving a fatal kiss. Herds of wild boars used to watch us from a distance. But the terror of the jungle, the tiger, had not shown up yet. We had to wait for quite some time. I had become familiar with snakes and scorpions while living in R. K. Patil's bungalow and also got stung by scorpions twice or thrice. But here, in Anandwan, it looked like their estate; there was a farm of scorpions and snakes as it were. We needed to be extremely cautious here. If we were to sit under a tree, we had to clear at least five or six square feet around first. Even the slightest movement of a leaf sometimes terrified us and caused panic.

While working here, there were things to watch and be wary of. The most common sight was the herds of deer. Once, we were stunned to see a deadly fight between a python and a giant lizard. It was a breathtaking sight. Both fought to the bitterest end. Finally, the python swallowed up the lizard, but after some time the lizard, tearing open the stomach, came out. The hunter was hunted in the end. We talked about it for the whole day.

The first cottage with a thatched roof was ready now and the patients were thinking of shifting into their new residence. It was around that time, that Vinobaji arrived in Warora accompanied by Gautam Bajaj and twenty-five other workers. They were on their way to Telangana as part of the Bhoodan movement. They dined with us and then we took them to see our new centre set up in the jungle, today's Anandwan. Baba always carried a kambal on his shoulder. Baba spread it on the ground for Vinobaji and his friends to sit on. Vinobaji was a vegetarian; his diet was no more than fruit and milk. We had decorated the hut, especially its entrance with wreathes of mango leaves. Our patients ceremoniously stepped into this hut with Vinobaji. He admired Baba for his work and before he left, gave us his heartfelt blessings. The parting words he uttered, are permanently carved in my mind. He said, 'There will be another Ramayana here, the Ramayana of social service!'

In a few days, the well was ready for use. We didn't have to worry about water now. Our hut was ready as well and we shifted into this new residence in the midst of the jungle. The rest of our things were brought in a truck. This was the beginning of Anandwan. Shifting and all that comes with it was not new for us and it had become a part of our daily routine now. There was a complete mess on the veranda. I could not find a single thing. Putting three stones together in a triangular fashion, I made the oven and finished the cooking. The natives – snakes and the like who belonged to the place first – gave us a warm welcome. We were not surprised, because, we had already acquainted ourselves with them by then. The house was not yet ready for use; there was a lot to be done and the work went on even while we lived there. It was a small cottage with a tiled roof. It wasn't very strong. When a monkey jumped onto the roof once, the tiles broke into pieces. Gradually another room was built, and now there was a separate kitchen. In this region, there was always shortage of water and clay. So it took us some time even to build a wall of nothing but sticks plastered with mud and clay. Then it was painted in slaked lime, which used to come off while sweeping. Out first guest in this humble lodging was Shankarrao Deo. Then came Dr Sushila Nair and Dr Wardekar.

Before Vinobaji left, he gave Baba hundred rupees. A gift from one fakir to another! This was exclusively meant for Baba whose health had deteriorated considerably because of overwork. Baba was in need of a nutritious diet, but in his meagre budget there was no provision even for milk. We kept two cows, Ganga and Yamuna. With the hundred rupees given by Vinobaji, we bought another, Narmada. Baba preferred to buy a cow rather than spend the money on milk for himself. Milking the cows was my duty. Baba, with the help of all the patients, busied himself in cultivating the land. The trees had to be cut down, the entangled vines, which shut out the sunlight, to be cleared out. The work seemed endless. However, Prakash and Vikas were very happy here, for the simple reason that they had free access to the treasure of the jungle—berries, tamarind and what not. Initially, they did not wander far from our house, but as they grew up, they got to know almost every corner of Anandwan.

What an enchanting place it was! Every season had something new to show. In winter, the garb of a misty veil lent to it the seductive charm of a ravishing bride. As the sun lifted the veil, thousands of flowers of widely divergent hues sprung up with smiling faces; while the trees laden with fruit looked like sages standing there since ages perhaps, eager to give whatever they had. They attracted flocks of birds, that feasted on their fruit. From a distance came the rhythmic sound of the woodpecker. Among the birds were, the common variety of sparrows, parrots and the golden winged swallows too. They lingered on until autumn came stealthily. The sharp winds and fall went hand in hand. Heaps of dead leaves for me to pick up! Such a simple job, but it tested my strength. Spring and summer had an altogether different look. It was red and saffron that dominated the surroundings. The first two months of the Hindu year, Chaitra and Vaishakh (spring and summer) look alike, especially in Vidarbha, except for the difference in the degree of temperature. This is the season of palas flowers. There is a flower almost on every twig. It looks as if fiery tongues have arisen from every corner. Summers are unbearable here. Scorching heat slackens the speed that characterises spring. It brings in sluggishness. In the beginning, when Anandwan was surrounded by thick forest, we could escape the hot waves. It was our favourite activity to pull up a bed under a big tree and lie down. Towards the end of May and especially in June, there came storms. There used to be little rain but the turbulent winds were frightening. It was difficult for the roof tiles and tin sheets to stay in their place.

Rains came towards the end of June and it used to rain heavily in those days. Rainfall has dropped considerably today. But it was a disaster then. Chandrapur, Bhandara, and Nagpur were specially known for rice. Rains were followed by other difficulties too. The rats would leave their holes – they were filled with water – and take refuge in our house and after them came the snakes. In the puddles, the frogs used to create pandemonium. Swarms of mosquitoes gave them company. The cottages used to leak and accordingly the bed had to be shifted every day. Despite all these inconveniences, Baba loved this season most.

Even today, this is his favourite season. It is in this season that you can experience the frenzy of the elemental forces. When the dance of thunder and lightning began, it was time for us to go out for a walk. Baba insisted on these ventures. He never liked to miss the touch of the slapping showers. Nothing like it! Our most favourite haunt was a pond nearby. It used to fill to the brim in the rainy season. A large banyan tree stood on its bank. We used to take the narrow dirt track by the side of the pond. Despite the busy schedule, we never missed the evening walks.

I found a few friends among the women who lived by selling wood. They would set out for collecting wood in the forest early in the morning. The whole day they used to pick up small twigs, dried stalks, tie them together in bundles. In the evening I used to see them pass by Anandwan balancing the bundles on their heads. I used to keep water, in a big earthen pot, ready for them. They rested here for a while. They came from the lower castes. There were the harijans, the scavengers, the trappers. I used to wonder at their smiling faces despite the odds they had to fight against.

The unexpected arrival of Dajisaheb, Shivajirao Patwardhan in Anandwan was a pleasant surprise for us. His turban gave him a majestic look and added a touch of profound serenity to his glowing face. I was reminded of Swami Vivekananda. Dajisaheb had a lot of affection and admiration for Baba. Once, when he came, I was giving Maya – who was a small baby then – a massage. He sat in front of me and looked on for quite some time. He did not say anything but tears came rolling down his cheeks. He looked at me and uttered a few words, 'You have showered motherly love on an unknown waif.' I said to him, 'Dajisaheb, this baby is a gift from god and I must take care of her, otherwise, he will lose faith in man. He is the one who makes the provision of food for every beak and in his world, there is no orphan. The evil in this world is the creation of those, who make a distinction between the self and other.'

A strange custom prevailed in Warora at the time. After the celebrations of Hanumanjayanti (which falls on the full moon day in Chaitra) were over, there used to be a weekly sale of cattle in Warora. This coincided with another big event—a lunch that was offered every year to all the beggars in the village, by the Marwari community. The recipients of this benevolence included the poor also. That year, Baba received a message from one of them that the leprosy patients from Anandwan were also invited to lunch along with the beggars. Baba was furious. This was an insult to the inmates of Anandwan. Baba is a short tempered man. This added fuel to his fury. First of all, our work at Anandwan was never intended to make the patients servile and dependent but rather, self-reliant. We wanted to boost their confidence and help them live with dignity. Baba is a staunch believer in his own creed that only work can build up confidence, a sense of self-respect in these outcasts. He also believes that charity destroys self-respect and breeds servility. Baba thought for a few minutes about that invitation and planned to attend the lunch along with me, and a guest from Wardha, Shri Devendrabhai Gupta. We reached there in time and Baba declared to the congregation, 'Three beggars have come, myself, Sadhana and Devendra. Please serve us lunch.' With these words we sat in the midst of others and refused to move. It was the turn of the host to feel guilty and they too joined us for lunch. Baba forgot everything and all of us enjoyed the special lunch. I have often wondered at the two types of beggars: those who are forced to beg and the others who choose to beg. The latter include the rich and the so called high-class people who continuously beg before God to give them something or other. How can they call others beggars? I am disgusted at them.

Anandwan and my children grew side by side, or together, you may say. None of the myths associated with the bliss of childhood in general, have any relevance to the childhood of Prakash and Vikas. What did we give them? Nothing, I would say. Generally parents, at least educated ones, pay attention to their children's health, education, and make provision for their future. We would prove to be the most unworthy parents, if judged by these criteria. We had neither the money nor the time to give them the best of this world. I remember their first day at school. That day Baba fell ill, seriously ill. In that tension, I forgot to bring them back from the school. My sister, Suma reminded me at around twelve o'clock that the children had to be brought home. We had admitted both of them in a school which was close to our home and anyway we could not have afforded the fees in other schools. One of the teachers used to come home to teach Prakash. I used to give him only a cup of milk. That too, because we owned a few cows—four of them. The milk was shared by our patients too. When Prakash fell ill, he would change the cold-water strips on his forehead himself. I could not even breastfeed him properly when he was a year old because I was bedridden for four months at Urali Kanchan. He did not get sufficient milk. He suffered from diarrhoea quite often. I used to give him kokam sharbat. He could not take solid food for quite some time. My heart bleeds to remember those days, his early childhood.

They went to school regularly, but they had no friends here in Anandwan, not a single one. They used to say to Baba, 'Baba, why do not you buy us a friend?' Baba used to say, 'We do not have any money. How can I buy you a friend?' Vikas used to say, 'Sell one road – the Nagpur road, or Chimur road – and bring us a friend'. Can you imagine the pangs of a child, who pines and pines for a friend? One day they brought a boy with them from school and told us that he was their friend. The boy was of the same age, but he was very lean and probably not fully grown for his age. All the signs of adversity were visible on his face. His name was Narayan. I later nicknamed him Narya. His father owned a small piece of land at Chinora, a small village two miles west of Anandwan. Vikas and Prakash used to go to school in a bullock cart. Narayan, who attended the same shool, used to walk to and from school; he normally took a shortcut. The three of them soon became friends. Sometimes he would come to Anandwan to play with Prakash and Vikas. I was touched by the circumstances in which he lived. I thought of keeping him in Anandwan. I consulted Baba about this. Baba said he had no objection provided his parents were ready. So one day I sent for his mother. She gave her consent and Narayan became an honourable member of our family. Between Prakash and Vikas, Narayan could not get along with Vikas much. He always used to threaten Vikas that he would leave Anandwan and go back to his place. On receiving this threat, Vikas used to hide his bag and clothes lest he might leave. Today Narayan is the agricultural minister of Anandwan. He has shouldered many responsibilities in the institution and helped Vikas. People call him Narayanrao today.

One day, Vikas and Prakash came home from school and started asking each of us our caste. He asked everyone—Baba, me, my sister, and a few others. While being admitted into the school, they were asked to mention their caste in the application form. Now they got a new topic to talk about with their friends. How could they have known what caste meant? Once, when the teacher was instructing them about ways of life, he told them all that they should never consume tobacco. On that, my children asked the teacher bluntly, 'Why do you consume it then?' The teacher had no answer.

Once, they went to a barber for a haircut. After the barber had cut their hair, he dabbed their face with powder. When they came home, they refused to take a bath because the powder would be washed off. Such a trifle as face powder and what excitement over it! Because, we could not afford it! Finally, I had to coax them to take a bath.

Most of the children in the school came from the working class. None of them came from educated families. Our monthly income was only Rs 150. We had a few cows and a bullock cart. Besides the two meals, I could not give them anything even to munch. I used to make chapattis in the morning to be had for both the meals. By afternoon, the container would be empty. I used to get irritated and sometimes even told them, 'Why did you eat all the chapattis? Now I will have to make them again.' I know, sometimes I was cruel enough to say all these things to them and would then wonder, not without regret, about what happened to the mother in me. I would cook in the morning only. In the evening, Baba used to insist on going for long walks. When the weather was stormy, we used to shut them up in the house and go for a walk. Then I used to cook only rice for the evening meal.

It was a night to remember; a stormy night in the month of May or June. Never before had I seen such an intimidating storm. It blew off the roof of our hut. I was milking the cows in the cowshed. Within half an hour the scene changed. Monstrous winds started flinging everything astray. The tin sheets that covered the cowshed, flew a mile away into the farm. Vikas and Prakash were alone in the hut. The winds played havoc; buckets of milk were spilt. I wanted to rush back to my children, but only a fool could have ventured out in the stormy weather. It spared nothing. What a purposeless dance of destruction! I could only pray to god for my children. As soon as the storm abated, I rushed to the hut. The children were not to be seen. Instead, I saw a heap of sand and lime; it had probably come off the walls due to the force of the wind. My pulse raced. As I looked on in desperation, not knowing where to search for them, Vikas and Prakash crawled out from under a charpoy. I hugged them and sat up with a blank mind for how long I do not know. Nonetheless, their presence of mind was commendable. They were lucky to escape injuries just by sneaking under a charpoy. In yet another storm, we sat up the whole night in a roofless hut. In the morning Balaji Patil came from Pisdure and repaired the hut.

Balaji Patil was a close friend of Baba, known for his hunting adventures. He sometimes came with his rifle. One of our patients Narayan was also a hunter once. The two went on expeditions together. Balaji Patil had to his credit a unique record—he had killed two boars with one bullet. It happened like this. He shot at one, the bullet went piercing through the boar's body and struck another one; both lay dead within minutes. A good shot indeed. Baba was impressed. He roasted them, asked me to prepare the masala, cooked it himself and took it to the people on the other side of Anandwan.

Prakash and Vikas were exposed to the dangers of the wild along with us. Prakash was only one and half years old when a black scorpion bit him. There was swelling all over. He writhed in pain. There was no medicine. The night seemed so long. As if this was not enough, the next day, a bigger one bit Vikas. Similar symptoms, great pain, life risked and our helplessness. The same scene was re-enacted. Such a lethal sting! I was horrified. I searched for the scorpion. With torch in hand, I cautiously ransacked the rooms and I found them—not one or two, but hundreds of them! It is unimaginable. I killed over a hundred with a brass stick. They were everywhere, hidden among the folds of clothes, or in big containers in which I stored food grains. In Anandwan, Baba too was twice bitten by snakes. Once, a furious monkey attacked him and he was quite badly wounded. You cannot imagine how the days were spent in the shadow of this 'natural violence'. Once, when I entered the trench latrine, I saw three snakes in three corners but somehow managed to come out safe. Once, at Kasrawad, during the Narmada Bachao Andolan, a snake fell on my head, when I opened the door. I thought it was a lizard but then it slipped down and I saw it slithering down and disappear in the same room. We had many such encounters with diabolic creatures.

I must tell you about another incident. We were living at Kasrawad then. Baba was to undergo an operation at Indore that day. He was advised to change the pace-maker. We were supposed to leave Kasrawad at three in the morning. I used to go to the river Narmada, for a bath early every morning. Accompanied by a girl, I went to the river in the dark. After my bath I would take a glass of water from the river and go to the Shiva temple on the top of the hill and burn incense and light the oil lamp. There was an iron door, which I used to close everyday after my evening prayers. That day, after my bath, when I came to the door of the temple, I saw a snake stretched across the door. I was taken aback and did not know what to do. We were to leave exactly at five and Baba is very particular about time. I was in a fix. It was the day of Baba's operation and I could not think of missing the daily ritual. It was, in fact, even more necessary on that day. I tried my best to drive away the snake; with the box of incense sticks, I tapped the stone slab. The snake responded, but it did not leave. It went to one side of the door. The door opened in the middle. So I pushed open the other side and somehow managed to pass through; the snake was just a foot away from me. I finished my worship and came out in the same manner. On such occasions, I have often felt that some unseen power has always protected us. Maybe, people's blessings and best wishes always shielded us against such odds.

The most awesome adventure was the one with the tiger. We were familiar with the roar which was often heard in Anandwan but we had never seen 'his majesty' in person. One day he entered our house and caught a dog and went away. We had four dogs in the house. We were woken up by the noise of the dogs' barking. Baba ran after the tiger in the darkness of the night. In that hullabaloo the tiger left the dog near Uttarayan and ran back into the jungle. The dog was seriously injured and died within a week. The tiger carried away all the dogs one after the other. In order to keep the tiger away, I used to fill an iron container with water at night and place it near the well to block his way, thus preventing him from coming any closer. In course of time, as the population of Anandwan increased, the tiger did not show up again. The only female dog left, Nisha, fell a victim to a herd of wild boar. The boars often appeared near Anandwan, and even destroyed the crops.

Anyone, who has seen Baba closely, will not fail to recognise the queer combination of qualities like action and reflection, labour and speculation, austerity and indulgence, dreaming and being rooted in the real world – the list is endless – and all these opposites are happily reconciled in Baba. They even compliment each other. Baba is inventive and enterprising. He is always eager to experiment with everything, not out of intellectual curiosity but always out of practical needs. Money was always scarce but it never stopped him from trying out new things. Sometimes, when I withdraw from the world and think about Baba's life, I feel it has been a perpetual experiment.

Baba has always been extremely careful about spending money. Far from being extravagant, he was always looking for ways to save money, whenever and wherever possible. Once, out of some savings, he bought cows – the desi ones, a common breed – but they gave very little milk. So he brought a few more from Punjab and Haryana. Baba himself could not milk them because of the pain in his hand. So he fetched a man from the village, from our own farm, to milk these cows. His name was Sadashiv Ghugul. But he also failed. It was a serious problem now; how to milk the cows. It was risky to try because the cows were tall and very strong. Then a rich Sikh gentleman from the village taught us how to milk the cows. Sitting on a stool, I used to milk them. Mind you, it was not easy. I had to endure their kicks, sometimes the bucket full of milk was spilt. The work used to begin early, at three in the morning—I had to prepare the fodder for them. Initially my shoulder joints and arms would hurt, but I soon became an expert. Just as I mastered the art of making brooms, I acquired the skill of milking the cows too, and I had to milk eight to ten cows at a time. There would be around sixty to seventy litres a day. Later on, Annasaheb Sahasrabudhe conferred the title 'The Milkmaid of Anandwan' on me. Vinobaji had already conferred 'Annapurna' and 'Yashoda'.

One evening, we heard the roar of the tiger; it sounded quite close, perhaps from near the well. Baba is a man of whims and fancies, sometimes totally unpredictable! On hearing that roar he said to Prakash 'Will you go and draw water from the well?' Prakash was only six. Fancy that! But off he went without a moment's hesitation. Baba heard the sound of the bucket going down into the well and the creaking of the pulley. When he came back, Baba, overwhelmed with love, gave him a pat on the back. Most people point out Baba's exceptional capacity for pity and empathy as characteristic features of his personality, but I think he is more fascinated by adventure. His capacity for taking risks is greater than anything else. That is why, when Prakash decided to step into the impenetrable jungle of Bhamragad, Baba was ecstatic. He even tested the patients' capacity for risks; he would have bets with them. One kilometre from Anandwan, on Chimur road, there is a place called Khairgaon. A small stream runs between the two places. The whole area was a part of the jungle. No one dared to go there alone, especially in the dark. Every day, after the evening meal, Baba would chat with the patients. After the day's work, it would be time to exchange ideas or distribute the duties for the next day. One day, Baba went to that stream and put a five-rupee note under a stone. When at night, all of them got together in the moonlight, Baba told them about the five-rupee note and said to them, 'Whoever has the courage to go there, and bring back the note will keep it for himself.' Everyone looked at each other. Finally, Vithoba got up, went to the jungle at that hour of the night, and brought back the note. Baba gave him a pat on the back.

Baba's maternal uncle (his aunt's husband) lived in poverty, but he was a man with a deep sense of self-esteem. He never asked for monetary help from anyone. I used to invite him to read the holy scriptures on occasions such as Hartalika or Wat-poornima. Women who came to listen to him, gave him dakshina. It would amount to something like twenty-five rupees. It was my way of helping him. Vikas and Prakash enjoyed counting all the coins. I used to take all the women in

Anandwan to the Devi temple during the Navaratri. We found some leisure, when people in Anandwan started celebrating the Ganesh festival in Muktangan. During Deepavali, the festival of lamps, I used to invite women for the traditional tulsi viwah.

Self-help being the motto of Anandwan, its members work without being told to; like charity, work also begins at home. It was Baba's duty to clean all the big utensils used for cooking. The utensils were often completely blackened with soot because of the fuel used in ovens. In the afternoon, it was Prakash, Vikas and Narayan who washed them. They used to play and tease each other and smear each other's faces with the ash used for cleaning the utensils. They fought too. Their pranks irritated me at times. There was no cook in Anandwan at that time. I had to cook for everyone, and do the rest of the work also. Some of our guests were very courteous—especially Chandraprakashji, Devendra Gupta and Prembhai, who used to help me with these chores. Among the kind souls, I remember Mama Kshirsagar and Bhau Ranade.

Things never remain the same. Time passes, and things change with it. I won't say that the days of the initial struggle and pain were over. But there was a change within and without. It was 1954. The number of patients had increased to a hundred. The barren land experienced the tremors when the young saplings shot up with pride. The joy of creation is infinite and it boosts up one's confidence. Our patients who were denied even pity, now held their heads high. They had created a world of their own, and they were self-sufficient. The most interesting thing that happened was that, the world outside, the same ruthless, indifferent world, now felt the need to connect with the lepers.

When a group of twenty-five workers, who were members of Service Civil International (SCI), an organisation working for the promotion of international friendship arrived in Anandwan, we were excited. A few more workers belonging to Rastra Sewa Dal, Maganwadi and Sewagram came along with them. There was not a single building to accommodate them. This was the first public camp in Anandwan. The first project they undertook, was the construction of a building. They started work in the most humble spirit and were eager to do anything, developing the land, preparing the mixture of grit and lime with the help of yoked oxen; there were no machines. Our patients also participated – in the well charted out daily programme – with tremendous enthusiasm. We were short of masons and carpenters and the local labour refused to come here. We had to get a few from Nagpur. Surprisingly, the students of the local school in Warora joined us. All these happenings had their side effects. The railway workers of Warora were inspired to dig a well for us. They worked day and night. Among the foreigners, were people speaking different languages such as French, German, Spanish, and English. They came from twenty-three different countries. But their hearts spoke the same language – the language of love – and that is why there was no difficulty in communication. The first three houses that were built were very simple, made of brick and lime, with a basic roof. Both in the rains and in summer, people used to take refuge in our hut.

The work went on for almost three and half months. I remember with gratitude the help extended by Kamaltai Hospet. She used to send nurses to our house. She herself used to walk all the way to cook for us in Anandwan. April came and the weather changed. It was terribly hot and Kamaltai stopped coming. Then, I had to take charge of cooking for all.

I told you, there were no cooks. In this camp, I shouldered the responsibility of cooking. It was not a joke. The students, who came from Warora used to bring fistfuls of rice everyday. Then came two women from renowned families to make the chapattis. Mr Chandawar from Maroda worked with me for sometime. A nice gentleman who was very helpful in the beginning! But after a few days, he turned his back. The programme was well charted out. The day began at 3 a.m. A pandal was set up. Ordinary ovens would not have done. So a big one was made – a simple technique used for large scale cooking – by making a deep furrow in the ground, it is filled first with wood, and then with sawdust and it is lit up with oil from the lantern. Cooking required all this preparation. Cleaning the rice was a pretty tedious and laborious job for me. So Baba went to every school and told the boys and girls to bring cleaned rice. People brought enough food grains with them and they lasted us for many days. We used to make dalia. On Sunday, tea was offered; our resources were very scanty in those days. Sunday was also marked by another programme—the sing-song.

Days went by. Now, we had a surplus of milk and vegetables. So we sent them to the market in Warora to be sold. But fear and ignorance about leprosy had gripped the people's minds so tightly that they refused to buy things produced by lepers. But there were some educated and cultured people in the village too. They showed the courage to buy the products of Anandwan, known as the 'leprosy colony'. Gradually, more people came forward to buy vegetables grown by our patients. One thing I must tell you is that Baba never compromised on the quality of any product. It had a desirable effect on people. There was an increasing demand for our products. Today, a large share of the vegetables required for Warora is supplied by Anandwan. Along with vegetables, fruits such as oranges, bananas, guavas, and papayas, and flowers such as mogra, from Anandwan have captured the market of Warora.

I specially remember three women in the SCI camp, who had come from abroad. They were foreigners, but showed interest in the Indian way of life. Among the three, Susan was eager to know more about Indian customs and traditions. She was a cheerful woman with a smiling face, and was very talkative! While she was at Anandwan, we received the news that my younger brother was engaged to be married soon. I told you that I was estranged from my family for some time after my marriage. But after the birth of Vikas and Prakash there was a considerable improvement. At least we were on talking terms and did not mind seeing each other occasionally. Baba was more eccentric. Even when he went to see his own father, he used to carry his own tiffin with him. He did not like my staying with my parents frequently.

Now that my brother's wedding was settled, it was an opportunity for me to be with my sisters and I was very happy. Susan insisted on attending this wedding. She was curious about all the customs and rituals in an Indian wedding and did not want to lose an opportunity to attend it. In those days, there was a regular train plying between Warora and Nagpur. It had a coal engine. This passenger train went very slowly, spitting black smoke all the way. We set out for the wedding. On reaching the railway station we found that the platform was over-crowded. It was the wedding season and naturally there was a great rush. I hustled Prakash and Vikas through the window and then the two of us managed to get in. During the whole journey to Nagpur, Susan never complained despite the discomfort. We got off at Nagpur, with aching bodies. During the wedding, Susan made an effort to find out the meaning of every holy mantra and the various rituals as well. She felt very much at home. After the wedding, we immediately returned to Warora.

Another guest-participant was a woman from Switzerland. Her name was Lalitamba. She had her peculiarities. She liked to be left alone. You may call her a loner. We had to make a special hut for her. It was the only hut within fifty acres of land. She lived there all alone. Once she saw me drawing water from the well and she fought with Baba. She argued that Indian husbands are very dominating, always bossing over their wives. According to her, drawing water from the well was a man's job. She was very conscious about women's rights.

The third one, Priscilla was influenced by the philosophy of J. Krishnamurthi. She insisted on Baba meeting him at least once. However, it was not Baba's sphere; sitting for hours in meditation was not his cup of tea. By nature, Baba is a karmayogi, a man of action and hot tempered too.

When she came, Baba became very ill with tuberculosis. He was shifted to Nagpur. Ironically, this was the only time I remember having stayed for long (one full month), with my parents in Nagpur. Baba was admitted to the medical hospital, five kilometers from my mother's house. Vikas and Prakash were too young; I would leave them in my sister's custody and go to the hospital. It was definitely not walking distance and travelling by an auto was out of question because I could not afford it. It cost six annas then. I used to walk four annas distance and then take an auto, which cost me only two annas. On my way back from the hospital, I followed the same rule. Money had to be saved like this. There were other methods of saving money. Actually, you do not need to learn them. Necessity teaches you everything. Before leaving my mother's home, I bought a dulai (soft blanket) because we had only the rough spun kambal which gave a prickly sensation. For the children, I bought a rajai for twelve rupees and when there was no money left, I sold it for ten rupees. With that money I came back with Baba and the children to Warora.

One evening, when Baba returned home, both of us could hear some heavy breathing from inside the hut. On looking inside, we were taken aback by the sight of a huge python stretched leisurely on the bed. Some people had to be called to kill this unwanted guest. There was no alternative but to kill snakes and scorpions. Later, Prakash mastered the art of catching them alive, and the killing stopped. At Hemalkasa, no one kills snakes. It seems more ghastly today to think of having lived in the midst of such deadly creatures. At that time, we had no choice. Circumstances made us bolder, you may say. I think adaptability, whether of body or mind, is a natural gift to man, usually lost sight of while living in comfort. Give up the comforts and you will know your potential and strength.

There is yet another zone where your dormant energies are activated—times of uncertainty and unpredictability. When faced with these evils beyond your control, a search for the inner strength begins. Moreover, the survival instinct is so strong in us that we learn to manage disasters, big or small, without ever being trained. There are no schools where this can be taught. I am talking about an individual's personal, private life. In public life one may think of disaster management in advance. As for myself, I learnt a lot in the school of life itself. Living with a man like Baba and all his idiosyncrasies, is like carrying a school with you for twenty four hours of the day.

Baba loves to play practical jokes. His jokes proved fatal at times. I was the first one to be exposed to what he would call his frolics. A glimpse into the following one will suffice. In those days, the board meetings were held in the houses of the trustees who lived in Warora. After the meeting, Baba had to walk five kilometres to get back home. The road went through a jungle. Once, after the evening meal, at about seven thirty, he went out. It was quite dark when he left. The clock struck eleven but he had not returned. Time ticked away, minute after minute. I lost my ease. Finally, I set out with a few patients, with tapers in our hands, in search of Baba. The darkness seemed impenetrable; the night, blacker than ever. After having wearied ourselves with the walking, we found Baba lying on the ground, with hands folded on the chest; there was no movement; the silence added to the suspense. How often have I missed a heartbeat on such an occasion! What must have happened? I tried to guess. Could it be a snake bite? Or did a tiger . . . ? Imagination travelled faster. I had always seen him bubbling with enthusiasm. To see Baba lying there motionless now! My mind refused to accept the unimaginable in that situation. At last I made myself bold and pinched his leg. There was an immediate reaction, almost a reflex action. Baba sat up and started laughing. Our faces were darkened with tension and he was laughing. I was boiling; anything might have happened to me, I thought. What if I had harmed myself in the fit of grief . . . ?

One day, a terrible stench was emanating from our hut. It made me sick. We found that it came from underneath my bed. There were two mattresses. When we removed the top one, we found a snake lying dead on the other. No one could tell how it came there. Whether it died a natural death or by an accident – perhaps, he could not bear my weight – remained a mystery forever.

Renuka's arrival created a ripple in our lives. She is the first among my god-daughters. Vikas, Prakash and Narayan were happy to have a sister. I used to give her an oil massage and bath myself. How many times these little ones made claims on my motherhood! I have been fond of children since childhood. Even today, I enjoy being with Gokul's children. Only they can tell you what innocence is. Theirs is a world without artifice, purpose and concealment. Theirs is the most natural response, and without any inhibitions. There is no diplomacy. How rare and lovely is this nakedness of the spirit!

Maya was found when Renuka was six months old in Salori, ten kilometres from Anandwan. Baba owns a piece of land here; it came to him as his share of the ancestral property. One day, two women who sold firewood, found a baby crying by the side of the road. They reported to the police who promptly brought her to us. She was a cute looking baby with thick hair and Baba took to her at first sight. We named her Maya. Baba brought a spirit lamp especially for her, so she could have hot milk at night. She liked to drink milk. Though she stayed with us only for about six months, she became the most beloved inmate of Anandwan, a darling of all hearts. However, her days were numbered. Perhaps, she could not digest milk and died of diarrhoea. Her death created a vacuum; we have not been able to get over this irreparable loss. Baba was drowned in tears. Rarely have I seen Baba weeping like this. We buried her under a tree. There was no one who did not weep that day; not a heart that did not ache on her death. For many days that followed, I used to pour a bowl of milk into the ground where we lay her to rest. The wound is fresh even today. To think of her is to make it bleed again. Memory has nothing to do with the duration of a relationship. It is drawn to where there is intensity and intimacy. She continues to occupy a corner of our hearts. There came yet another girl, whom we named Bijli because it was the day on which electricity came to Anandwan for the first time.

Prakash, as a child, roamed around only in his shirt. He felt more comfortable in this 'bottomless' condition and walked about with a majestic gait. He was always attracted to birds and insects. Once he saw two of them, sitting on a stone; for him this was a new species. He lifted the stone and came to me. 'Indu, look here. See what I have brought,' he said to me, and insisted on my having a look at them. I looked up and would have screamed in fear if he had not held it in his hand. There were two giant scorpions, flashing their diabolic tails with more than enough poison for ten of us. I snatched the stone from his hands, threw it away, and hugged him as I prayed to god. I could see, in a minute, what destiny held for my children in future. But why blame destiny? Wasn't it our own doing? These encounters with the underground creatures became a daily affair. They showed up unexpectedly. They had a free passage everywhere; during lunch from under the wooden seats, or in the bathroom at a very difficult moment. There was no place they could not enter. Gradually, we got used to it but our guests had a tough time. Most of them used to pack up before they were scheduled to leave, giving some excuse or the other. I do not know how, but Prakash and Vikas had formed a strange habit—they used to ask every guest when he or she would be leaving. We felt embarrassed then. If at all they took to someone, especially one who entertained them, they would do everything to prevent them from going; the easiest way was to hide their chappals.

Whether we lived in the kingdom of insects, birds, and animals or they came to stay with us, it seemed that neither of us could get away from the other. In Anandwan, monkeys came very rarely. They watched us from a distance. There was more of curiosity than nuisance in their conduct. But one of them attacked Baba once. Unfortunately, it died within three days. The doctor advised Baba to take injections and Baba flatly refused. I teased Baba saying, 'The poison in your body has killed the monkey. You do not need to take the injections'.

Besides these uninvited guests from the animal world who could enter into our house at any time, there were people who were difficult to deal with. Once we were about to go to bed when a strong smell of bidi roused Baba's curiosity and he opened the door to find out where it came from. There stood eight to ten trappers with sticks and spears in their hands. When they were questioned about their purpose they answered that they were out hunting. Baba warned them not to show their faces again and they disappeared in the darkness of the night. Even the women who broke stones for a living gave us a lot of trouble. They casually pilfered from wherever they went. They picked up anything that was handy. They did not spare even the vegetables in our farm. One day our patience and tolerance ran out; Baba's fury knew no bounds and he took them to task and told them never to come here again. From that day, they disappeared. On another occasion, Baba caught a man stealing cotton from our store. But he did not hand him over to the police. He believes more in moral change than in punishment as a corrective measure. He gave him a sermon on morality and let him go.

We had our share of meeting good people too. It is difficult to remember each and every one of them, but some did stand out with their peculiarities. Mrs Jakate, who was a member of Uttarayan – our home for the aged – donated one thousand rupees for building the well in Anandwan. Besides, she also expressed her desire to donate a piece of land near the Ram Mandir in Warora. However, the land was jointly owned, so we did not accept it. Mrs Jakate was a widow and followed all the rules of widowhood—wearing a particular type of sari, shaving off the head completely, observing all the rules and the rituals of cooking. She was orthodox. Once, she came to our house for lunch and I had to observe all those rules of cooking for her—wearing a special sari while cooking and not touching any one until the cooking was done. When she died, Baba performed all the last rites; he gave the ritual bath to the body, then draped it in a new silk sari; her body was carried from the village of Warora to Anandwan in a cycle-rikshaw. Baba held the body during the procession, and people sang bhajans. She was cremated under a bel tree. The gold she wore, was handed over to the officer in charge of the panchayat.

Mr P. B. Bhave, the well-known Marathi writer, once visited our centre with his wife. He was ready to donate twenty-five thousand rupees to build a temple in Anandwan. Obviously, Baba refused to accept this proposal. The secular framework in which Baba works did not allow it. In those days, there were no images or idols of god in our house; no puja ghar, nor the typical carved, wooden case for god. We later got a case, and that too at the insistence of Parvatibai Patwardhan. We were criticised for our disrespect for custom and tradition many times. Though I was a believer, I treated it as a personal preference. Baba never subscribed to it. Mrs Bhave, however, was pleasantly surprised when I applied kumkum on her forehead when they were about to leave.

Human nature is a very strange phenomenon, and unpredictable too. You often meet people who frustrate your attempts to understand them and defy the labels you attach to them. My younger sister, Ratnaprabha – known as Baby – got married to a professor. All of us went to Nagpur for the wedding by the regular passenger train. Bhau Ranade came with me and Baba was to join us later. When we got down at the Nagpur railway station, the ticket collector bumped into Bhau. In fact, he was not at fault. But that was enough for Bhau to flare up.

The two began quarrelling. Standing there with the children, I watched the war of words that went on for quite some time. The detached observer in me was stunned by Bhau's force. What a big fight over a trifle, I thought. Quarrelling must also be an art, in which Bhau excelled.

There cannot be a wedding, at least in India, without the razzle-dazzle, hurry and bustle and of course a lot of work too. In the midst of the crowd, I saw two women servants working very hard. They were specially employed to wash all the dishes that lay there in a heap. It was winter and in that cold weather they were working their fingers to the bone, late at night. I decided to join them. Eyebrows were raised at my voluntary help. I did not bother. I too share this trait with Baba—when the call comes from the heart, there is no other consideration but to act at your will and plunge into the work. Public approval was not something we sought. We never lived in the world of images, so there was never any question of living up to them, even though they are mostly false.

We were supposed to leave early next morning. Since I worked till late that night, I was late getting ready and we were behind schedule when we reached the station. Baba, along with the children and the Pol family got onto the train and I went to buy tickets with Sudhakar. Just then I heard the whistle and got on the nearest compartment. As the train moved, I asked a fellow passenger, whether it was the train to Chanda. When he told me it was not, I jumped off from the running train and fell on the platform. The train went by and then I came to know that it was the right train after all. I had the tickets in my hand and Baba travelled without them. I reported to the stationmaster who was kind enough to call the Wardha railway station and brief the stationmaster there. I rang up Mr Jog. Kisha came and arranged for my bus to Warora. The train was delayed, so I reached first. I went home and prepared dinner. Baba, however, could not forgive me for the mess and flew into a fury. The male ego was hurt.

In 1956, a woman called Leela came from Greece. Her actual name was Orvilla; after she became a nun, they called her Sister Leela. We accommodated her in our own hut. With the partition made by tying a sari she tried to make herself comfortable. It was not easy for her to cope with the rats that moved freely in the hut. They did not spare even the bed. The first night she spent emptying a whole matchbox. The next morning, she had a big fight with Baba. She complained that we purposely kept her in the outer portion so that we might enjoy our privacy. But, within a short time she came to know that the other side of the partition was not safe from the little culprits either. She then apologised.

Leela stayed with us for a year. She was amused to see me and my children sleeping in the same bed. How could I tell her what it meant? What a gap in culture and values! When the children went to school, I used to go with little Renuka in my arms, to the well to wash clothes. Putting her on a charpoy under the tree, I used to finish the washing; carry Renuka home first and again go back to collect the clothes. Later on, Leela took over this job and with some effort, somehow managed; but she used a lot of soap and still could not remove the dirt from the clothes. She excelled in other things though. She was good at darning. She used to stitch my old, worn out saris by patching the pieces together. This was the scene in our quarters; anyway, the general standard of living of people in those days was not very high. Very few could have been marked 'rich'. Salaries were modest; and yet there was a sense of happiness and contentment which seems to be missing today despite more money. My old saris were never wasted. I made frocks out of them for the milkman's daughters. Once I got thirty rupees as prize money for writing in the special coloumn of a magazine called *Stree*. With that money I bought a new sari for the wife of one of our workers. Most of them worked on meagre salaries without ever complaining. Their sincerity and tenacity was indeed commendable. It was really amazing. They commanded our love. At that time our sources of income were limited. We used to get wheat and chillies from a nearby place called Goraj, and rice from Baba's ancestral farms in Salori. It was strictly utilised only for our institution.

Of all that Baba suffered from, headaches were the most painful. All well-known doctors including Dr Ginde examined him but failed, both to diagnose and to cure. Once they tried lumber puncture during which, due to some technical lapse on their part, Baba came to have severe and permanent headache. Headache is very common, you may say, but Baba's was very uncommon; in that the pain was unbearable, and no medicines worked. He felt as if someone was pounding on his brain. He became increasingly sensitive to sound. I finally handed him over to Balkoba for two months. They took him to Urali Kanchan, near Pune, for some naturopathy treatment. This too, proved ineffective. He came back to Warora. We built a separate hut for him in the midst of the jungle in front of Uttarayan. He shaved his head. Everyday, I would massage ghee made of our cow's milk into his scalp. Vomiting accompanied the excruciating headache. He had to be admitted to the Nagpur Medical Hospital. He was on a liquid diet for nine days; we fed him with a tube. There were continual bouts of vomiting—the tubes often came off, causing him immense pain. On the tenth day he asked for food for the first time. We gave him a few spoons of dilute toor dal. After a fortnight, we returned to Warora. During this illness, sister Leela and and

P. R. Bhide (Swami Vidyananand) called us from Delhi regularly and enquired after Baba's health.

In Delhi, Sister Leela arranged a meeting with Indiraji. She wrote to Baba inviting him to Delhi. Baba went in his usual attire; a pair of chappals made from a tyre, and unshaven. Sister Leela was not happy with this appearance. She bought a coat for Baba for sixteen rupees and a pair of chappals too. She even took him to a barber for a shave. Now he was ready to see Indiraji, she thought. Indiraji spoke courteously and asked Baba about his work. She even escorted him to the car when the meeting was over. Leela wrote in her telegram 'Baba has conquered Indiraji'.

I must say that in all the difficult times that tried our mettle again and again, it is my faith in god that gave me the strength, and even saved us from time to time. When Baba went to Mumbai for a major operation, I sought to invoke the almighty in my own ways—reading the scriptures, observing vratas and performing pujas were part of a regular routine. My anxiety led to a number of such pious acts, propitiation rites, fasts and the like. There was a big pool behind the school. Now the area is crowded with people, but in those days it was a jungle. Near the pool was a big banyan tree. I decided to read Vinobaji's Geetai eighteen times and do 108 pradakshinas around the tree. I did not even think about how much time it would take. My youngest sister Suma was with me. Early in the morning, I left for the jungle. I cleared a patch of ground and sat down to read the sacred book. By the time I finished eleven readings, the sun had already set. No one knew about my plan. They came searching for me in the jungle with lanterns. I had finished the reading when they arrived and my pradakshinas had begun. They waited until I had finished and all of us went home together. My Satyawan was in Mumbai, fighting a battle for his life, and I prayed, like Savitri, for him. My prayers were answered.

Our work had taken roots now. Patients came regularly, and there were visitors too. Geetabai, Kaushalyabai and Vanhere came from the leprosy home at Dattapur. They had the experience of working in the hospital and extended all their help here. Geetabai worked efficiently under Baba's guidance at the dispensary in Anandwan. She volunteered to do jobs such as dressing wounds and distributing medicines to the patients. There was no separate kitchen for the workers at that time. I used to cook for all of them until 1964, when the college started and a separate kitchen was constructed. Once I went with Kaushalyabai and Geetabai to listen to kirtana. All of us were so absorbed in it that we did not realise how time passed. It was twelve when it got over. There was no electricity in Warora then. We crossed the jungle and came to the bridge; no sooner had we crossed it, than we realised that a truck was chasing us. There were only three of us in the cart, and all women. They kept focusing lights on us. They overtook us, and stopped at Nagpur Square; we changed the path to bypass them and went towards the railway station. Nana got off and came back with fifty men, all carrying spears. The men in the truck did not expect this. It was their turn to be scared now, and they took to their heels.

In these trying conditions and times of hectic activity, there came some rare moments of comic relief. Once, the brother of Tarabai Modak came to Anandwan. He was a naturopath. He spoke confidently about nature cure. We handed over five patients to him as an experiment. He reduced their diet to coconuts and groundnuts only. The experiment went on for one and half months. The patients soon started complaining of toothache. Some had more serious problems; their teeth were becoming loose from their gums. One by one, they absconded. We could not stop laughing at his peculiar and failed experiment.

There were moments worth cherishing for life. Moments of selfless love of humble folk made us forget our toil. It made us stronger too. In 1956, I had to undergo an operation; it was a minor surgery on the nasal bone. I went to Ghataprabha with all my little ones, five of them. Many times people avoided us for peculiar reasons—our appearance, our friends, our radical and anti-establishment views. On our way back, we stopped at Pune where Raosaheb Patwardhan insisted on having lunch with us. To be very frank, I always feel embarrassed when it comes to interacting with the 'highbrow'. I feel suffocated in their presence. When work forced us to travel to distant places, we always stayed at public charity houses. I never forgot to ask waiters to pack us the leftover food from our order at restaurants. We had learnt our lessons from the poverty in which we had chosen to live. The first one was against wastage. I can never tolerate the wastage of food. I get terribly upset to see people wasting food. The most miserable of the victims of poverty are the children. It has greater dimensions than merely suffering the want of something. Katu, the brother-in-law of Narayan used to milk our cows. He had two daughters, Girija and Asha. Girija and my daughter Renuka were in the same class. My sister used to stitch frocks for Renuka. I once gave an old frock of Renuka's to Girija. You know how it is with children. She was so happy with the frock, her face beamed with joy and the next day she wore it and went to school. In the evening when she returned, she was crying. I asked her what the matter was, and she told me how the girls at school teased her for wearing Renuka's old frock. I did not know how to console her. The horror of such economic inequalities claimed the simple joy of a little one. The next day, I purchased two metres of cloth and had two frocks made for Girija.

The incident I have just described may be a trifle for the readers of this book, but it cost me my peace of mind for some time; and in fact, was a lesson for me. We strictly observed economic equality in Anandwan. After Vikas and Prakash became doctors, they received only Rs 300 extra as compared to the menial workers. Today, the situation has changed. With the arrival of grants from the government and due to some unreasonable demands made by some of the workers, it is impossible to maintain that same economic equality at Anandwan today. It pains me to admit it.

After 1957, Baba set up a number of medical centres in different villages. He visited each of the centres once or twice a week. Patients flocked to these centres in large numbers. His day would begin at three in the morning, earlier than the early bird's. I had to keep his tiffin ready by four, when he set out. If, by any chance, I was late even by two minutes, he used to go without it. At home, I would atone for the delay by fasting for the entire day. Sometimes he arrived late at night. His legs would hurt from walking long distances. Since he had no assistant in the clinic, he had to work overtime. His hands hurt terribly too, from continually giving injections. Everyday, I would give him an oil massage when he returned. He worked day and night. None of the doctors were ready to stay overnight in the leprosy hospital. So it was quite taxing on Baba to do everything alone—it was difficult to get doctors to work for the lepers; most of them flatly refused. It became a one man show—cleaning the wounds, picking maggots, dressing and bandaging, cleaning the bedpans and all other routine matters in a clinic. Consequently, his own health deteriorated. He would suddenly clench his teeth as if in a fit, or his pulse would drop causing him to faint. His health became a cause for worry for me. However, a most faithful well-wisher, Dr Sainani used to rush to my aid even at midnight. There was some relief when Geetabai joined us.

To think about the days gone by is to be filled with wonder sometimes. Where did the strength come from while we fought against such a variety of odds, I often ask myself. Consider the health problems alone. They were serious enough to have to take up all our attention and distract us from our work. The inconveniences we had to put up with could have been the major deterrents. As far as I can reason out, I think both Baba and I had the tenacity and resilience that saved us from sinking into impotent dejection or self-pampering frustration. In fact, our sense of pleasure and elation were never associated with comforts or achievements on the material plane. Moments of success never made our heads swell with pride. We remained firmly rooted to the ground reality. That is why the institution could grow in many directions, gathering new skies in its fold; nestling hundreds who were rejected by the world. Leprosy was just the beginning—a tiny trickle, I should say. Soon it grew into a spate. Between the trickle and the spate are the years of struggle, labour, isolation, and convergence. The love shown to us by all those known and unknown souls, made our tasks easier though. There is no doubt about this. Their love had many faces and names too. No barriers could have stopped it because it was as spontaneous as ours. The faith that there are some good souls in the world and the good fortune of having met some of them was enough for us to carry our work forward.

Annasaheb Sahasrabuddhe once arrived at our house with seven or eight guests. He was accompanied by the counsel of Israel and his wife, and some other people. They arrived late at night. I had to cook for all of them. I do not know how but I burnt my hand; there were big blisters and they hurt. However, the burning problem before me was how to milk the cows in the morning. There were eight or ten of them. Since milking them had been my job for years now, the cows could easily recognise my hand. If anyone else tried to touch them, they would kick. Anna helped me that day. The next morning at three we went to the cowshed. I sat down facing the cow. Anna, hidden partially behind me, stretched his right hand. I put out my left hand and the two of us somehow managed to milk all the cows successfully. Anna never lived like a guest in our house. Like a member of the family, he used to share all the work in our house – whether it was cleaning, washing, filling the water barrel or any other – he was ever ready to do them. His circle of friends included Devendrabhai Gupta, Prembhai, Subramanyam and quite a few Gandhian social workers.

Baba Deshpande the novelist and his wife Vimaltai came to Anandwan quite often. When they came, Vimaltai used to take charge of the kitchen. She used to make the chapattis and allow me to rest. Some of my happiest memories are associated with Dajisaheb and Parvatibai Patwardhan. The credit for the fact that we have idols of gods in our house goes to Parvatibai; if she had not insisted on it, our house would have forever remained a forbidden place to god. Baba would have never allowed me to have them. He is not so much opposed to the idea of god, as he is to rituals and traditional forms of worship. He is perfectly at ease with the abstract conception of god. On the other hand, my frame of mind calls for material images of the eternal, and ritualistic and ceremonial worship too. Baba found his god in those who were rejected. It was his inborn compassion that prompted him once to bring home a mentally challenged man. Baba was on his way to Delhi for a conference. The train was delayed. As he stood on the platform, he saw an old mad man rolling on the platform, smeared in his own excreta. Baba immediately brought him home and asked me to boil some hot water. Then he bathed the man himself, and after ensuring that he would be taken care of, left for Delhi. In Baba's absence, we had a tough time managing him. The stench was nauseating. His name was Ganpat and he stayed with us, in a hut in front of ours, for quite a few days. Geetabai would keep a watch on him and I would feed him.

Baba's sympathy flowed, uninterrupted, to everyone and everywhere that it was most wanted.

SIX

Our trip to the Himalayas was one of the most memorable journeys in our life. A lifelong experience, I should say. We had received two thousand rupees from someone in Philippines, for the travel. It was in 1958–1959 that we went to the Himalayas. Mahadev Ambekar, Suma and our children accompanied us. We visited holy places such as Haridwar, Hrishikesh, Manasadevi and Neelkanth Mahadev. Vikas, Prakash and Narayan could travel with half-tickets, Renuka and Bijli, free of charge. The sight of the Himalayan ranges brought eternal peace to my mind. If one wants to experience a momentary reunion with nature – a very primordial bond indeed – one must go to the Himalayas. The bond does exist, though it seems to have been temporarily severed due to man's thirst for learning and scientific knowledge.

The serenity and calm that surrounded the Mahadev temple left a permanent impression on my mind. The journey was arduous. The path that led up to the temple was the most difficult part of the journey. The Shiva temple was down deep in the valley, at least fourteen kilometres from our camp. We left the children in the lodge and set out for the temple at about four clock in the afternoon. It was a hard climb and by the time we reached the temple, it was quite dark. The doors of the temple were closed. We had to awaken the priest. He was shocked to see us there at that hour. It was not his fault. Nothing could have stopped us from such a venture. Not even the fear of wild animals. So intense and indomitable was our inner urge and our faith! We had a bath in the ice-cold water at that hour of night and worshipped Lord Shiva at leisure with floral offerings. Early next morning we made for our lodgings and found our worried children waiting impatiently for us. Once they saw us, they were relieved.

Returning from the Himalayas was not so easy. The mind was constantly looking back, lingering all the while in those spots of blissful silence and its whispers. I think anyone who goes to the Himalayas, will have a similar experience. The simplicity of the people living there is unforgettable. I remember, with gratitude, the gracious and endearing inn-keeper, who used to have lunch with us during our stay. Curious to know more about Maharashtra, he indulged in a friendly conversation with us and came to respect Baba for his work.

On our way back, we visited Delhi, Agra and Mathura. In Mathura, we were separated from each other in a crowd. Baba and Mahadev moved ahead, and Suma, the children and I were left behind. It was difficult to spot the two of them in that huge crowd. When our search for them was rendered futile, we went to the police station. The policeman announced our names on the loudspeaker. Thankfully, Baba heard the announcement and rushed to the police station.

There are some other interesting incidents that took place during this tour. We went to the river Yamuna to wash our clothes. The turtles had established a colony in the river. Never before had I seen such big turtles. Their statue-like stillness and hard grey backs deluded me. Thinking they were rocks, I thought of washing my clothes by banging them on the hard surface, but suddenly they started moving. It took us sometime to realise what they were. Call it naivety or ignorance, but these experiences have their joys; simple ones that cost you nothing and that keep you eternally fresh in mind and spirit. I have found places, people and things to be equally fascinating. Flowers, birds and animals, whether domestic or wild, have always fascinated us as they attract children. I am not a philosopher and Baba has never indulged in empty speculations; the world of abstraction is not for us. I am not talking about universal harmony. What I am telling you is what we have felt in our pulses, long before it transformed into a thought—the offshoot of momentary sensations.

Baba's interest in raising cattle is well-known to everyone. He took a special interest in raising cows and oxen. In this region of Maharashtra – the annual festival of the oxen – Bailpola is celebrated with great pomp. We had in our stock, a pair of very strong oxen. Well bred cows were specially brought from Punjab. On the day of the festival, I enjoyed getting the oxen ready for the procession—dressing them in frills and painting their horns. These humble and hardworking creatures that served us without complaint had to have their day. As a token of our gratitude, we fed them special food like puranpoli on this day. Our patients helped me with the preparations for the celebrations of the day. In the evening, Baba used to take them round the village in a ceremonial procession. Our pair of oxen were always the centre of attraction for all. You might wonder, why I am telling you all these things; perhaps, not worth writing about at all in such detail. To be frank, I can never forget the significant contribution of these dumb and docile animal friends of ours, in transforming Anandwan into a fertile profitable land. Perhaps, they worked harder than men and were more loyal too.

Among these faithful and hardworking friends, was Laxman, a young male calf. He was quite plump. His majestic gait could not have passed unnoticed. If by chance, he was unleashed, he would wreak havoc everywhere. He spared nothing, not even the huts. Like a turbulent wind that gushes forward to destroy everything, Laxman made everyone quiver when he appeared. If people chased him he was doubly provoked and then no one had the courage to face him again. But he had one weakness, which we realised rather late. If a woman came his way, he would become quiet and docile. This change was so obvious and sudden that everyone wondered whether it was the same Laxman. Later on, whenever he got out of our control, we sent women to get a hold on him. Many people in Anandwan will tell you interesting anecdotes about Laxman's weakness for the feminine.

No less moving is the following account of Ganpat's death. We used to go to Nagpur quite frequently, especially to purchase goods or material for our institution. Once, on our return, we found a large crowd of people round the corner, where the grocer's shop stands today. On enquiry, we were told that a patient called Ganpat had expired. The people close to him were mourning, and some others had started making preparations for the funeral. Without wasting a minute Baba rushed forward and after quickly examining Ganpat, gave him an injection. To everyone's surprise, Ganpat got up at once and called for Baba. However, after three days, he died.

Trepidations, tremors, uncertainties and doubts are associated with all beginnings, I think. Whether in personal or public life, we could not have escaped them either. In the early phase of our leprosy centre, coping up with the challenges was not easy. Transforming the barren land into a cultivable one was, in itself, a mammoth task. There were two hundred patients now. Even for essential goods, Baba had to travel to Nagpur for which we had to depend on public transport. In 1958, we received a van and that was some help. Baba now went to Nagpur, once a week, for the shopping. He would shop for everyone. The articles he bought included everything from kumkum to food grains. Baba tried to remember everything that the poor patients asked for. You will perhaps laugh at some of the things they wanted—bangles, cheap artificial jewellery, tooth brushes, soap etc. I once accompanied him on this weekly visit. Naturally, I was eager to meet my parents. My house was just two kilometres away from the market place. My mother used to make Baba's favourite dish on such occasions and keep it ready. If she failed to keep time, Baba would leave. He has never compromised on time. He will not tolerate even a minute's delay.

Gradually, more patients poured in. Baba had to work overtime. He did not allow anyone else to attend to the patients. His services included giving them bedpans when needed, picking the maggots from their wounds, and dressing and bandaging them. Our institution had now taken shape. The land was being cultivated. Farming had begun. Vegetables were being grown for our daily use. There was enough milk for everyone. It was at this juncture, that many important people visited Anandwan. Among them were Dhebarbhai, Shrikrishna

Jaju, Chandraprakashji and Madalasa Agrawal. People had started taking cognisance of the work that Baba was doing in this remote corner of Maharashtra. A friend of sister Leela, Freda Bedi wrote an article on Baba. It helped rouse people's curiosity about his work.

Baba's experiments had borne fruit. There were signs of the institution taking a definite shape. But all this hectic activity demanded a heavy price. Those who have seen Baba closely know that he is a workaholic. Some of you might say that he exploits himself, or that he is a fanatic of sorts. There were times, when I used to wonder where the strength came from or what mania this was. I knew that there are people in the world, very few perhaps, who revel in sacrifice. But none of my conjectures were true. Every guess was rendered futile, because Baba's personality defied my logic. Soon, I realised that the source was within him. How shall I name it? Shall I say that there was something in him that clamoured for fulfilment? Most probably!

It was love of the good and the beautiful that dictated the terms in every sphere of his life and our life together. And he never spared himself, when it was a question of discipline. I was talking about the price we had to pay for the work we did in Anandwan. Baba's health deteriorated as the work progressed. In fact the two have always had an inverse relationship. A permanent pain in the back was his reward for his incessant labour, though it was a labour of love. Health emergencies cropped up so many times that they soon became part of the routine. I remember our visit to Tapowan. It was Dajisaheb's love that took us there. Parvatibai's hospitality was overwhelming. On our way back, when the train reached Wardha, Baba complained of severe pain in the chest. It was a Sunday. The train was over-crowded; there was no place to lie down. Finally, when he could not bear it any more, he went and tried to make himself comfortable in a corner. He quietly lay down, resting his head on a sack of nails. Nothing could be done until we reached Warora. A message was sent to Dr Sainani and a bullock-cart sent to fetch him. His treatment gave Baba some relief from the pain.

Baba's back-ache has a long history. It first began with a snake-hunt. Once, while returning from the well at Uttarayan, with a pitcher in one hand, I saw a snake stretched across the gate. I did not notice it at first, but as I went close, it raised its hood all of a sudden. I screamed out for Baba. Baba killed the snake, but in the process he jerked, and sudden sharp pain shot down his back. It aggravated with time and has stayed with him. We tried many medicines and kinds of therapies. Once Dr Kamaltai Joshi from Nagpur brought Mr Karmarkar, an ayurvedic practitioner with her to treat Baba. Can you imagine the remedies he tried? He heated iron rods and scalded Baba's back. And he did this many times. It was really a test of endurance for us, the observers, but Baba sat still throughout the ordeal. What was the outcome? Only blisters! It is possible to write Baba's life-story in terms of his illnesses alone and the unheard of remedies he tried. Whether we invited them or they had chosen us, I do not know. But something or other was always happening. Even I could not escape it. Once there was a widespread contagion of mumps in the town. Along with Vikas, Prakash, Narayan, Renuka and Bijli, I fell a victim to it. For four days I lived only on milk.

Soon after this, Annasaheb Sahasrabuddhe came one day to meet Baba who had just returned from the farm. They got ready for an evening walk. Considering my health, they decided not to go far. But they got so involved in their conversation as they walked that they did not realise how far they went. I lagged far behind. This happened many times with Baba. I could not keep pace with them. I got cramps in my legs. I had no energy left to walk. I prayed to god for a vehicle and lo, there appeared one. Some government officer was passing by. On seeing Baba he stopped and all of us returned home in his vehicle. I thanked god for answering my prayer.

In the history of any institution, there comes a time, when people come seeking after you. There was a time when people used to avoid us; we were ostracised for our unorthodox views and actions. Around the late 1950's, the scene began to change. Many people started taking interest in our work. One evening in 1960, while I was in the house with the children and Baba was busy with something in the courtyard, a voice, sonorous and masculine, was heard. 'Is Amte Guruji in the house?', he asked Baba. I did not blame him for not recognising Baba. Perhaps, Baba's attire – only vest and underwear – deluded him. I came out to see who it was. It was my turn to be surprised. There stood no other than Acharya Atre himself. Hours passed by in conversation! He was all praise for Baba and equally stinging in his comment on the indifference of the government towards leprosy. Only he could have said what he said—'Unless the ministers get leprosy they will not come to Anandwan. Baba, you are god on earth and Sadhanatai, a goddess.' He was too liberal in his praise for us, I thought. After going back, he wrote an editorial on us. The flow of words in his conversation was stunning. He had a roaring voice that perfectly suited a man who invited controversies. There was nothing that he did not shine in. He was at home with everything—politics, education, the arts, literature, poetry, parody, theatre and what not? He was the pride of Maharashtra, a versatile man, and a rare kind.

The change in Baba's image in society was noticeable now. People began to see him in a different light. This was reflected in the domestic sphere too. Our relatives, who had never looked at him positively, now realised their errors in judgement. The mist of misunderstanding evaporated gradually. The following letter from my grandfather, written in English, underlined this change:

> My dear Babasaheb,
>
> It is with the same emotional spirit, which failed to express itself the other day at Warora in words, that I am now trying this evening once again in letters. In a way, it is better in the case of a lawyer (as I happen to be) who is generally supposed to have a heart far away from his tongue. I am however sorry, I may not succeed even in letters also, because as the saying goes, 'words fail when the heart is full.' I really do not know how to discharge the unforgettable obligations with which we have been burdened. I am aware of what you did on the previous occasion few years ago when Sau. Baby was married and I have seen what you did this time. I must say that chiranjeevi saubhagyavati Suman has been rightly styled as 'God's child' and because she had been so, she got 'God parents' like you and Chi. Sau. Indu, and all concerned, including myself have to be grateful to you both for ever, and I am sure, whatever you have done for your God Child will not go unrewarded.
>
> I was extremely sorry that there has been a lot of misunderstanding spread about you. It is really a pity that our own people should behave in such a way and try to disturb cordial relations. I was very much shocked when I saw that I was also being

connected with the mischief of which, I had not even the least idea. I do appreciate your feelings when I feel the pain myself. I, however, feel that we should not attach much importance to this mischief, which is the creation of petty minds and weak ears and will die out in due course. Clear conscience fears no such mischief however pinching it may be, and I hope you will not allow yourself to be led by it and tax your brain, which is already heavily burdened with other more important matters. I need hardly say how pleased I was at the good luck, which has come to Chi. Suman. I have been quite aware of the anxiety of her unfortunate mother; and I have seen how she has breathed a sigh of relief now. Our only prayer note should be that God will bestow upon His Child and her new partner a long, happy and prosperous life.

Though I have been undoubtedly happy during my short stay in your ANANDWAN, I must admit, I have not left the place without a feeling of regret and disappointment. You have been asking me to visit the place for the last several years but I could not fulfil my promise, which still remains unfulfilled, as I could not enjoy the real pleasure of ANANDWAN where life is really worth living; a life full of service and sacrifice where one can experience and have the darshan of God that is sought in vain in Haridwar, Kashi and Rameshwar. I am really proud of the creator of ANANDWAN and his partner in this great task, Sau. Indu who has brightened the names of both the families. May

God bless you both with a long and happy life to achieve the fruit of your great sacrifice, which is unique in itself and an ideal for others who pose to be public workers. I do not wish to add anything more but cannot also close without a warning, which I think, I have the right to sound to you. I have noted with great concern your capacity to work with utter disregard for your health, which is more valuable to others than it is to you. I hope you will agree with me when I say that both of you now belong to millions of people for whose sake you have lifted this great burden and as such you are their valuable property, if I may say so. In the circumstances it is your duty to honestly preserve their property with all possible care, to complete the work which, I suppose, has been entrusted to you by God.

I wish and hope to be able to take some chance to come to ANANDWAN once again. I was equally glad to be acquainted with your friend Shri Padmawar and shall be pleased if you come to me with him some day. Please remember me to him.

With affectionate blessings to you all.

Affectionately yours,
S. G. Ghule

We received our first donation in 1960. The Indian Ambassador to Switzerland, Mr M. V. Vellody and his wife, who were familiar with our work, came in contact with a Swiss institution called Swiss Aid Abroad. They knew that this institution had donated liberally to constructive projects all over the world. Mr Vellody acted as the bridge between us. He promptly provided all the information about our work to Swiss Aid, and as a result, we received thirty thousand rupees by way of donation. The most commendable thing about it was that the Swiss school children had raised all this money by skipping one meal. With this money we could undertake the 'tin can project' in Anandwan. This was a historic event. The inmates of Anandwan, until then, had confined themselves to agriculture and cattle-raising only. Now they stood face to face with the challenge of technology. And with Baba's indomitable self-confidence and constant encouragement, they could overcome their lack of technical skill and knowledge. The project was inaugurated on the 28 November 1960. The target now was to produce articles of domestic use such as oil-lamps, ladles, sieves and tin cans. The hands that were to produce these useful things were the hands of the diseased, the disabled, and the lepers. Pandit Jawaharlal Nehru wrote a letter congratulating Baba on his achievement.

A turning point had come. More people were eager to join our project now. Impressed by Baba's work, Sushilabai Kelkar, who had just retired from Sewagram, was drawn towards Anandwan. Her husband was a leprosy patient. He too joined our office. Among such dedicated workers, were some doctors who regularly arranged medical camps at Anandwan and extended their services to our patients. These camps were sponsored by Gramodyog Sangh, Sewagram and Maganwadi.

Meanwhile, my younger sister Suma got married. The wedding was arranged at Anandwan. This was the first wedding held in the leprosy colony. It was because of Dr Sadhaphale (Suma's husband) that this first wedding at Anandwan could take place. He had booked a marriage hall in Nagpur, but on our request, changed the venue. At the time, he was engaged with some research in the Department of Agriculture, Government of India. His simplicity and unassuming nature impressed us the most. All our companions attended the wedding. He became a member of our family—the greater family of Anandwan, I mean.

The next year, nine public weddings were held at Anandwan. Eight of the weddings were of our friends in Anandwan. The ninth one was of Baba's close associate from Bhadrawati, Shridhar Padmawar. He willingly agreed to have his wedding, along with the patients, in our premises. In fact, it was my proposal that the patients be allowed to marry. Baba helped them rediscover their lives and I worked for their conjugal rights and the right to a family life. Knowing fully well that sex is as important as hunger, and that denial of the same would lead to immoral and deviant behaviour, I insisted on their marriages. Baba was strongly opposed to the marriages, but I was firm and refused to give in. He too would not yield so easily. He fretted and fumed. And I could only ignore his growing irritation and aggression. I had made up my mind not to surrender to his tantrums this time. Eventually, his rigidity melted and he consented to my proposal. This opened a new chapter in our patients' lives. It was a pleasure to see them setting up their homes and enjoying their family life with their children. I think the only remedy for irritability and stubbornness—characteristics of a bachelor (Baba was a confirmed bachelor once upon a time)—is wedlock. Sindhu, Shankardada's wife, gave me the credit of bringing this warmth of the hearth and the breeze of domestic happiness into their lives.

Many things settled down by now. The institution was established. We enjoyed our work. But that was not enough. The stuff, of which Baba is made, always demanded more—enough was never really enough. He wanted to bring the two worlds together—our world of the diseased and the disabled, and their world of complacency, comfort and indifference. The tin can project provided the opportunity for this. In 1960, the first get-together for the friends of Anandwan was organised. It was an attempt to build a bridge between the two worlds. We sincerely felt that the people on the other side, living in a secure world, should at least catch a fleeting glimpse of the hundreds of phoenix in Anandwan rising from the ashes of their wishes and hopes, once extinguished by the curse of leprosy. We wanted them to be witness to this historical moment and participate in the creative frenzy of these deformed fingers. All preparations were made for the production of the tin cans. The raw material was purchased, the machinery had arrived and above all, their minds were overflowing with energy, hitherto untapped, and waiting to scatter itself in—it really did not matter whether in tin cans, sieves or something else.

We decided to inaugurate the project in this first get-together. Dr Cuttat, the Swiss ambassador, was present on this occasion. Among other dignitaries, were Shankarrao Deo, G. N. Dandekar, acharya Bhagwat, acharya Jawdekar, Prema Kantak, Kamaltai Hospet, Mr and Mrs Korgaonkar and other members of their trust. At the time of the camp of 1954, six rooms were built. We could accommodate some of the guests there. Others made themselves comfortable in tents of tarpaulin. The number of people who attended the camp was as high as two thousand. They came from all over Maharashtra to see this experiment at Anandwan. Cooking for everyone fell into my sphere. Geetabai, Kaushalyabai and Sushilabai shared these responsibilities with me. We began our work a month in advance. Cleaning rice and other food grains consumed a lot of time.

It was a convention at Anandwan that each one wash her own plate after the morning and evening meals. Dr Cuttat too insisted on washing his own dish. He refused to be treated as a guest. At night, the cultural programme started on time, but I was busy serving dinner. There was no end to it. However, Dr Cuttat would not allow them to start the programme until I joined them. Finally, when I reached the hall, he escorted me on to the stage. I was overwhelmed by his courtesy and respect for me. He even made a speech and every word he uttered expressed his sympathies with our work. We wanted to felicitate him but we did not even have a shawl to offer to him. So finally, we presented him a kambal. He was so moved, that he held on to both of us for quite some time. 'I will plead your case when I go back', he said, at the end of his speech.

This get-together had a desirable effect. Not only did it bring together the inmates of Anandwan and the complacent society outside, but also helped to change their attitudes towards leprosy and its victims. We found a permanent friend in the Swiss Aid. This relationship ripened by leaps during the reign of Dr Schenellman and Pierre Oppliger.

We were now convinced about the double utility of such camps and decided to conduct them every year, for youth from all over India. It continues to attract them even today. It was intended to inculcate the love of labour and thereby plant the idea of dignity of labour in their minds. We trained our children, Vikas, Prakash and Narayan in this tradition of labour. They had their first lessons in our 'broom culture' at home. Whether it was dishwashing, cleaning, or scrubbing the floor, they did their share of the work willingly. I sincerely feel, that the young need to be taught to respect and love honest labour and to never feel ashamed of it. Our ten-day camps were initiated with this purpose and they have borne fruit. Many young boys and girls have been inspired in these camps.

When your readiness to do labour is coupled with help from others, it does not take time for dreams to materialise. In 1956, Mr Jog, the proprietor of Jog Industries, donated hundred acres of land near Nagpur to us. This project was named after their son, Ashok. In setting up Ashokwan, Baba's capacity for hard labour was tested. It involved, first of all, a daily walk of three miles from Gumgaon railway station to Ashokwan. He used to take the morning passenger train and come back late at night. Once, exhausted from the day's work, he lay down under a tree and soon dropped off to sleep. A passer-by noticed a giant scorpion quietly resting on Baba's chest. Before Baba could wake up, he had picked it up with a pair of tongs.

In 1958, the Ashokwan project started functioning. Mr Jog supported it fully. He had risen from a driver to be the owner of a balloon factory. Besides, Baba also knew many ministers from the central Varhad region. With the help of Vinobaji, we could procure fifty acres of land. But the real problems lay ahead. How were we to cultivate this land? It was a forest. The wild trees, standing in a file, as if to resist any intruder; the soil, completely barren and rocky. To make matters worse, there was shortage of water. It was really a test of Baba's strength and capacity. He used to set out early in the morning to take the four o'clock train; I had to keep his tiffin ready by that time. With the jar of water and a cloth bag full of medicines in one hand, and the tiffin carrier, a bed sheet and the kambal in the other, he trudged his way to this open-air centre. From Gumgaon, the walking exercise began; four miles to and fro. He selected a spot – under a tamarind tree – where he would carry out his daily medical practice. In course of time, Mr Jog, with the help of the patients, set up a small hut. He extended his help in many ways—bringing drinking water for Baba, sometimes sprucing up the mud-floor of the hut with cow-dung. Baba had no assistant; he would get completely exhausted by the end of the day. He even neglected his meals whenever there was a rush of patients. Again in the evening, the same exercise of walking, and on reaching Warora, driving his bullock cart home. Sometimes the tiffin carrier used to come back with the food untouched. On such occasions, I gave up my meals too. Fasts were a part of my life; both kinds, the voluntarily ones on sacred days, and the occasional ones as described above. Today, even at the age of eighty-eight, Baba stands on his own. He is independent. The credit partly goes to my fasts.

At Ashokwan, we mainly focused on agriculture and livestock, especially on raising cows. Anandwan is industrialised but Ashokwan is committed to its initial schemes even today. Not far from Nagpur – only twenty kilometres – it serves as a rest house for us. We halt there whenever we come to Nagpur on work. Until yesterday this project was going slow but Vikas has infused a new life into it now.

In 1962, a new colony of leprosy patients was set up in the close vicinity of Anandwan. It was called Muktisadan. It was our good fortune that we could get the national saint, Tukdoji Maharaj to inaugurate it. Muktisadan is a sister concern of Anandwan. Fifty couples from among the patients there have been rehabilitated here. They are mainly engaged with farming, poultry and related vocations. This project could materialise because of funds raised by the Swiss, in response to Dr Schenellman's appeal to them. The fund was used for the housing construction. In addition, an agricultural organisation in Australia supplied the capital for buying agricultural equipment. To crown these efforts, the State Government of Maharashtra released a large piece of land, almost 250 acres.

Baba's creative urge led him to these widely divergent experiments. His surging fancies would not allow him to rest.

His eyes were always set on new horizons. Even today he dreams of new things, as if each were his first dream. And his insight and foresight about which I spoke earlier, kept him grounded as well. The dreams he sees, have the exotic charm of lifting one above the rut, and the irresistible lure of the warmth of their practicability. Leprosy was only the beginning. If I were to describe the journey of his life in just a few words, I would say that it is a series of beginnings; or shall I say that every end had the potential of a new beginning? He went on lighting lamps and I willingly took on the task of feeding the flame. The honesty of his purpose and the frenzy of his creativity commanded this total submergence on my part. His ventures became *our* ventures. I was never afraid of losing my identity. On the contrary, it was like renewing myself. There were occasions when we fought too. I did put my foot down or made myself clear. I never had to sacrifice my right to hold opinions on any issue and he was gracious enough to accommodate my dissenting voice.

That is not all. The graph of the emotions he is capable of, has many irregularities. Like love, his fury is uncontrollable. You are familiar with the Chinese legend of the fire belching dragon. In his fury, he can find a rival in Baba, who can be as hot as a volcano. Once, while travelling to Somnath in our jeep, I read the line written on the back of a truck, 'Highly inflammable. Handle with care' and I could not help laughing to myself. Baba did not know why I was laughing. Finally, he asked me the reason. I pointed out to the line written on the truck and said to him, 'I think we should also write that line on our jeep when you are in it.' He too joined in the laughter.

However, there is no questioning his love, immeasurable as it is. Since the very day after our wedding, he has never had lunch without me, though it was against the custom. But he never bothered about social norms; he never allowed anything or anyone to stand between him and me. In love, there was no adjustment, no compromise.

There is yet another thing, about which Baba is incurably strict—in matters of punctuality. He cannot put up with even a minute's delay. Once, I was late due to my daily puja and he went off by the bus at the appointed hour. I had to take a truck in order to catch up with him.

Baba never suffered from any kind of inferiority complex as far as I know, except perhaps when he came to my parents' home, and was compared with the other sons-in-law in our family. I was also different from the other girls in not dreaming of a prince charming on a white horse. I wanted my life partner to be unlike others, with something special and unique about him, and I found this in Baba. I was educated; I had completed the first year of college, and people were pained by my choice; they even made bold to say, 'Was there a dearth of better boys in this world?'

What attracts me the most in Baba is his honesty, truthfulness, loyalty and transparency; and none of these have been cultivated deliberately. All these qualities are as natural to him as light is to the sun. Baba had written letters to English actresses like Norma Shearer and others, and he showed me all these letters before our marriage. But the fear and the doubts, that most women would have felt, did not touch me at all. On the contrary, the trust and faith that he commanded right from the beginning, became the solid foundation of our relationship. In terms of age, these talented actresses could have well been his mothers. I was convinced about Baba's spotless character. I had no fear, no jealousy, no suspicion. On reading his letters to them, I felt proud instead. He could not have been disloyal even in his thoughts.

The thought of setting up a college for the students in Warora was Baba's foresight and his instinctual understanding of the needs of the society. There was no college in Warora. Students had to go either to Chandrapur or Nagpur for higher education. It was expensive too. So most of them preferred to look for jobs after their matriculation, rather than go on for higher studies. Even the most deserving candidates were deprived of college education because they could not afford to spend so much on it. It is not in Baba's nature to watch these things silently. Whenever he finds a challenge, he throws himself into it and then there is no limit to which he cannot push himself. I have seen enough of his fundamental instinctual submergence or submission to a cause. Only he could have had the vision of a leprosy institution running a college for the healthy and the privileged.

But, between this vision of the educational centre and its realisation, there was a shadow. There were rumours that it was exclusively meant for victims of leprosy and that the faculty members too, are from among the lepers. Baba had to undertake a tour of the district of Chandrapur and campaign in order to lift the veil of misunderstanding and doubt. The third Service Civil International camp in Anandwan satisfactorily complimented these efforts. This was attended by stalwarts, such as Professor Deo, D. S. Jajurley, and Professor Prakash Shende who was introduced to us by Professor Roy and who became the first principal of our college. Thus, Anand Niketan College of Arts, Science, and Commerce was started with the combined efforts of the inmates of our leprosy colony and the well-wishers from the larger community outside. The campus vibrated with a youthful energy. Dr Schenellman wrote to us, 'Our friendship is strengthened further by this new venture'.

The next year saw the addition of an agricultural college, which was affiliated to the Punjabrao Agricultural University in Akola. In the beginning, students mainly came from the neighbouring state of Andhra Pradesh, but gradually students in our region too realised the importance of the systematic study of agriculture. The sons of landlords and farmers could, now, be systematically trained in farming, which, till then, was mostly based on traditional methods. They could experience the difference between the two methods and their respective merits and demerits too. There were difficulties on other fronts as well. There was no cook in Anandwan. The number of inmates including the professors was about forty. Until the cook joined, I had to shoulder responsibility of cooking for everyone. Even after a month of his joining, I helped him make chapattis.

The same year, a school for the blind was started. There were five teachers. Soon blind people from the neighbouring villages also came. This school brought a ray of light into their lives. Parents thronged to the school to admit their children. We found a very able principal in Mr Mukundrao Vaishampayan. A sudden encounter with leprosy brought him here—he had read about our centre and came directly to us when he learnt of his illness. He came from Pen, a small place in the district of Thane in Maharashtra. He is an ideal and dedicated teacher which is why we could safely hand over the children to his care. He became the first principal of this school. The affection with which he looked after the children is commendable. He always reminds me of the venerable Sane Guruji. He had a knack of getting things done smoothly by his colleagues. Those who worked with him never had a feeling that they were being bossed over. On his retirement, he became the trustee of Maharogi Sewa Samiti. His valuable guidance is available to all at Anandwan. Now, Mr Sudhakar Kadu looks after the school.

Today, Anandwan runs a school for the deaf and the dumb as well. Ever since, the curve of progress has been rising. The college results too, have improved considerably.

During all these years of growth and expansion for Anandwan, Baba's health deteriorated considerably. As far as our work was concerned, we were able to overcome all the difficulties eventually. At least, we were able to stay and keep things on track. But Baba has been completely helpless in matters concerning his health. And it was never one problem so much so, that sometimes I wonder how he manages to do all these things despite his failing health.

In the summer of 1964, Baba suffered from a severe sunstroke. The summers in Vidarbha are terrible. Continual hot waves give us the feeling of being in a furnace. Baba spent most of his time out in the sun. Whether it was working on the farm, or digging the well, he was always exposed to the extremities of weather. We did not have a cooler at home at the time. He had high fever. A gentleman named Shirpurkar lent his cooler to us. The professors from the college ran to my help. They sat with him turn by turn, and changed the cold water strips. I had to see to their breakfast and hardly found any time to look after Baba. His condition was quite critical. Finally, slabs of ice were brought from Chandrapur to use them to cool his body temperature. Baba's younger brother, Madhukar, who was also ill (suffering from abdominal pain) was with us at that time. My nursing duties were divided between the two of them. After a fortnight, Baba recovered from the stroke.

My mother, who was very fond of Baba, was very upset by Baba's continual ill health and, being a staunch believer in god, she depended on her spiritual ways of healing—vratas. She was a devotee of the saint of Vidarbha, Shree Gajanan Maharaj of Shegaon. She promised to offer one thousand modakas at his shrine on Baba's recovery. All of us spent hours making them in such huge quantities. Baba's timetable being fixed, he did not even wait for the ritual to be completed and left for Ashokwan. I joined him the next morning and we left for Anandwan amidst heavy rain. The river was overflowing and we were delayed by four hours.

There were battles on other fronts too, and they took different forms and were fought on different fields. In 1962, Bapuji, Baba's father, became very ill. It was the month of April. Vikas and Prakash were appearing for their matriculation examinations. Bapuji could not even drink water. Baba travelled every day from Warora to Nagpur, so I stayed with Bapuji. Vikas and Prakash, along with Narayan, cooked for themselves and went for the board examinations everyday. They used to go in a bullock-cart for the exam. One day, just as the cart was passing underneath the bridge, a train passed over the bridge. The sound of the train distracted the bullocks, and they, along with cart, left the track and went straight into the stream. Prakash broke his hand; he had three more exams to write. I was shocked to hear about all this. Leaving Bapuji, I went to see the headmaster, and requested him to provide a scribe for Prakash. He offered the help of a boy from the eighth standard. Finally, Prakash had to write his papers with the pain in his hand. Both passed their exams—Prakash with a second class and Vikas with first. Vikas excelled in languages, whereas, Prakash scored well in Maths. There is a strange combination of qualities in the two brothers. I think the best of Baba is distributed equally between the two of them. Vikas has derived from Baba his communication skills, mastery over language, and memory; and Prakash, his endurance and courage.

In 1964, Bapuji passed away. He died of throat cancer. I cannot describe in words his suffering, pain, and his endurance.

I never heard a groan from him. Perhaps, he foresaw his death. However, his equanimity was exceptional. It was my good fortune that I could at least nurse him in this last phase of his life. Baba spent more time with him in Nagpur. It was during this period that all his misunderstandings about me were cleared. He showered all his love and blessings on me. How can I forget the day he departed for his heavenly abode? In those last moments, I was the only one sitting by his side. During this last illness, he insisted that only we be present in his room. Baba composed a beautiful poem *Conquering Death* for his father.

After Bapuji's death, Baba's mother came to stay with us in Anandwan. Once upon a time she had concentrated all her hopes on Baba and had felt extremely delighted when he decided to marry. She had without hesitation, given me the credit for this metamorphosis in Baba. But now she had changed. She suffered from a stroke of insanity. She was no longer part of the normal world now. When I was around, she used to get furious and would abuse me. I had nothing but sympathy for her. I used to feed her with my own hands everyday, during which time, she would be quiet. Somewhere deep in her psyche, she held me responsible for the thieves' attack on Baba before our marriage. She was fond of Vikas and was all right when he was around. She passed away in 1969. This was the greatest loss in Baba's life. Baba has written about her in his book, *My Mother's Insanity*.

Often, just as we were drawn towards people, sometimes, strange people were drawn towards us, for reasons known only to them. Take the case of Tukaram. Before he joined Anandwan, he was sentenced to life imprisonment having been charged in a murder case. In the same prison, Tukaram had met Dr A. C. Lagu, who had been charged with the murder of his patient. This was the most famous court case in Maharashtra. Dr Lagu brought shame to the medical profession by this black deed. The two murderers came to know each other in prison. Tukaram was released first, and being a leprosy patient, came straight to us from the prison. He worked as a driver for our four wheeler, the bullock-cart. He used to escort Prakash and Vikas to school everyday. He worked sincerely. After a few years, when the Hemalkasa project was undertaken, he went there with Prakash. It was a matter of coincidence that Dr Lagu, after being released from jail, also came to Hemalkasa. The two met again. However, Dr Lagu did not stay for long. He soon went away. But Tukaram stayed with us until he died. He married a tribal woman called Mainee (also a leprosy patient). She had a son from her first husband, Pandu, called Pandu Pongati. This boy is a gem of a person. He has studied medicine and become a doctor and joined Prakash on the same project. Tukaram died a miserable death—he died of bear-bite but all his dreams for Pandu have come true.

I also remember an old gentleman called Tatya Bhake, who came to stay in Anandwan during the sixties. He was a moody person and short tempered too. He was fond of Prakash. I had a tough time looking after this sixty-year old child. After he left, he wrote me a letter that was filled with his appreciation for my tolerance and diligence.

Baba is often compared, and rightly so, with the mythical sage, Vishwamitra. With sadhana, Vishwamitra became a Brahmarshi, Baba has also turned his back on comforts and chose to live as a shramashri. Like Vishwamitra, he too undertook to do new projects. This was the time when Anandwan was well established, but Baba was dreaming of setting up a workers' university. A real worker, according to him, is a person who combines in himself intellect, mental power and physical strength.

He was looking for adventurous young men with the zeal for experiment, as prospective members of this university. In other words, he wanted intellectuals not to feel ashamed of physical labour and labourers to use their minds. All his thoughts and efforts were now concentrated on this dream flower.

SEVEN

The bond is primordial,
Between the creative impulse,
And mother earth
Who cradles all future.
O, for the day
When youth shall plod
These miles of emptiness,
From end to end they will ride,
Scattering their dreams
In the hills and the dales,
Renewing their bond with the mother
And make it a blissful bower.

Baba was in need of the kind of young men and women, described in his own poem above, to set up the workers' university. Initially, Dhule was thought of as the best place for this project. Baba went there with Dr Wardekar to survey the location too. I lost my ease at the thought of Baba being tossed between Chandrapur and Dhule, and of the heavy toll he would have to pay in terms of health. Thank god, my fears did not materialise. Vasantrao Naik, the then Chief Minister of Maharastra, came forward with a helping hand, offering 1,950 acres of land near Mul, in Chandrapur district itself, for this new project. We felt relieved, but it proved to be momentary. The farmers in the vicinity of Somnath refused to surrender the land. They openly protested against it under the leadership of Chandawar. I had tremendous respect for Mr Chandawar, the person. In the S.C.I. camp of 1953, he had shared some of the work in the kitchen with me.

In a country like India, where a majority of the people are ignorant and illiterate, how easy it is to become a leader! Religion, caste, economic inequality, or social injustice—select any one of these attractive issues and begin your cacophony against the establishment! That is all you need to become a leader. Spice up your speech with a bit of rhetoric, and people follow you like sheep. You can become their leader overnight. I wonder how many leaders really take the trouble to study the problem from the various perspectives.

The local leaders were upset by this deal and strongly opposed our acquisition of the land for our project—they claimed that they had a right to this land and about 600 acres of land was already being cultivated for quite some time; though it was, in fact, usurped by them. Another reason for their opposition was the utilisation of water from the nearby Umary stream. The farmers feared that we would use all the water for our project. In fact, the local leaders had planted this fear in their minds. Baba tried his best to explain how baseless it was, but in vain. It is easier to talk to a single individual and make him understand your point of view and even persuade him to accept the same finally, but, when the same individual becomes part of a mob, his psychology changes. He allows his reason and conscience to sleep, and anger begins to rule. In no time he becomes violent. The beast, lurking somewhere in his unconscious, emerges.

This agitation went on for three years. Baba even risked his life on a few occasions. Nevertheless, in due course, the storm subsided. Among those who actively worked towards a peaceful resolution, were prominent social figures like Anna Sahasrabuddhe, Dada Dharmadhikari and S. M. Joshi. Ultimately, Vinobaji succeeded in bringing about a truce. We had to surrender 600 acres of the total land given to us by the government, but at least, there was an end to the problem.

The Somnath project had become an obstacle race right from the beginning. The workers' university, on the other hand, had become Baba's passion. It was no longer a passing fancy. And once something becomes a passion with him, he will even stake his life to fulfill it. He not only dreams, but has also the necessary capacity and the creative frenzy to turn them into reality. Nothing he did was without frenzy, be it in love or war. If he takes to something, he will take on anyone or anything.

This project not only tested his patience but his legs too—walking up and down, meeting people, summoning up all his strength, both mental and physical. He finally succeeded in acquiring 2,000 acres of wasteland, a jungle which was the natural habitat of wild animals; tigers, wolves, all kinds of snakes and vipers, giant scorpions and a variety of deer and rabbits. Do you know what we saw here on our first visit? When our bus reached the temple, we saw water trickling from the rocks above. The temple was on the top of a hillock. Being tired and hungry, we stretched our legs and sat down for lunch at the foot of the hill. After lunch, we climbed up to go to the temple, and saw pieces of meat scattered inside. A tiger had just claimed two monkeys for his lunch.

We spent the night in the open. Our prospective residence lay two and half kilometres ahead. In the beginning, we used to walk this distance, carrying bags full of necessities and medicines along with one or two of our patients. There was not even a dirt track. We had to wait for a year to make a working road for the jeep, and there was no guarantee that the jeep would not get stuck in the marshes. We once had that experience too. The jeep simply refused to move. There was a distance of five kilometres at least left to cross. We left the driver with the jeep, and went barefoot to our house in the darkness of the night, finding our way through the ferns and wild hedge-rows, and thorny bushes. The next day, we had to bring a tractor from Anandwan to pull out the jeep from the marsh.

With the development of the Somnath project, we began to feel the shortage of residential units. We had to make do with small huts with tin-roofs or the tiled ones or tarpaulin. Using cement and bricks was out of question. Electricity came after 1972. Till then, we managed with these humble lodgings. It was our favourite pastime to spend the night in the jungle with only a kambal. Do you know why? Only to see the tiger! We deliberately chose spots near streams or ponds and preferred to lie in wait for his majesty's appearance.

Somnath is situated next to the famous Tadoba forest in Chandrapur district. It is known for its rich wildlife. It was named after the famous Somnath temple in Saurastra. Near the temple, is a natural spring and a gomukh from which water drips throughout the year. Surrounded by a dense forest and vibrating with the wildlife; nothing else was required for Baba to set up camp right in the heart of the jungle. Tigers, bears, leopards, bisons, deer, wolves and rabbits, made their presence felt occasionally. Baba chose a vantage point for himself from where he could see the tigers easily. Tigers dominated this territory. People were scared even at the thought of seeing one. In order to drive away this fear, Baba deliberately invited such encounters by spending the night out, getting closer to their haunts. To tell you the truth, he had many narrow escapes.

The adventures of Rupa, the tigress Baba kept at Somnath, are thrilling. Baba would sometimes take her out for walks. During one summer camp, she left her cage and came straight out into crowd of participants who ran in all directions in fear. From inside their rooms they watched Baba and his rival with a glistening body and rolling eyes. Baba survived this deadly fight but both of his hands were ripped. A tiger is known to have a natural tendency to attack moving objects. She chased a boy who was running. Perceiving the danger, Baba tried to rescue him. Holding her paws in his hands, he tried to push her back into the cage. She too was furious and before she entered the cage, had her revenge on Baba. His hands and shoulders bled profusely. The next day the mother of that boy came to see Baba; she kept crying. There is no dearth of such tales of adventure; there are so many to recount.

Many big trees had to be felled as we carved out space for ourselves; a colony of humble cottages. Then came the concrete structures. As conditions improved, we moved into the new houses built in cement and concrete. All our faithful friends – snakes, scorpions, and monkeys – exercised their right to shift with us into our new house. The monkeys often used to steal lumps of dough kept ready for the chappattis. There was a common mess for all the workers. In 1967, we conducted an open-air camp for school children as an experiment. The next year, the first well organised camp was arranged. There was an overwhelming response from the youth of India. About 1400 young boys and girls participated in this camp. During this camp, Baba announced the 'Knit India' programme. The simple message given to the youth was: hands are given for construction, not destruction.

Preparations for this camp, the first of its kind, were made in Anandwan. Vikas and Prakash were studying medicine at Nagpur at that time. Narayan brought all the necessary goods from Anandwan, in trucks. Temporary residential units were set up. The name by which this summer camp is known today—Shram Sanskar Chavani, a camp intended to inculcate the idea of the dignity of labour, was first given during this 1968 camp. Prefixed to this title, was the term Antar-bharati. Five students and a teacher were invited from each state. Among others who attended this camp, were Shyam Patwardhan, Divakar Agashe, Latabai Patankar, Kumar Saptarshi and the members of Yukrand, Dr Anil Avachat, Pareet Guruji, Chandrakant Shah and Chandrakant Patgaonkar. Right from the first year, this activity drew many people to the camp. And ever since, camps are regularly being held here in summer. There are sufficient cooks today, but in those days, I had to make chapattis in hundreds. In the sweltering heat of the summers, many participants would fall ill with high temperature. Nursing the sick came to me naturally. Gladly did I play the nurse and sometimes even the doctor to them. There were so many things to take care of—preparing breakfast, making sharbat from raw mangoes, nursing the sick, changing cold-water strips, cooking arrangements and what not? However, the campers – young boys and girls from all parts of India – enjoyed it all.

Somnath thus became a rendezvous for like-minded people, a centre for interactions between people on both the sides. Many well-known personalities from different spheres attended these camps. It is difficult to remember all the names; people like George Fernandez, Mohan Dharia, Shankarrao Deo, Sadanand Varde; literary icons of the day such as Vasantrao Kanetkar, Narhar Kurundkar, Vishram and Malati Bedekar; people like Sant Tukdoji Maharaj, Yadunath Thatte, Devdatta Dabholkar,

Damu Bele, Devendrabhai Gupta from Sewagram, Anna Sahasrabuddhe, Mama Kshirsagar and Smita Patil.

In its early phase, there would be two successive camps. The first one, meant exclusively for students who appeared for their S.S.C., took place in April after the board examinations. It was a fifteen-day camp. Sadanand Varde, Murlidhar Shah and Chandrakant Shah used to guide the participants. The activities included cultural programmes too. The second camp too was for fifteen days, in the month of May. Now it has been reduced to seven days only. It included cleaning, clearing the hedges; farm work such as making beds by removing the boulders, bandharas on a small scale, followed by camp fire at night and sometimes a nightly jungle trail. Baba used to spend hours telling them about his adventures.

Since we were called upon to surrender about 650 acres of land we had to revise our original plan of setting up the workers' university. A new concept was taking shape in Baba's mind. He was continually thinking about some activity that would foster the process of building man. The most interesting thing about Baba is that he will give every thought a fair chance to translate itself into action. The key to success in any undertaking lies in the immense enthusiasm, the zeal and the diligence that is required for it. Baba, fortunately, has all three. So, the trial began. The young people, who joined this programme, came here to conduct agricultural experiments. We provided them with all the equipment and the land. Baba handed over charge of this scheme to Shankardada and his wife, Sindhutai. He spent most of his time at Somnath now, but occasionally visited Anandwan.

Sindhutai was a woman of substance. Under her systematic guidance and discipline, workers like Arun and Hari shaped very well. Shankardada could not recover from the shock of her death. Parting becomes more painful when you have to suffer it in old age. It is easier to bury your pain when young. No doubt, Shankardada was mentally paralysed when Sindhutai passed away. He is the shaping spirit behind Somnath. The credit for the systematic development of this project goes to his committed and selfless support to its goals and interests. He was one person who understood the essence of Baba's words, 'the future of our institution depends upon the future of the Somnath project.' I must say that in his hands Somnath was transformed into a gold mine. However, the picture has changed over the past few years. The yield from the land has fallen considerably due to continual droughts, affecting our self-sufficiency in food grains. The land produced everything that we needed once upon a time. In order to cope up with the shortage of water, Vikas has undertaken the cleaning of tanks and removing silt to enhance their storing capacity. That is his one-point programme now. Shankardada had a stroke of palsy and is no more. His son, Vijay, looks after the workshops conducted there now, whereas Arun and Hari have taken over responsibility of Somnath.

As memories about Somnath crowd my mind, there is a temptation to ramble. So many things happened here. We had made our home in the midst of the wilderness. Therefore, encounters between the civilised and the untamed were bound to happen. Given the chemistry of Baba's mind, no external stimulus was required to provoke him to a feat of courage. Wanderer as he is, he went where his mind and legs took him. During the first few months of our stay here, there were no roads of any sort because no one would have ever thought of coming to such a deserted place. Some women used to come to collect wood in the jungle. Except for their foot prints and ours, there were no visible signs of any kind to make out a road. Cooking was done near the pond and in the evening we returned to our cottage two kilometres away, carrying a pitcher of drinking water on our head. Baba would do anything to see the tiger and put his cot in the open space, well equipped with the mosquito net. He was not afraid of the tiger, it was mosquitoes that he dreaded the most. As darkness fell, swarms of them poured in from all sides. One day his desire to see the tiger was fulfilled. There was not one, but three of them. Except man-eaters, tigers generally do not attack people. Baba and the tigers, stood face to face. They gave each other a fixed stare. Then Baba took off his sweater and covering his face, crawled on all fours. The tigers must have taken Baba for a strange creature and ran away into the jungle. Some of those women had seen Baba and the tigers. They came telling me that the tigers had eaten Baba up. We were all so anxious, but Baba soon returned to our relief.

My religious fasts were always the cause for skirmishes between me and Baba. Often, I renounced even food that could be eaten during the fast. One day, the two of us fought over this as usual. I have told you about Baba's anger. That day he got so angry that he left for the jungle. The clock struck ten at night but there were no signs of him returning. Now it was my turn to feel worried. I grew more anxious as time passed. In the dense forest, it was not safe to take a stroll even during the day. I dared not step out at that hour of night and search for him in that impenetrable darkness. However, of the two equally powerful instincts, love and fear, love emerged victorious. I set out combing the jungle, when the rest of the world had quietly surrendered to sleep. I took a round, searching the jungle, looking for traces of his presence; even the faintest one would have done for me. Mumbling a prayer to god, I returned home, thinking that he must have returned by now. To my disappointment, the house was empty. I waited for sometime, and again set out with trepidation, my heart beating faster than usual. I was lucky to find him this time. Both of us returned home quietly.

On another occasion, we were caught in a storm. I was on a fast but Baba was in high spirits and felt up to a jungle trail. I found it difficult to deflect his enthusiasm by telling him about my fast. I kept mum and joined him though I was almost dragging my feet for want of food. We crossed the reserved forest, came upon the stream, and went to the hut, our favourite haunt. On our way back, a storm broke out unexpectedly. A storm in a forest is something else—the wind and the lightning were competing with each other in speed and sound. The trees trembled in fear. I wondered if Shiva's tandava would be much different from this; or was it nature's fury? In that sound and fury, we made our way home by the slippery path – strewn all over by thorny bushes – rendered invisible by the enveloping darkness. I was completely exhausted that day.

There were other interesting things to see as well. I have been a devout worshipper of Lord Shiva all my life. It was customary for me to offer leaves of the bel tree to Shiva. My daily instalment of these leaves took me to certain parts of the forest, where, sometimes, I used to see herds of deer. I used to bathe in the lake on top of the hill and go to worship in the temple. In the beginning, we used to burn the bushes to prepare the ground for our cottages. On realising that it was hazardous for the birds, we stopped doing this.

Associated with Somnath are other tales of adventure and romance too. Ajit came from Goa and stayed at Somnath for some time. Later, he joined Prakash at Hemalkasa where he met Dorothy, a German girl. She fell in love with this Tarzan; the two of them got married and went away to Germany. One of our efficient workers was thus kidnapped!

Who will forget Abhimanyu? His is a tale painted in dark colours. He was a young, talented worker who was introduced to us by Jawahar Kotecha. This happened in the early years of Somnath. Baba had made temporary staying arrangements in tents of tarpaulin. There were eight or nine patients with him. A well was newly dug. I had not yet shifted there but often went to stay with Baba. At that time, fleas were a big problem and many of us fell victim to the viral fever they spread. I was down with fever at Anandwan. Abhimanyu too had the same, and had to be admitted to the Nagpur Medical Hospital. An edict was sent to Baba. There was no telephone connection in Anandwan, or at other centres. The rivers were flooded. The chances of Baba getting the message were bleak. Vikas left the message at Mul, with Dr Vasantrao Wankar. The flood held him up too. They shifted me to the Nagpur Hospital by train. On getting the news, Baba rushed to Anandwan and then to Nagpur, driving his jeep through more than ankle-deep water. I had a narrow escape but Abhimanyu quietly succumbed to death in two days. That year, in the summer camp we cherished his memory by naming one of our colonies at Somnath after him.

Vikas and Prakash studied medicine at Nagpur Medical College. They stayed at the Ramakrishna Mission. Ashokwan was too far from Nagpur to travel up and down daily. We had no means of transport of our own in those days. When they were to leave for Nagpur for medical studies, I was reminded of their first visit to Nagpur as four- and five-year olds. I was amused to remember the commotion they had created when we went shopping. This was their first visit to Nagpur. They had never left Anandwan till then. They were never exposed to the 'high culture' of the cities, its mannerisms and etiquettes. My brother took us to a shop. I could have hardly imagined the pandemonium they created in the shop. As soon as they stepped into the shop, they laid their hands on everything. They were thrilled. They had to open every jar and peek into every tin or can. The shopkeeper watched their pranks helplessly. To top it all, they insisted on buying everything they saw; not only biscuits and chocolates but, buckets, jars, glasses, cans, and what not. I felt embarrassed with the thought of what the shopkeeper must be thinking. This must be his first time he had uncouth customers like us in his shop, I thought. My children, with their rustic innocence and inquisitiveness, were misfits in his urban world, perhaps.

In the fifties, we had an opportunity to spend some time with G. N. Dandekar. The off-beat track he chose made his life exciting and thrilling. He ran away from home when a child, to join venerable Gadgebaba's special movement of cleanliness in the villages. At a young age, he completed the Narmada Parikrama. He was a true follower of the varkari culture in Maharastra, wandering from place to place, visiting forts of historical importance. With his enriching life-experience and sweet words, he commanded respect from everyone. At that time, he was busy writing two of his books, *Yashodhara* and *Dnyaneshwar*. Sometimes he read out chapters from them to us. Later, he wrote a novel about leprosy, *Anandwanbhuvan*. A moving piece of writing indeed! Once, an interesting thing happened during his stay in Anandwan. He was completely absorbed in narrating one of his experiences during the Narmada Parikrama. It was all about his encounter with a tribe of monkeys; how, despite his efforts to drive them away, the whole tribe was approaching him even faster. Just then, somebody said in a suppressed tone, 'They must have been females.' Everyone burst into laughter and he too joined in.

People kept dropping in, from far and near, leaving their impressions behind. Mr David Scott and his wife came all the way from Australia to forget the sorrow of their son's death. They found solace in the lepers and admired their indomitable courage to weather all kinds of storms in life. When they got back to Australia, they sent us some wheat for the institution. After ten years, a son was born in their family again.

We came across many virtuous souls, who belonged to different stratas of society. Take the case of Mahadev Pimpalshende. He came from Bordi, a small place not far from Warora. He was a very sharp and diligent man. Taking into consideration his aptitude for, and skill in agricultural work, Baba, with the help of his acquaintances, arranged for him to go to Australia. On his return to India, Mahadev went to Chindwada and conducted agricultural experiments. His tragic end put an end to all his efforts. We were shocked to learn that he was killed in an encounter with burglars.

Anandwan became a home for many destitute children by providing them with shelter and education. Vinayak and Baccharam have grown to positions which might have seemed impossibe once. Both of them are intelligent and with their hard work and dedication they have done themselves proud—Vinayak is now a lecturer in chemistry in our own college and Baccharam is working in the Dapoli Agricultural University. He came to see us with his family once. Years have passed, but the bond of love is still intact.

It is difficult to put every name on record. But they have left their mark behind. We have been drawing on the love of such people ever since we stepped on this road. It was our good luck to have met people who showered love on us. They are known by their peculiarities.

Mr P. Y. Deshpande and Vimaltai Deshpande frequently visited Anandwan. I remember with gratitude, the help extended to me by Vimaltai in cooking, whenever she came. Another talented young man, Ramesh Gupta, adorns our portrait gallery. Master of words and gifted with fine imagination, he took it upon himself to crystalise Baba's seething ideas into beautiful poems. The publication of the first volume of Baba's poems, *Jwala aani Phule* (Flames and Flowers) was the fruit of his filigree work. Poetry is not my cup of tea; however, I do like to read and appreciate them. I think, a poem happens spontaneously, without effort; something like the inner turmoil pressing itself out in words, unawares. Take any form, from the vedas and the upanishads to the religious verse of our saint poets, the spontaneity is remarkable. When the poet's words penetrate the outer region of our reason, and come to roost in the heart – not an easily accessible domain – it takes no time to feel his life's vibrations, his commitment and his loyalties. The poet's mind is forever young; it loves to sport with the known and the unknown untiringly; that is why poetry remains forever fresh, forever young. It is free from the curse of staleness. Whether it is Ramayana or any other form of poetry, people continue to read and re-read it.

The well-known writer, V. S. Khandekar, an icon in Marathi literature, wrote the preface to Baba's first volume of poems. He had respect for Baba's work. Quite a few letters were exchanged between them. He expressed a deep sense of anxiety over Baba's back-ache in one of his letters. He wrote:

> I was in Pune and Mumbai recently and returned on the 13th. Received your letter dated 8th. I was overwhelmed by your best wishes. I took them as blessings, since they came not from an ordinary

man, but from a karmayogi like Baba. Wishes become blessings when they are preceded by life-long sadhana. I still cherish the desire to write something, that would inspire posterity, though I suffer from bad health and weak eye-sight.

I felt deeply worried to read about Baba's battle with his back. Nevertheless, his courage and endurance are inimitable and commendable too. It makes me think. Why, of all the persons, this should happen to Baba, I ask myself. Is misfortune a necessary evil for the enrichment of the soul? You can't find the answers in any book of philosophy.

I was delighted to know that the Somnath project is feathering forth. I could see it a minute, spreading its wings. I will have to wait, until I undergo the eye operation, to see it budding with my own eyes. I was happy to know about Sandhiniketan. The seed that was sown when Anandwan was set up, is sprouting new leaves.

I can only pray that Baba gets well soon. Let the young draw inspiration from his creatively nourishing thoughts!

My kind regards to him.

Yours sincerely,
V. S. Khandekar

Madhubhai Pandit came to Anandwan during the same period. In him, Baba found an educated, efficient and disciplined worker. He is a saraswat brahmin. His wife, Nalinitai was a lecturer in economics. She was also actively involved in the workers' movement. Madhubhai worked in the share market but there was a social worker in him. He was a member of Sewadal. When he joined our institution, Baba found a breathing gap from his work. He is the member of our trust today. He is old now but attends the summer camp with the same vigour.

Meeting people who came from different fields and regions and with different socio-economic backgrounds was an enriching experience. I cannot tell exactly why they were drawn to us or why we formed intimate relations with them. But there was something very special about each of them. Nilu, alias Niranjana Gavankar was a nuclear engineer and a member of Sewadal. As a participant in our summer camp, she came to Somnath one day and fell in love with the Anandwan family and became our permanent friend. She had a talent for writing and was gifted with a sweet voice too. She settled down in the USA later, and built her career there. She wrote to us regularly. One fine morning she left America and returned to India and then to Anandwan. We found in her the same old friend, with the same intensity of love and affection. She actively contributed to the development project of Somnath, designed by Vikas. At present, she is engaged with film production. I am sure that with her perceptive intellect, she will excel in everything that she ventures into.

The publication of Baba's poems, *Jwala aani Phule*, brought an unexpected shower of love and a gift of long cherished friendship in our life. P. L. Deshpande wrote a long letter to Baba. He complimented Baba by describing it as Fire Flowers. He wrote:

> This is not the type of book to be read once and put away. One has to read it again and again. A great work of literature has the power to cause you some unease. That, which puts you to rest, is

> inferior literature. You and Ramesh Gupta have left enough to tease me out of my wits like an insidious worm in a fruit that gnaws at its core. I find my brain swimming in the vortex, that the thoughts have created.

P. L. Deshpande and his wife, Sunitabai, have become members of our family. He is not only a great writer but also has a golden heart and a splendid soul! He has donated liberally to many institutions and never even mentioned it to anyone. A very cheerful, endearing, family man indeed! He gave one lakh rupees as donation for the development of Muktangan, the open-air theatre for the deaf, the dumb, the blind, the physically handicapped and the lepers. In Warora, there were no theatres to screen movies. Except for the occasional keertanas, there was no other entertainment available and even when there was, the lepers were not allowed to enter it. The idea of setting up Muktangan, the open-air theatre, to give their hidden talent and art a chance originated in this alienation and deprivation among the inmates of Anandwan. Now, they had a platform to explore and experiment with their own potential; it is worth noting that they made the best of it. They could act and direct a skit, or try their hands at costumes and make-up or be a back-stage technician; in other words, they could learn and have fun. The historical plays came in handy, and they also enacted stories from the puranas. They performed Dandar as well. P. L. Deshpande was deeply moved by their will to live and their zest for life. Their vibrance made a lasting impression on him. He allowed his sympathies to flow freely by contributing substantially to this project.

We found permanent friends in P. L. and Sunitabai. Both of them came here whenever they wished. Together, we have shared many moments of excitement, pure laughter, and adventure. Once, Sunitabai wanted to see a tiger. So we set out early one morning. Baba, Vikas, Prakash, P. L., Sunitabai and I left Somnath in the darkness of the early dawn, in a jeep. Baba's gaiety knew no bounds on such occasions. He has the mind of a child, who is delighted to show his precious possessions to guests. We had only these sites of rare beauty, the flora, fauna and aura of untamed purity to show to our beloved guests. It was a privilege to take them around. Baba always snatched the opportunity. We had entered the Tadoba forest. This forest is named after a lake, which is at its centre. We drove around the favourite haunts of tigers. However, there was a strange calm that day. Hoping that the tiger would come to drink water we skirted the lake too, but in vain. It seemed, as if the tiger had decided not to show up. Baba was becoming angry. He fretted and fumed all the while as if somebody had failed to keep his appointment. Everyone could make it out from the way he answered our questions; the others being guests, he directed all his anger at me. P. L. tried, with little doses of his characteristic humour, to bring down the temperature. How would the tiger know that Baba had come with a famous and beloved writer to see him, I wondered. And even if he did, he was not a rasika that would rush to see his favourite author. Stealthily, the evening came, the sun tilted westward and lo, the treasure of the jungle stood before us, unexpectedly. He showed off his shining yellow back with black stripes and was a feast for our eyes! Baba was tempted to drive back and take a closer look but P. L. and Sunitabai protested hard as we were travelling in a jeep without a hood. On our way back home Baba returned to his normal self and was again filled with excitement. The precious child still lives in Baba's heart. P. L. and Sunitabai visited us often. We enjoyed their visits not only to Anandwan but Hemalkasa too. They in turn showered their love on Prakash and Manda and their tribal family.

Once upon a time we were the 'outsiders' in our society. Now there was a constant flow of the 'insiders' into our institution. They came from everywhere, from far off lands too. Who needed the other more, is not a question to be asked nor to be answered. More important is the fact that bridges were built between the two worlds now. At least the traffic had begun. The year 1963 saw the arrival of Count Arthur Tarnovsky in Anandwan. Polio had claimed both his legs. He had travelled with the *Reader's Digest* group, all over the world in a wheelchair, to survey the facilities given to the physically handicapped in different parts of the world. Our friendship was sealed soon and he too, like our other friends, kept coming back to us. After returning to England he created awareness among his people, raised funds for us to help our cause. He is old now but comes every year to Anandwan with his son. It was through his financial help to Sandhiniketan that we could construct the hostel for the handicapped children.

Divorce and remarriage are quite common amongst Europeans. However, here in India such a thing is not so common. Consequently, the inmates of Anandwan were confused to see Arthur bringing a new wife every year. No explanation would do for them. They were extremely critical of him.

Arthur's book on Baba, *Unbeaten Track* inspired Mary, an old handicapped lady, to come to India with the help of Community Aid Abroad, an institution in Australia. Her son had written to us. I went to Nagpur to receive her at the airport. She stayed with us for many days and died within a few days of her return to Australia. After her death, her son wrote a very moving letter to us in which he said, 'My mother's last wish was to visit your institution. I am grateful to you for fulfilling her desire.'

Our well-wishers came from different spheres of life. The respectable Tatya Shirwadkar alias Kusumagraj deserves my public acknowledgement of his generous donation on his birthday. I always loved to write letters and writing to people like him doubled the pleasure. At that time, it was almost a venture to write to such an eminent poet in Marathi. On the receipt of his donation I wrote to him:

> Anandwan
> Dist. Chandrapur,
> 12/03/71.
>
> Respected Shri Tatya,
>
> Baba was extremely delighted to receive the donation you directed to us. It was kind of you to remember to pass on your birthday gifts to Anandwan. Both of us are grateful to you for the same.
>
> Baba's commitment and dedication to his undertaking remains as steadfast as ever. He is the last one to bother about failing health or feel bogged down by growing disabilities. This has become a routine matter for him now.
>
> The thought of the plight of the tribals of Bhamragad makes him eternally restless. His mind has already reached the wilderness of the impenetrable forest; the body is wriggling, in earnest, to follow the same path. The camp at Bhamragad is the only thing he is thinking about at present.

Baba stayed behind. I returned yesterday to Anandwan. I ventured into writing to you because he asked me to convey his feelings to you. The terrible pain in his hand prevents him from writing. He only signs the letters now.

I have never met you. However, your deep sense of concern for our work has elicited this response from me. I could not help writing a few words to you. I extend an invitation to you to find some time to come over and stay with us.

Many happy returns of the day to you from both of us.

Regards to Mrs Shirwadkar.

Yours Sincerely,
Mrs Sadhana Amte.

Around this time, Narayan got married. My first daughter-in-law, Kalawati, Narayan's wife, came home. It was a pleasure to do things for her. In fact, I have always loved all my daughters-in-law as I would have my daughter. Kalawati came from Bhadrawati. Ours was a joint family then. Narayan chose to work on the farm and has done so till date. He has always shown prudence in everything he does. His eldest son has completed law and the youngest, has just graduated.

The year 1971 arrived with a different agenda for us. Baba's health problems had become acute now. He was, perhaps for the first time in his life, forced to listen to his groaning body. It had become a necessity now, though he had always dismissed it as a luxury. Severe pain in the neck and the back made even simple movements impossible. He was advised to go to London for an operation. It was not a joke. Above all, where was the money to come from? The amount required was as high as one lakh, sixty thousand rupees. However, Yadunathji Thatte voluntarily came forward to collect the fund and he did it. He advertised it in a monthly called *Sadhana* as well as in the newspapers. Many people – friends, well-wishers – contributed to this fund. They came from all sections of the society. We were overwhelmed by their love and sense of social commitment. Among them, were mail carriers, labourers, bus conductors, and college students too.

The news of Baba's operation sent my mother into depression. My father was known to have suffered from severe back pain. Naturally, she became very sensitive about this issue. Her anxiety as well as fear about the operation is reflected in the letter she wrote to me from Hyderabad:

> Chi. Sau. Indu,
>
> My blessings to you.
>
> Your letter informs me that you had been to Mumbai and that Baba's health has deteriorated considerably. Now listen to me, you have to cancel the operation at any cost. Tell him that it is risky and you do not want to take any chance. Tell him not to overstrain his back. Give him injections and medicines. You are all mature, think about what I am saying. I think, it's only a matter of his having a bad time, an evil conjunction of stars. I have complete faith in Mata Jagdamba, Saint Gajanan Maharaj and Lord Krishna. You have to be with him all the time. You are probably in two minds, but I know that you are strong and capable of handling the situation. I am your mother but I

can't do anything except send my blessings for a happy, healthy, and prosperous long life.

Do not leave Baba even for a minute. My blessings to you!

Long live your marriage.

Yours,
Aai.

But we decided to go ahead with the operation. This was Baba's first trip to a foreign country. You won't believe me, if I tell you how ill equipped he was for this journey. When it came to a tour in India, we used to carry our things in a tin trunk. Our clothes were made of home-spun handloom fabric, of Khadi; we continue to observe this code strictly even today. It was a serious problem before us—where to bring the suitcases from? Finally, Vishram Bedekar and his wife, Maltibai came to our help; they offered us their bags and clothes too. At London airport Baba was in trouble; he could not recognise his own suitcase. When everyone else had collected theirs, Baba picked up the one that remained. Baba stayed at Arthur's home in London. First the doctor tried lumber-puncture but due to some technical mistake, the pain doubled. Madhubhai called me up from Mumbai telling me about Baba's condition and that I should get ready to leave for London. I had to go to Chandrapur to get a passport and to Mumbai for the visa. I felt worried and found myself by Baba's side even before I left for London. Sixteen hours felt like sixteen ages. Madhubhai stood by me like a brother in everything. Both Baba and Arthur came to receive me at London airport.

It was a major operation and there was a risk of Baba being paralysed. There were difficulties on the practical plane too.

Baba had lost a great deal of weight because there was no Indian food at Arthur's place. When I reached there, I could at least cook for us. In the meantime, Yadunathji wrote to Appasaheb Pant, who was India's ambassador to England at that time. His wife came and took both of us to their house. We stayed with them for two months. On the 26th of December, we celebrated Baba's birthday without any pomp or special ceremony.

Dr Walsh, Dr Ginde's guru, was going to perform the operation at Wimbledon. It was Christmas time. People in London were busy preparing for it. I could not hide my anxiety though. On the day of the surgery, I was asked to sign the forms. There was no one to turn to or to console me in those stressful hours. After Baba was taken to the operation theatre I turned to a small chapel in the same premises and read parts of Vinobaji's Geetai in front of the idol of Jesus. I was not alone really. My god was with me. And the nurses and other staff members of the hospital were very loving and helpful. They tried their best to allay my fears. The cook in the house of Mr Pant was a very endearing person. His loving care made us feel more embarrassed, since we were not used to such hospitality.

The operation was successful. During this period, I was in touch with Anandwan only through letters. The same day I wrote to Vikas:

> Atkinson Morley Hospital,
> Wimbledon, London, S.W.
> 1/12/71.
>
> Dear Vikas,
>
> Baba was operated upon this afternoon. Every thing went on smoothly, says Dr Kashyap from India

House. Arthur, Mary, and Mrs Pant were with me. Baba looked at us. He cannot speak because of the oxygen mask. He has a cut in the neck, on the left side. They are taking care that the blood does not coagulate. He vomited blood. It was painful. They are giving him injections regularly; antibiotics and sedatives, I think. All the staff are very efficient and co-operative.

The nurses want me to go home. But Baba wants me to stay in the hospital. He talked to me a little time ago. I think I will have to leave for home. Going home is an ordeal for me. They have taxi service. The drivers keep on changing. They ask me the address. It is twenty miles from the hospital. I pray to god for my safe return. The grandeur of everything frightens me.

Baba receives all possible aid promptly. But everything is uncertain until things return to normal. Last night he could not sleep. He was talking about you all the time. He remembers everyone.

The night before the operation was literally the darkest night for both of us. He talked in such a way, as if he was saying goodbye to this world. I had to control myself, and him too. We got up early in the morning and had our bath at five. The day dawns at eight here. People generally get up at that time.

I had never imagined that such a thing would ever happen to us in life. They say that we will have to stay in the hospital for two to three weeks. Under the influence of anaesthesia he felt no pain, but now it is unbearable. The doctor says, it will continue for about a year or so. Earlier, he could not lie down on back, and now, he cannot sit up even for five minutes.

The doctor says he is improving and there is nothing to worry about. Baba is still using the oxygen mask. The doctor says, 'He is breathing the air from India.' He has a fine sense of humour. He must be above sixty. Anyway, they are all very nice to us. It may be that they have seen our photographs and read about us in Arthur's book, especially the chapter called 'Amte's Miracle'. I think that is the reason, behind the nurses' courtesy.

With love to all,

Yours,
Indu.

Madhubhai was our connecting link with Anandwan while we were in London. He was busy collecting money for Baba's operation and at the same time kept in touch with Vikas and Prakash, who were doing their M.B.B.S. at Nagpur Medical College. He was so patronising to them that we were relieved of anxiety over domestic matters. The concern and the sense of responsibility he showed, during these days of our isolation from our family, provided solace to us. How promptly he informed Vikas and Prakash, in detail, what was happening to us in London! The following letter, which he wrote to Prakash, speaks of his involvement and his presence of mind.

Bambuli Niwas
Mahim, Mumbai16
11/12/1971.

Dear Prakash,

I sent a telegram to Advocate Pawade, so that you would have the latest information about Baba and Tai. Did he ring you up? I am also enclosing the letter that Tai sent on the 3rd. Another one is expected today or tomorrow.

Mr Pant sent me a telegram asking me to send one thousand pounds. I had sent six hundred and fifty two, a day before. The Reserve Bank is asking for bills to issue more pounds. I gave the message to Tai over the phone. But, the bills have not arrived yet. In view of this delay, I have given the guarantee in writing, to the Reserve Bank, so that I may be allowed to submit the bills later. They have issued a voucher for 349 pounds. Sadhanatai has asked me not to send the money immediately, but I have decided to send it on Monday.

Prime Minister Mrs Indira Gandhi has sent a cheque for five thousand rupees and Yashwantrao Chavan for two hundred and fifty. Donations are coming from far and near. Kamani Trust has contributed five thousand and two more came from Excel Indusries, a phosphorus making company from the Kutch region. We have fifty thousand rupees in our bank account today.

Kumar and Deenanath wrote to me from Somnath. Deenanath has decided to work at

Bhamragad. I met Dr Schenellman at the airport on the 4th. He was enquiring about the workshop to be conducted at Somnath.

Shankar's speculations about food grains for this year are encouraging. He thinks, it will touch something like twelve hundred quintals. The seasonal yield of vegetables at Somnath is going to be high. We must be in touch with the brokers at Chandrapur.

Do write to me.

Yours,
Madhubhai

You may wonder, why am I telling you these trifling details. There are reasons. Trivialities are a part of everyone's life; even the great cannot escape them. We never identified ourselves with the great. In fact, we are closer to the humblest of the humble. We had more to share with them than with anyone else. Hierarchy was something we never bothered about. Our life is full of such trivialities. Moreover, I believe that important truths are revealed in small things. They tell us about human nature, about their values, their way of thinking and feeling. Without going to school, you learn a lot about life; learn without the burden of having to learn.

Now look at me. Going abroad in the circumstances in which we went; at a time when it was almost a question of life or death, every little thing mattered. We depended completely on charity, not from one or two people but hundreds of them. The practical problems I faced, during our stay in England, had a frightening dimension. Whether it was daily travel from home to the hospital and back, or the financial crunch, or food, I could not help worrying about these routine matters.

When Baba was hospitalised, I used to get up early, bathe, finish washing, and set out with my lunch box for the hospital; return around eight in the evening, then inform Baba of my safe return. The taxi drivers were very polite. I had to spend twenty Shillings a day on transport. Once, on my way back, I could not find the house. The driver started grumbling. I could only pray to god. You cannot imagine how I trembled with fear at the thought of losing my way. But after wasting a considerable amount of time, I reached home safely.

In the hospital, they prepared non-vegetarian food and naturally, Arthur feasted on it. We ate the rice that I cooked at Arthur's home. We had paid £1,200 towards initial payment for the operation. Every afternoon people came to see Baba. Tea and biscuits was the least we could offer them but the thought of increasing bills made me restless.

Despite the series of troubles we waded through, we enjoyed our stay in London because the love they showered on us was immeasurable. I do remember those cherished moments even today, when the Christian fathers and nuns came to see Baba or when they prayed collectively in the church for Baba's recovery. Sister Leela, who came to see Baba in the hospital, organised these prayers. She loved Baba no less than his own sister. We got a golden opportunity to attend the musical concert of Ravi Shankarji and have lunch with him. I told the music maestro that my nephew, Raju, Suma's son, worships him as his guru.

I cannot express my gratitude to Appasaheb Pant in words. A perfect gentleman with a golden heart! Cultured and simple at the same time! He made our stay comfortable and pleasurable.

During our return journey, our flight was delayed. So, we spent the night at Smita Patil's mother's house in London. On reaching Mumbai, we stayed with Madhubhai.

Yadunathji accompanied us during the journey from Mumbai to Anandwan. People knew about Baba's return. They crowded on the platform at Nandgaon station. The venerable Saint Tukdoji Maharaj was travelling on the same train. He mistook the people carrying the garlands in their hands and shouting in joy, for his own followers. When the train stopped, he discovered the truth and came to Baba and patted him on his back in admiration. Do you know what he said to Baba? 'Had you been a yogi or a saint, you would have snatched my bread from me.' At Manmad, they had arranged lunch. They asked me about Baba's diet. I told them that except for chillies, anything would do. They brought non-vegetarian food. I felt embarrassed. Again they had to run around for a vegetarian dish. We had to face a similar situation in Sangli later. I started giving clear instructions to people about his diet.

People were very happy to see us in Anandwan. Their faces were brightened and could not contain the joy they felt on our return. Every line on their face spoke of their happiness. The London hospital waived the operation charges in recognition of Baba's work for leprosy. The amount – one lakh, ten thousand – that we had collected for Baba's operation, was finally deposited in the account of our Trust. My air fare had cost us around eight thousand rupees. We raised that amount by selling a piece of our own land at Salori and deposited the money in the account of our Trust.

The year 1972 saw the beginning of a new phase in our life. Baba set up a small centre at Nagepalli. This was the year of severe drought in Marathwada. Villages were vacated on a large scale as the people left in search of better prospects. Baba conducted a two-month camp for the youth of this region. It turned out to be our gain; we found two dedicated workers in Jagan Machakale and Dada Panchal. Fortunately, the government of Maharastra donated twenty acres of land for this project. A cottage stood by the side of a small stream in a short time and Mangilal came forward to shoulder this responsibility. Soon Jagan replaced him and has since been in charge of this centre.

Nagepalli lies midway between Anandwan and Hemalkasa. It became a halting station for all of us when Prakash decided to set up his Lok Biradari Prakalpa at Hemalkasa. Jagan acted as the messenger between Anandwan and Hemalkasa. The distance was sixty kilometres, and the means of transport was only a bicycle! Sixty miles on a bicycle, fancy that! In addition, he had to cross the river Bandia. It was an ordeal, which he had to face not once or twice, but a number of times. I must say that Baba's dreams could become a reality only because of such dedicated, frenzied young men like Jagan.

Initially, they lived in humble cottages beside the stream. During the rainy season, the floods submerged their huts and they had to set up a temporary camp. Jagan got married to the daughter of a resident of Anandwan. Mukta, with her ever-smiling face, proved to be a perfect match for him. Their hospitality, to anyone and everyone, is par excellence. Jagan is a wonderful man; always at ease, come what may and gifted with an enviable equanimity combined with a rare capacity for toil. He had to wait until 1983 to move into a safer and better house. He is not only the messenger but also the maker of so many beautiful things. With his inventiveness, he transformed the face of this project. It became a self-sufficient unit with poultry, live-stock and vegetable farming under his guidance. He could provide vegetables to Hemalkasa in its early phase, when a school was started for the tribal children. In course of time, the strength of the school increased and to make up for the shortage; vegetables are now sent from Anandwan and

Somnath. In my first stay at Nagepalli, a king cobra had made its appearance and until the jungle was cleared, it became almost a daily sight.

Jagan also set up a dispensary for the tribals at Nagepalli to provide them with at least first aid. He has the skill of establishing a good rapport with the people around. Today he is running a tailoring school for the tribal women at Nagepalli and the nursery has provided means of livelihood to many young men.

Around this time, Vishram Bedekar and Malatibai paid a visit to Anandwan. They enjoyed their stay at Anandwan and Somnath immensely. The letter they wrote on their return unhesitatingly expressed their sentiments. Every word they wrote, carried the stamp of their emotions and feelings for us. Both of them believed in astrology. Before they left, they asked us for our horoscopes. They wanted to show them to some good astrologer. In the letter they informed us about the astrological finding about the two of us.

> 4 Dec 1972
>
> Accept my greetings to you.
>
> We reached here on 27th. Before we left, I had made two commitments and I am writing about the same.
>
> I could contact Shri Uplekar by the phone after two or three days. Even Nalinitai complained about her failure to contact Shri Uplekar. Importantly enough, he enquired about the documents, the vehicle you will be sending and the person you will be sending it to. It is better to inform him in advance.

We held a discussion on the horoscopes you had given us. I am sending herewith the findings about the same.

Your birth chart is rated very highly. The blossoming and flowering of Baba's career after marriage was made possible because of the powerful stars in your chart. This is the reading of the astrologers, I hope Baba will not get angry with this. In other words, the house dealing with married life in Baba's chart is very strong. It indicates a major role of his wife throughout his life. Your marital status will last longer. Baba's stars predict a very long life. During our stay at Anandwan Baba had said to me, 'If you and I live for two more years, I will take you to Bhamragad.' It means I will have to take care and keep myself healthy at least for two years. Baba's health will improve gradually in the next fourteen months. They also say that he will never feel the dearth of money. Wherever he goes, money will come to him, it will be generated.

If there are any other problems to be consulted upon, do inform me. I want my friend, Kavish to see Anandwan once, and he too is eager to see it. He is a novelist of good calibre, besides being a short story writer and an essayist. He never gets tired of writing. He has already translated the speech I gave at Somnath, into Urdu and Hindi and is thinking of publishing it. He has taken from me Baba's recorded poems along with my interpretation of them. Listening to our account of this trip has already inspired the writer in him. Once you get through Prakash's wedding, tell me what time will be most suitable to bring him to you. The first or second week of January suits me well.

Bye.

Convey my regards to Baba and Bhai.

Vishram Bedekar.

In the same letter Malatibai had written the following lines:

Greetings to you.

My mind is still occupied with the thoughts of Anandwan and Somnath. Whenever you find time, do send me a copy of Baba's poems sung by Rupatai. I have the recorded version of Baba's poem *Shrinkhala Pai Asu De*, I want the other two that she sang. I have also recorded the blind boy's song. I do not know what it is but something in me is urging me to write. However, it is not so easy to capture the two of you in words.

Your horoscope speaks of a long partnership with Baba. The root cause of all his trouble is the position of Mars in his birthchart. Nevertheless his lifeline is long and strong. I was happy to learn that. I know, Baba will laugh at these astrological readings, so please do not tell him about it.

My kind regards to him and bhai, love to the children.

Yours,
M. Bedekar

The get-togethers of the friends of Anandwan have attracted many well-known personalities from time to time. We had the opportunity to have in our midst: music maestros such as Kumar Gandharva, Vasantrao Deshpande, P. L. Deshpande; writers like G. N. Dandekar, Narhar Kurundkar, Ram Shewalkar, Sunitabai Deshpande and the poet of poets, B. B. Borkar. Among other stalwarts are Dada Dharmadhikari, Chandrashekhar Dharmadhikari, Rahulji Barpute and Chinchalkar Guruji. B. B. Borkar is Baba's favourite poet. Once Borkar wrote a letter to me, only four lines. It was no less than a poem. He wrote:

In your arms, a storm
Long held by you;
A bow to you I owe,
A father to you, though.

What is the requirement of a sustainable human relationship? Mutual love and trust! What else? A bit of tolerence too. It does not cost much unless you make a fuss over identity. Had it not been true, there would not have been such bridges built in no time, with thousands of unknown people, great and small. We had nothing to give and yet we have received so much love. What other things do we need to live? And is there anything else worth living your life for? These relationships are the calyx that holds the flower of life. Little things suffice to nourish and make it strong; just trifles. We have experienced it time and again. People who came for annual camps and gatherings, often used to leave behind their possessions in their rooms while leaving. It was my duty to collect them, label them and take care of them until their owners' next visit. They had a pleasant surprise and felt happy to have them back after a long interval. They also kept their promises even in trifling matters. Once, I asked Mr Kurundkar to name the sixteen ingredients of some special paan. He did not know all of them at that time, but he never forgot to inform me about the same in the letter he wrote. The answer was not important but the fact that he remembered it spoke of his sincerity.

EIGHT

The idea of setting up a centre for the tribals at Hemalkasa had already taken root in Baba's mind. The successful completion of projects such as Anandwan, Somnath, Ashokwan and Anand Niketan college of Arts, Science, Commerce and Agriculture had now given a definite direction to the work Baba wanted to do in his life. Completion often brings stagnation. However, the word 'stagnation' does not exist in Baba's dictionary. The inexhaustible source of energy that you find in him, has never allowed him to rest. He was not made for the beaten track. Every day brought new dreams, new hopes, new plans, and new ways of realising them. Did I not say, that the leprosy colony was just the beginning?

In the early seventies, he became very restless with the thought of the plight of the tribals in Gadchiroli—the Madias and the Gonds. He spent sleepless nights over this. Insomnia has been Baba's faithful companion all his life. Whenever he is possessed with some idea, sleep is the first thing to elude him. Not the quixotic ideas, but those dipped in passion. Likewise, idea and reality are strange bedfellows, but Baba always sought for a happy union between the two.

Baba had already surveyed the land, and selected a spot, from where a river ran at a distance of two and half kilometres. He had to surmount a number of difficulties to acquire this part of the forest, which was the natural habitat of the wild animals such as tigers, bears, wolves, swine, panthers, snakes, scorpions and the like. The location for this project was picturesque. However, when it came to staying there, the circumstances – lack of any means of communication with the outer world, complete isolation during the rainy season, a good distance away from any big town, lack of means of transport – all made it quite difficult. It was thus necessary to have diligent and devoted workers who would be ready to stay at Hemalkasa, since it was an isolated place in the interiors of the forest. During the Somnath project Baba was accompanied by many dedicated workers. It is difficult to remember all the names but some of them were Kumar Shiralkar, Deepak Dikshit, Rupraj Nagesh, Hatkar, Ravi, Mukunda, Sharad Kulkarni, Deenanath, Manohar, Mohan Tandon, Ajit Mankarnekar, Gulab, Kalyan, Arun Belsare and Rajanikant Pot. Baba was not one to be discouraged by thoughts of difficulties, real or imaginary. Instead of wasting his energies brooding over them, he would always utilise it to surmount them. I have never seen him being in two minds over any issue; it may be because he is essentially a man guided by the heart, a true romantic, sensitive to sights and sounds. It was not a surprise to anyone that he was drawn to the virginal beauty of this forest in Bhamragad.

The river Vainganga previously divided this region into two parts. The one beyond is known today as Gadchiroli district. As we ramble away from the river, on the other side, the forest envelops us from all sides. The teak wood bars the entry of the sunlight with all its might, leaving the soil with the eternal yearning for a caressing touch of a ray of light. The roaring streams of the rivers like Indrawati, Pamul Gautami, Pearlkota and Bandia girdle around it almost like a python coiling around its prey. You watch everything anxiously, with eyes stunned and your heart pounding. Small figures pop up suddenly, from behind the trees, dressed in colourful feathers and myriad beads of stone. This is their world; far from the one, in which we live and love to live. This is the world of the untamed where the vipers and the tribals are its legitimate citizens.

This was our first view of Hemalkasa. Today, things have changed considerably. Baba had first seen this territory in his college days and he fell in love with it. Moreover, the thought of the plight of the tribals had percolated too deep to eradicate from his mind. Prakash was doing his M.S. at Ghataprabha then. Being the director of the State Co-operative Bank at that time, Baba occasionally visited this place. It took him no time to sense their immediate need for health facilities. They needed a doctor who would stay on against all odds and adversities. Baba tested Prakash. Yes, he neither dictated nor requested him. Once he found that Prakash sounded positive on this issue, he started with his plans and worked them out in detail. Vasantrao Naik was kind enough to offer fifty acres of land for this experiment. However, there was another hurdle to overcome. Prakash was engaged to Manda, who was a doctor and had completed her course in anaesthesia. If she was to marry Prakash soon, then her consent was essential. She was working as a lecturer in Nagpur Medical College at that time. We felt relieved when she willingly gave her consent to join Prakash on this project.

In 1972, the wedding took place at Anandwan. It was a simple wedding. There was nothing special for lunch except fried rice. Mama Kshirsagar chanted the holy verses for the sacred rite. Prakash and Manda bowed to the dalit for their blessings. No gifts were exchanged. I felicitated five married dalit women with coconuts.

Manda came from an educated family. Her father, Mr Deshpande was a lecturer in the agricultural college in Nagpur.

Her mother was a teacher in a D.Ed college. All the inmates of Anandwan attended the wedding. Baba composed a couple of verses on this occasion.

Life be tested in total surrender,
Love, in sacrifice;
Woodward the two went
To try their fate;
New was the day and new the skies,
And left for tomorrow, the worries.
Now was the time or never, they said,
Waters of Indravati, they waded;
The river swelled with the pity they poured,
And the love they scattered;
A hand raised to bless the twain,
Woodward, the two went.

Manda resumed her duty in the medical college immediately after the wedding. Prakash left for Hemalkasa all by himself. Renuka was doing a course in nursing at Matru Sewa Sangh in Wardha. She too decided to join Prakash. The first four musketeers at Hemalkasa were Prakash, Renuka, Ajit and Nagesh. They set up their huts on the bank of a stream; a few leprosy patients gave them company.

Manda had signed a bond with the college. It was only after a year that she could join Prakash at Hemalkasa. Before she came to stay permanently at Hemalkasa, I wanted to take her there once. She came from a different background, perfectly urban and sophisticated. In her family too, like mine, there was a strict code of conduct. And here she stood, on the edge of a forest—a boundary that divided the two worlds. Perhaps this was her first visit to a jungle, and she had chosen to make it her permanent abode. Nothing but love for Prakash could have dictated such an adventure on her part. Prakash stayed alone for nine months.

We made all the preparations. We had to travel by truck, the only vehicle we had in our institution. We loaded all our necessities for the journey—grocery, vegetables, raw bananas, drinking water, bedsheets and blankets. The odyssey had begun. Our first halt was Perimili, near the river Bandia. We stayed with the Madias. This was a common practice in each of our trips to Hemalkasa. With us in the shed were Madias, who travelled with their hens, goats, and sheep. In the bleak light of a lantern, we spent the night together. On one such visit, it started raining at day break. Completing the morning duties was an ordeal; first, the open-air toilet, and to make matters worse, the incessant rain. Manda was new to all this. We resumed the journey. Forty kilometres by truck to reach Bandia! And not without crossing another river, Konari. The water was running over the bridge, we were told. All the vehicles were held up. Manda did not know swimming. Prakash had come to receive us. He took Manda on his back for a round in the river. We were all very worried till they returned. Prakash, too, like Baba, is adventurous. The next day we reached Bandia. The road to Bandia was not an easy one. At another place, we ran out of drinking water. There was a tank nearby but the water was not safe for drinking. We saw insects floating in it. What were we to do? A moment's thought and down went the bucket! We used a piece of cloth as a filter. Then, we boiled the water and quenched our thirst. This was not the end to the problems. The bridge on the river Bandia too, was submerged in water. Prakash had come with a bullock-cart. How, do you think he knew we were coming? Jagan, our most reliable messenger, rode to Hemalkasa, on his bicycle, two days in advance. We crossed the bridge on the bullock-cart. That is not all. The last phase consisted of twenty-five kilometres on a bad road; six hours of strenuous driving in the same cart, being knocked about every now and then, before we reached our destination. We were too tired to cook now; we had to make do with the left overs that we carried. We stayed there for four days, during which time Prakash took us around the jungle.

The earlier visit to Bandia was also dotted with many thrilling incidents. That time, I went with Baba and Biju Pandit came with us. I remember the night when we had to take refuge in the dried up river basin. Everyday we would scour the jungle as much as we could, and return to the base camp in the river basin. Once, we met a driver sweating from fear because he had seen a tiger in the jungle. He felt better when we talked to him. He was stunned to hear about our ventures in the jungle. Perhaps, he had seen a tiger for the first time. In the evening, we visited the villages, Hemalkasa and Koyinguda, the former occupied by tribals called the Madia Gonds and the latter owned by the feudal chiefs. We stayed there for three days. On our way back, we spent the night at Perimili in a ghotul, a sort of a guesthouse of the tribals. Every tribal village must have a ghotul. Sometimes, I wonder at their customs and social norms. There is a lot to learn from them, I think. This guesthouse accommodated another family along with their hens and sheep that day.

I still remember the days when the Bhamragad project was in its nascent stage. For the first fifteen days the cooking was done on the bank of the river in open air. It was a regular practice to take a bath in the river and walk down to Hemalkasa. It must be at least a two and half kilometres' walk. There was not a single hut at Hemalkasa, not a drop of water to drink. A cart loaded with barrels of drinking water was the only alternative.

Many a time, cooked vegetables turned sour by the evening. The heat was scorching. Sometimes on finding worms in the curry, we had to make do with chapattis and pickles only.

All these journeys to Hemalkasa are full of exciting moments, of suspense, fear, pain, wonder, longing and so much more. Of course, we never bothered about such things. I think, what matters is your readiness to face anything, your strong desire to go on. If you have the will, you can put up with physical pain too. Once, a thorn got into my foot and was excruciatingly painful. Hours passed before Manda could do something. She took a safety pin, sterilised it in boiling water, and pierced the blister round the thorn. It bled profusely but I was immediately relieved of the pain. This was done in the light of a lantern.

My mind is crowded with the innumerable incidents associated with my visits to Hemalkasa. During the early phase of work I had many shocking revelations. I had taken lots of old saris that I had collected from my friends, for the tribal women there. Never in their life, had they seen, such a long piece of cloth as a sari that would cover the whole body. They were not to blame, because the very idea of wearing such a dress was new to them. Reluctant as they were to adopt this new style, they cut the saris into pieces and dressed themselves in their own style. It was my turn to be enlightened about poverty and ignorance. A sense of gloom crossed my mind. Mind you, these tribals had never seen a soap in their life, and when they were given one, took it for some eatable, and started eating it. Prakash and Manda made their first appearance here against such odds. It became a tryst with the tribals for life. Imagine, for seventeen long years they lived without electricity. I used to visit Hemalkasa during Ganesh Chaturthi every year. And there was never any dearth of shocking experiences for me. It was a different world altogether. But when the time came to say goodbye after my temporary stay, it would be tears all the way. Nothing is worse than the pain of separation! I think the feeling could not have been different from mine on their side either. Manda and Prakash were joined by a few dedicated co-workers who went through similar rigorous experiences while setting up our centre at Hemalkasa. The thought of leaving little Digant, Aniket and Moksha in that wilderness sent tremors down my spine.

On another occasion, Manda and I were travelling in a truck, and met with an accident. The front of the truck was completely damaged. Both of us received head injuries. Pieces of glass had to be removed from our heads. It was a miracle that we survived this accident, they said.

Various things happened through all these early years of work at Hemalkasa. The risk and the dangers also had different faces, different forms. On another occasion, Shanti, Ramesh and I set off for Hemalkasa a day before Ganesh Chaturthi. This was the day of the special fast in the name of Lord Shiva. The journey was marked by halts at Nagepally, and then at Burgy. The river Bandia was flooded. The waters, surging with tremendous speed, would not allow us to cross. The ferryman initially refused to take us across, but finally, we persuaded him. As the boat moved along the current, we held our breath in fear as we were being pushed far below our destination. Even the thought of the boat being capsized or getting drowned had frozen me for a few minutes. There was yet another hurdle to overcome. After a few hours of walk from Bandia, we came upon another stream at Kudkeli. It was raining heavily. This stream was flooded too. We waited helplessly for the waters to subside. Prakash had already been informed of our arrival, but there lay many streams between us. Neither of us knew, where we would meet each other. Stealthily the evening came, and the fear in my mind grew darker and darker. The probability of encounters with bears and other wild animals was high. Just then, unexpectedly, a cyclist showed up. He was a gentleman and led each one of us, turn by turn, through the gushing stream. While in the middle of the stream, Shanti was almost swept by the current, she even asked us to leave her, but somehow we managed to pull her out. On reaching Dudepally, we found that the road had disappeared into a big pothole. Climbing down and up again we made for Tadgaon, literally groping our way in the darkness of the night. We were relieved to see the lights of the jeep. Prakash had come searching for us. It was eleven, when we reached Hemalkasa. We prepared a meal, and went to bed late in the night.

Do you think that the tribals gave us a warm welcome when we stepped into this wilderness to set up a centre for them? They were suspicious for the obvious reasons. We were strangers and belonged to a world they had never known. Their hostility was natural. Finding a way through this dense forest was perhaps easier than finding a way to their hearts. Their's was a way of life, that was completely controlled by blind belief. They had their own laws and their own methods of settling issues or finding solutions or remedies—even in trivial matters like the common cold, for example. They held 'good souls' and the 'bad souls' responsible for everything. They used black magic, sorcery, and some other esoteric methods for curing diseases. They consulted a holy man, who chanted mantras for everything. He was their priest and enjoyed an important position in their life. He was the most wanted man and was always busy. The reason I am telling you all these things is that when Prakash and Manda came here and set up their dispensary they had to wait for patients for days on end. The tribals had more faith in the priest than in Prakash, his rival. Prakash did not know what to do with his time, which seemed to stretch endlessly. You will laugh to know what he did; he chopped wood, or carried bricks from one place to another, and if that was not enough, he would go exploring the forest, allowing his legs to guide him.

The construction had begun. The contract for making the bricks was given to a local person. Bhau Nagelwar came with his assistants for the building and construction. Shankardada also paid regular visits. Some of the tribal people were now making bold to visit the dispensary—at least traffic had started between the two worlds. Renuka helped Prakash in the dispensary since Manda was pregnant for the first time. I was away for Madhubhai's daughter Shama's wedding in Bombay and rushed back to Hemalkasa, aware that I had to cross the river Bandia before it swelled up. It was a very short stay there too—just three hours. I had to be back with Manda at Anandwan. I packed my meal and got on the bullock-cart. As we reached the banks of Bandia, we sensed danger—the water was rising. There was no alternative but to wade through the water. The ferrymen must have thought us mad to take on the furious Bandia. I closed my eyes but I could not shut my mind to the force of the river. By god's grace, we reached the other side safely. We were on the outskirts of a small town. Our chapattis were wet. The villagers provided us with a cot and we left the chapattis to dry before we ate them. The night passed and early in the morning even as the rains continued, we set out for Nagepally. Baba, who was waiting for us, had our lunch ready.

Digant (Pilu) was born on the 9th of August. This good news reached Prakash via Nagepally, through Jagan, of course. Pilu became seriously ill when he was fifteen days old, and had to be admitted to the Nagpur Medical Hospital. Manda and I had to look after him. Prakash was beyond our reach, as the rains were pouring in—it looked as if we were living on different planets.

Rains in this region are so heavy, and the roads, if at all there were any, were always blocked. Prakash came to know about Pilu's illness after a few days. What could he do? Hemalkasa was totally cut off. You can't even imagine the condition of the roads. To tell you the truth, there were none. I remember having crossed the river Bandia in waist-deep water between the years 1974 and 1983; there was no bridge on the river then. We used to leave the jeep at Kandodi, and cross the river on foot in the rainy season. Sometimes, the jeep would get stuck in the swamps and would not move, until all of us got off and pushed it. This was the routine for many years. Even a pilgrimage to a holy place could not have been so difficult, but the yearning to see them inspired me to face any challenge. For seventeen long years they lived without electricity. I refused to use fans and coolers during this period in Anandwan. On every trip to Hemalkasa, I used to take wheat flour and vegetables for them. The rainy season was the worst time of the year—no roads, no electricity, no vegetables, no fruit, no wheat flour and above all, no communication of any kind. Complete isolation, in the vast wilderness. Except for potatoes there was hardly anything to eat. It was no use storing things. They would rot very quickly. Fungus appeared on the things in no time. The weather spoilt everything. Even tea leaves did not last longer than a few days. There was no one to make chapattis. Whenever I went, I used to grind wheat in the grindstone. Only half of the flour could be used. The rest, being rough, had to be discarded. I think Prakash and Manda had to work harder than us. Their challenges were far too trying, and yet there was never even a faint murmur of complaint from them.

Pilu was a year old when he contracted cerebral malaria. This time, I stayed for four days with them, and was happy to have been able to spend some time with little Pilu. I was about to leave and had almost boarded the truck, when a man came running to tell me that Pilu had suddenly become unconscious. It was a test of my endurance to see Manda's agony. Dr Bhate, who was at Hemalkasa then, began some treatment, but it did not work. It was only in the evening that he opened his eyes. The next day I had to leave for Anandwan, but I had left my heart at Hemalkasa. It took quite some time for them to diagnose this as cerebral malaria, which was widespread in this region, and even today it beats every other disease in terms of its casualty rate. Almost everyone has had to face it.

It was agonising for me each time I had to leave this place. As Pilu grew up, it became increasingly difficult to leave him there. He too, would start crying when the time came to say goodbye. He had never seen lady's finger. The first time he tasted it, he was so excited that he refused to eat anything else that day, and went to every house and told them about it. He is my first grandson, and has stayed with me longer than any other. Vegetables were a luxury for him. The very thought of this filled my heart with pity. It was a common practice for me to sleep in one room with my grandchildren and the orphaned children.

The penchant for adventure drew a few more young boys to Hemalkasa; Vilas Manohar and Jagdish Godbole came from Pune and Mohan Tandan from Gadchiroli. Then came Mukunda, who belonged to Nasik. He took charge of the school in the beginning. What did he not do to bring children to the school? He used to comb villages around on foot, looking for prospective entrants, coaxing them to join the new school. We had to be extremely cautious during the harvest time, because human sacrifice was common and rampant among the tribals here, especially since the sacrifice of little children was a regular propitiation rite. Besides, the number of dropouts and 'runaways' was alarming in the beginning. We had to offer incentives to bring them back to school. It took time to get them to sit in one place and copy alphabets. It was an open-air school. Another Shantiniketan! A bunch of them, sitting under the trees, struggling to master the numbers and initiating themselves into formal education! My visit was normally scheduled around Ganesh Chaturthi and they used to wait impatiently for me. They also put up cultural programmes during the festival. In the beginning, the classes were held up to fourth standard, then extended to the seventh, and today we are running a full-fledged high school up to S.S.C. and a junior college too.

Sharad Kulkarni also joined us around the same time. He took on the responsibility of our medical sub-centre at Nelgunda. When another sub-centre was set up at Lahiri, Mukunda volunteered for this work. He stayed there for a number of years with his wife and children. The next ones to join Prakash, were Gopal Phadnis, Shekhar, Sitakant Prabhu, Joshi, Godbole and many others, who came and left. Gopal is the headmaster of the school today. Kanna, an old student of this school, has completed his M.S. Pandu has completed his masters in medicine when he joined our centre. Sudhakar Barsai is studying dental surgery. Quite a few of them have joined the teaching profession, and are doing valuable work in the field of education of the tribals. To me, their future seems very bright.

One fine day, Vilas came from Pune. He had planned to stay here for a year, and he became a permanent member of our family. He married my daughter, Renuka. He took interest in agriculture. He has written a beautiful book, *Negel,* on the animal friends at Hemalkasa. Renuka started with the dispensary and then became a teacher in our school. She was very fond of sports and excelled in some of them. Even after joining the school as a teacher, she cannot help going and playing with the children sometimes.

In course of time, three brick buildings were constructed, and all the workers shifted into them. Except for Prakash, all of them were bachelors. They had a nice time together—joking and teasing each other, or spinning yarns. I often wondered at their smiling faces. None of them ever showed the faintest shade of discomfort of having to work in adverse conditions, or of pride that they were doing any extraordinary work. Everything was normal, and each one of them, composed. Baba was very fond of this group of young men, and enjoyed spending time with them, whenever he went to Hemalkasa. Long drives to a green patch by the riverside, or into the interior of the forest, with all of them, was his favourite pastime. The cook would prepare the meal in the jungle and time passed in revelry over books, jokes, poetry, and what not.

The education of the tribals was education for the young workers too. Teaching in the school was not enough. After school was over, many odd jobs consumed their time; they would go to the jungle to collect wood, load bricks in trucks or carts, repair water pumps in the nearby villages and so on. They had to be men of many trades. Some of them liked to distribute articles and goods such as salt, kerosene, and seeds among the native tribals. Once, Prakash spent the whole day repairing pumps in the sun. When he came back, he looked so tired and pale, and said, that he would faint any moment. All the workers shared this spirit for work, which in a sense was unusual, but they did not even mention it; never indulged in futile discussions over what they did, nor gloried in their acts of kindness. When the children in the hostel fell ill the workers looked after them, as they would have cared for their own children. The serenity of this place, and this absence of consciousness of what they did, became a source of inspiration for Baba and me. Hemalkasa became our favourite haunt.

The health centres in the different parts of the jungle received a good response in due course. Medical aid was now available to the people in their villages—Hidur, Kothi, Lahiri, Nelgunda, Yechali and Mirkal. Mukund, Sharad, Shekhar and Kishore took all pains to run these centres. When they left, the leprosy patients took over, and successfully contributed to the work for the upliftment of the tribals. Later on, when the government set up its own primary health centres, these sub-centres were closed down.

Prakash and Manda concentrated on their work now. There was no fixed timetable for it. Whenever the patient came – be it mid-day or midnight – they rushed to help them. The patients came from long distances, sometimes they had to be carried on homemade stretchers—a pair of bamboos, a sling of cloth or rope at best, or on the shoulders at worst. They trudged their way, barefoot, in rain or sun, and in the shadow of the fear of attacks from wild animals. They walked fifty miles at times or more. Prakash and Manda had succeeded in persuading them to give up their blind beliefs and brought them to embrace modern medicine instead. Malaria and diarrhoea topped the list of common ailments. Cases of bear-bites were not less frightening. The patient and the accompanying relatives or friends made themselves comfortable under a tree in the open ground in front of our house. Today we have a well-equipped hospital building, but the patients prefer the open ground to the cosy hospital wards.

Prakash is a simple man, untrimmed and without affectation in speech and action. He possesses the highest sensitivity to pain and an incomparable capacity for endurance. In these only

Baba can compete with him. All his co-workers have displayed similar qualities of perseverance and recklessness, when face to face with danger. More amazing for me is Manda's capacity for acclimatisation. How natural it was! There was not even a ripple. She hailed from Nagpur, an urban setting. From Nagpur to Hemalkasa! What a distance, not in terms of miles but in terms of culture and surroundings. It was a journey back in time, perhaps, to choose to live among the tribals of the soil of Hemalkasa. How gently she closed one door and opened another, as if it was just entering another room of the same mansion. I often see myself in her; but she is a better version. She went a few steps ahead of me. She is an ideal wife, I think. Without friction, she managed to forego her artistic talent. She used to make beautiful idols of Ganesh in clay during the Ganesh Chaturthi and paint them; she also enjoyed decorating them during the festival time.

With a smiling face, she welcomes the guests at Hemalkasa; her hospitality includes breakfast and tea that she makes herself. Here, there is no 'help' to take care of these things, no servants to answer your calls at the ring of a bell. She combines in herself all that is required of a doctor, wife, mother, hostess, and cook. Her excellence and grace exceed all the best words in my stock. Behind every great man there is a woman, they say. I believe, that without such a consort beside him, no man can reach the heights of glory. She is his first friend, counsel, and critic. Manda has nestled the whole of Hemalkasa under her wings.

It was summer. I had been to Hemalkasa. It was the season for making paper there. All the paper mills in this region run in full swing. Obviously, this calls for cutting the large scale of bamboos. There is a demand for labour, which is brought from Andhra Pradesh and Madhya Pradesh. There are labour camps. Prakash and Manda are over-burdened during this season.

During this visit, I was witness to their hectic schedule. Manda left for the hospital at seven in the morning and came back at two-thirty in the afternoon, hurriedly finished her bath and lunch, and went back to work again to return only after sunset. After the day's tiring work, there is nothing as pleasurable as lying down to drop off to sleep, while counting the stars in the sky above. But Manda had no right to this. Even at midnight patients came—a village girl in labour pains, Manda would rush to her rescue. She treated such cases as emergency and spent the remaining night expecting the entry of the new life into this world. This was her routine throughout summer. Let me tell you, there was never a sigh nor any sign of irritation from her. I feel proud to say, that she is foremost in my list of role models today.

Prakash, on the other hand, is doing a lot more than just treating the tribals for their ailments. They often bring their disputes to his court too. He is their mentor, and they have faith in him, and accept his judgement without complaint. He does everything quietly, without ever mentioning it to anyone, not even to himself, I am sure; I do not know what to say about conceited people, who take credit for trifling things, and boast of little nothings. Manda and Prakash are indeed too humble; and shy too, I should say, though they have been honoured with many national and international awards.

Prakash has never practised yoga, but he has reached the ultimate stage in it. These are not my words, but the compliment given to him by Purnimatai Mandlik, the wife of Vishwasrao Mandlik, the chief director of Yogavidyadham, the well-known yoga school at Nasik. The most deadly animals also take to him easily and enjoy his company immensely. I think, love itself is the greatest yoga, that keeps you eternally fresh and sane. The whole universe is contained in these four letters.

It is more than two decades since Prakash and Manda entrenched themselves in this wilderness of Hemalkasa, fighting, not for their survival, but, to bring a ray of light in the life of the tribals. Their reckless absorbtion in their work speaks for their tryst with the tribals. Their only weapon was love. They kept their needs to the minimum. They command my reverence for what they are and what they do.

Sundays were mostly spent in exploring unknown places around. Once they went to Bijur, a nearby hill. There were large bee hives underneath the big boulders. They were frolicking as usual, when all of a sudden, the deadly bees flew about in all directions; they came in swarms, darkening the upper air for a while and then lashing at everyone mercilessly. Everybody ran. There was total commotion. Kalyan had the presence of mind to carry Pilu – who was very small then – to some distance from the bees. He and Vilas covered Pilu at the cost of severe injuries to themselves, though, Pilu too had his share of bites. Renuka was lucky to have escaped. She gave the message of the attack to the patients at the centre, and all of them started in search of Prakash and Manda. They found them in a most miserable condition; both of them lay unconscious on the ground. Only then did the bees leave. Among the wounded soldiers, were Jagdish, Mukund and Sharad. Manda and Prakash had to be brought home in a bullock-cart. After some time, Prakash regained consciousness. He helped himself and others, and treated them. The next day, their faces were swollen and they suffered from diarrhoea. The effect of the bite lasted for a week or so. Before they set out for Bijur, the local people had warned them against tigers and bears. And here they were almost finished off by the bees.

When Pilu was a little boy, he had no companions except for Savitri, the daughter of our cook, Lakhan and Rani, the young bear. He would do nothing but whimper in his loneliness. When the school was set up here, he found company in the children of the Madias.

He studied up to the third standard here, and went to Anandwan for further education. Pilu was good at chess while at school. Someone had explained the game to him once, and he took to it within a short time and mastered it. He was not even ten when he played with many of the guests who used to come to Hemalkasa, and beat them too. He enjoyed playing chess with everyone. People appreciated his talent for chess.

Prakash's second son, Aniket (Anu) was born soon. He stayed here at Hemalkasa. He passed his seventh standard, and shifted to Anandwan after that. But, he was a misfit there. He was so used to life in the jungle that he longed to go back and waited impatiently for the vacation. He often became homesick. On seeing the film Sant Dnyaneshwar he cried his heart out, especially when the parents of Dnyaneshwar committed suicide by jumping into the river. He refused to eat that day and insisted on going back to his mother. For many days after that, he did not eat properly and longed to be back with his parents.

Anu took to the wild animals just like Prakash. Once, an interesting thing happened. Manda had taken Anu to Nagpur. She visited her friend, who used to teach in a school there. At that time, the interviews for admission to the school were going on. She was asking questions to the little ones. She asked Anu a question for fun, 'Can you name some domestic pets?', to which Anu promptly replied, 'tiger, bear, crocodile . . .' All of them were amused. How could he have made the difference between the wild and the domestic? These were the only animals he had seen, since he was born. For him, they were far from being wild.

In the early days of our project at Anandwan, countless number of snakes were killed while clearing the ground. But Prakash changed everything. He mastered the technique of catching and handling snakes. It was at Hemalkasa that I saw the most poisonous snake, the agya manyar, sixteen times more poisonous than an ordinary one, deep yellow with black stripes. It is rather sluggish and so there is less probability of its biting anyone. However, if it does, the road to heaven is made clear.

The tribals in Bhamragad, on seeing how much Prakash loved the wild animals, started bringing them to him as gifts. In return, Prakash gave them his shirt or some other item of clothing. He had already changed his dress style, ever since he went to work among the tribals. To make them feel at home, he started wearing only shorts and vest. He parted with most of his belongings, meagre as they were, to build up confidence and trust in the minds of the tribal people. As he succeeded in persuading them against hunting animals, the number of animals in his menagerie went on increasing. In the beginning, most of them had taken shelter in Prakash's house. They had free access to any place, even the wooden swing, which became their favourite resort. But the guests had problems. The unexpected arrival of a monkey, showing his row of teeth, would scare them; or the sight of a pair of bear or tiger cubs entering the house as they sat leisurely in the swing, would make them tremble in fear. Naturally, the presence of all the wild animals filled the house with a strong smell, not to say the stink. Manda put up with all this, without complaint. Later on, they were all put in cages.

Everything has changed today; there are no traces of this early struggle anywhere. The shimmer and shine have changed the face of this little village completely, but the Hemalkasa that lures me is the old one, in which the shadows of darkness loomed large in the light of the lantern and the birds flitted from tree to tree making strange sounds.

NINE

In 1977, Vikas got married. The wedding was celebrated with great pomp. His wife, Bharati, the daughter of Bhausaheb Vaishampayan, an MLA from Aurangabad, had once visited Anandwan with her mother. In our very first meeting, she impressed me. Her father was a man of principles and stood out among politicians with his moral earnestness, borne out by his characteristic simple living. He was a man with clean hands, although he was in politics, and never misused his power or position. Naturally, I was drawn towards Bharati, and dreamt of having her as my prospective daughter-in-law. I could see in her not only a suitable match for Vikas, but also thought of her complementary role in our work. Before we met her, we had advertised in the matrimonial column. How much salary, do you think, Vikas drew at that time? Only Rs 250 per month! That was his honorarium from the trust. No girl would have accepted the conditions in which we lived. A meagre salary, and staying and working with the lepers all her life! It was difficult. There was no other alternative, so we resorted to a marriage bureau and to advertisements. A message went to her family and we received a positive response.

The wedding was arranged at Aurangabad. We hired a bus and went there with few people; some trustees, and a few workers. Bharati's father offered us the bus fare but we refused to accept it, at which he felt hurt. Even Govindbhai Shroff was disappointed. However, the wedding was conducted in the old vedic style with elaborate rituals, respecting the wishes of the Vaishampayan family.

Bharati contributed substantially to the medical service in our hospital. She has a special interest in paediatrics and gradually women from villages around Anandwan started coming to the centre with their children. She has done a course in yoga from the well-known institute in Nasik and is running a yoga centre. She believes in the principle, 'prevention is better than cure'—an idea made possible through yoga. She successfully persuaded people to try yoga for fitness. Hundreds of people in Anandwan, as well as people from outside, have benefited from the centre's activities. While Vikas and Bharati engaged themselves with the increasing work in Anandwan, their children, Sheetal and Kaustubh, had to fend for themselves in the same way in which Digant and Aniket, did. Sheetal has passed her MBBS and Kaustubh has done CS. My grandchildren are lucky not to have spent a miserable childhood as my sons did, but the fact remains that their parents too could not give them as much time as parents normally do to their dear ones.

It was in the same year, if I remember correctly, that Marianne, a charming girl from Germany, came with her husband to Anandwan. She came and within no time became a member of our family. She found no difference between her home and Anandwan. She was already married, when she came, but she insisted on performing the wedding once more in our style, with the bridal costume, holy mantras, and elaborate rituals. I think, there was something Indian about her personality. The first time she came to Anandwan was before her marriage. She used to spend the whole day playing with the blind girls, doing their hair . . . . How easily she identified herself with the people here! Sumitra, a physically handicapped girl, commanded her special attention. They grew closer day by day. She showered all her love on Sumitra. The unexpected death of Sumitra left Marianne with a broken heart. She sent a large amount of money in her memory. With that money, the construction work at our Salori project was completed. Marianne's interest in Hindu customs and rituals took her to people's houses, and she asked them hundreds of questions. She even tried to learn Marathi. Whenever she comes here, she makes it a point to speak in her broken Marathi. And she comes to us regularly—every alternate year, even today, with Barnard, her husband, and her daughter. We are her Indian parents, she says. She has not yet seen the rest of India. Her route is fixed; from Germany to Bombay airport, and from Bombay to Nagpur, and then straight to Anandwan, into our arms. No halts in between, no detours anywhere. And she follows the same route on her way back. Her love for both of us is an enigma for me. What bond or bridge is there, I do not know.

Among the people who were attracted to Anandwan in the late seventies was Dr Arvind Bawadekar, a renowned orthopaedic surgeon from Bombay. He could finally find time out of his tight schedule, to visit Anandwan. He had heard about us long before he came. The bond of friendship between us was sealed in the very first visit; the next year, we were in his hospital in Mumbai for Baba's back operation. I still remember with gratitude his hospitality during our stay there. He remained a member of our board of trustees until he passed away recently. I have nothing but admiration for his commitment to work despite his battle with cancer. He set up a hospital at Gondavale, which provides medical aid to thousands of the poor and needy. We lost in him, a faithful and loving friend. He has set an example of selfless service to humanity. He is one of the rare species that embrace life and death with the same equanimity.

It is not without reason that Baba says that we are affluent in love. The bees, that hummed around Anandwan, brought honey of different flavours. Ramesh Gupta and Gopal Shah had a talent for writing. The press in Anandwan published a magazine called *Antarbharati* in those days. Ramesh and Gopal looked after it. When Ramesh left, Gopal shouldered the responsibility single-handedly. During the eight or nine years he was with us, he tried to give a definite shape to the printing section. This magazine provided many young and committed workers a platform to voice their opinions. Under Gopal's guidance, many of the young boys in Anandwan acquired the technical skills required in printing. His wedding with Mrunal took place at Anandwan. He wrote down Baba's poems too. He has settled down at Bardoli now. The letters he writes to us are drenched in his love for us and smack of his longing and affection for Anandwan.

Baba's foresight in building bridges between Anandwan and the privileged world beyond, had commendable results on the practical plane. Interactions between the two proved beneficial to both. There was no dearth of pain in our world, be it disease or deprivation. What was needed was a friend who could provide a balm, a friend in pain! We looked for such pain-friends in the world beyond. This has been the motto behind our life's work. This is the time-honoured value, and we were drawn to wherever it was respected. Artists in general and literary artists in particular have always contributed to it substantially. Beyond the aesthetic pleasure, Baba and I valued this inherent quality in the written word. It was with this view, that we extended an invitation to hold the thirty-fourth annual literary meet of Vidarbha Sahitya Sangh in Anandwan. I felt honoured in welcoming them to this congress. I got an opportunity to voice my thoughts on this occasion. I am not a writer, nor do I claim to have a refined aesthetic sense. However, whatever I have read so far, has been the anchor in my life. I believe that pain has been the fountainhead of great literature starting from the Ramayana and many other classics down the ages. There is a challenge, inscribed in pain, whether a sigh or a sob, that appeals to the human in you. Does it not? I spent many of my days surrounded by pain and felt enriched. What surprised me was the confidence that it will all end happily. I consider it my good fortune that I was able to witness hundreds of such transformations in Anandwan; and an even greater fortune to be a part of it. There is no fear of losing a friend-in-pain. A relationship born out of pain is sealed for eternity. It pulls down all barriers—caste, religion, nationality . . . I have experienced it. A wounded bird could inspire a work like the Ramayana, they say. What to make of the wounds of the leper, the destitute and the deprived? Not to mention that we owe our creativity, in word or work, to them. Are we not blessed in their pain? Shri Gangadhar Pantavane presided over this literary meet and honourable Shri Laxmansastri Joshi was the chief guest. Ten years ago when we hosted such a literary meet at Somnath, it fetched stalwarts like Vishram Bedekar and Narhar Kurundakar. Memories of these events also crowded my mind as I decided to write.

If the seed is strong enough and the ground fertile, it takes no time for the tree to grow in many directions. Uttarayan, a sort of home for the aged, owes its inception to the magnanimity of Dada Kulkarni from Gondia. Being familiar with poverty, he decided to share the burden of the misery of his fellow beings by setting up this home for old people in memory of his mother; it became our bank of wisdom. This was followed by another project, Gokul, a home for orphans. The incident that led to the realisation of this project is worth narrating. In 1979, a woman found a newborn baby at the Warora railway station and brought the baby to us. On seeing that little one, I was immediately reminded of Maya. Mr Dharav, a treasurer in our office, and his wife, took the responsibility of this few-days-old entrant. She was named Dharati. Today, she is studying in Anand Niketan College. Dharav and his wife Anjani showered their love on her.

This was the inspiration behind Gokul. Money came from hundreds of tiny hands; school children from Mumbai donated one rupee each from their own gift-money. Prakashbhai Mohadikar, the founder of Sane Guruji Kathamala, was the shaping spirit for these school-going children. Gokul thus became the first project, run by the children for children. How time passed in bringing up these little ones, I did not know. What a pleasure it was to do all those odd things for them! Giving them a bath, doing their hair, dressing them, sleeping with them—quite a lot of work but not without its pleasure, helping them smile, or allowing them to rest in my arms and let worries pass by. A girl called Ranjana gladly shared many of these tasks with me.

The workers at Hemalkasa went one step ahead—each family adopted a child. Gopal and Prabha looked after Dheeraj, Prabhu and Chatura parented Pankaj, and Prakash and Manda adopted Arti. Saroj Kathale, the headmistress of our school for the deaf and the dumb, mothered Prerana from among the first members of Gokul—Niraj, Prerana, Shivaji and Akbar. Prerana's wedding was celebrated with great pomp and she was happily married to a boy worthy of her goodness. There was Niraj fostered by Mr Kadu, the headmaster of the school for the blind, and his wife Suman. He recently passed his twelfth standard examination. Suraj is no less than my grandson. All my relatives are very fond of him, especially my younger sister Suma who has been taking a special interest in him. The two others were mentally challenged and commanded love from all, more than any other child did. I wonder if they would have received so much love from their real parents, for the number of children in a family used to be large in those days. I have nothing but admiration for all these mothers and fathers. Blood can't be thicker than water. What other proof do you need?

The wedding of Z. Prabhakar is one of the most memorable events for all the residents of Anandwan. He was very close to everyone because of his simplicity and unassuming nature. His straightforwardness and transparency attracted many to him. He stood out among all the friends of Anandwan because of his informal approach and rather aggressive kind of love. Everyone knows his boundless love for all the Amtes. His faith in Baba and love for Prakash was expressed in little acts too. Only he could have brought fish curry for P. L. Deshpande from Nagpur during his last stay in Anandwan. His love for Vikas was mostly expressed in endless arguments on many issues.

The second volume of Baba's poems, *Karunecha Kalam* (Pity's Pen) was published around this time. In this volume there is a beautiful poem on Sane Guruji who influenced Baba as much as Mahatma Gandhi did. This time, Suresh Dwadashiwar from Chandrapur dressed Baba's meditations in words. He is the chief editor of the daily, *Loksatta* today. He is a prolific writer. When I think of Suresh, I often wonder, who is greater, the man or the writer. The world is full of people who make a lot of noise about little acts of charity. Suresh is an exception to this. His pen was mighty enough to do justice to Baba's thoughts. Between Suresh and his wife Jaya, who works as a lecturer, and Anandwan there exists a bond of love. We bank on it, whenever we feel like. His is the first claim on my motherly love.

Another daughter of mine, Bijali, (Renuka was the first) got married to Vikas Muthe, Prakashbhai Mohadikar's nephew. Vikas worked in a tourist company before the wedding. Now he has joined Anandwan and looks after the guests and visitors. Bijali teaches in the school for the deaf and dumb.

Baba's strict adherence to his principles tested my mettle many times. He never compromised with them. There were never any exceptions. My close blood relations were often the ones on trial. Once, on our way to Hinganghat, I asked him to take another route so that I could meet my people. He promptly replied, 'I can't spend public money on your private visits. This truck belongs to the institution and has to be used for public work.' I said, 'I will bear the extra expenses on fuel.' When we reached the place, people gave donations liberally. Now I could justify my visit, but Baba would not listen and I had to pay for the extra distance. I paid for private phone calls too. Baba used to write accounts late at night and paid for the extra consumption of electricity from his pocket. My brother's wedding was arranged at Nagpur. Dada Kulkarni made arrangements for our stay close to the wedding hall. There was an unexpected storm accompanied by thunder and lightning. The bus that was hired for carrying the luggage along with the bride and the bridegroom did not come. It started raining but I did not dare to ask Baba to lend our bus to my brother. It was the property of the institution and Baba would never have agreed to such concessions. Finally, I asked my brother to donate Rs 101 in return for the bus service. Baba never used a single pai from the public money for private work. We observed this rule, religiously until 1990, when we left Anandwan for Madhya Pradesh.

In 1980, I brought my mother to Anandwan. She felt embarrassed to come and stay with us; old fashioned as she was, how could she have brought herself to stay in the house of her son-in-law? However, on Baba's insistence she finally agreed. She was old and had become very weak. She could hardly leave her bed. Her fragile frame and sinking health were warning enough of her approaching death. Even she had a premonition, I think. I was away for two days at Hemalkasa and kept thinking about her. I saw her in my dream telling me that she had embarked on a long tour, asking me to return immediately. What will you call it—telepathy, intuition, or coincidence? Without wasting time, I rushed back to Anandwan. She was eagerly waiting for me, I thought, and felt relieved on seeing me. She gave me money to buy new clothes for everyone. It was her way of acknowledging the kindness and love of all those who served her during this period. Baby also came from Nagpur the same day. The countdown had begun. She often went into fits of delirium. In one of her moments of consciousness she said to me, 'I had been to Shegaon to worship at the altar of Shri Gajanan Maharaj.' Then she looked at all of us and closed her eyes never to open them again.

The loss of a mother is the most irreparable loss. For every daughter, whether young or old, her mother is the safest roost. She is the only one, with whom one can share all worries and cares. The courage with which she brought us up and shaped our lives after my father's death is simply admirable. None can repay this debt. As she lay dead, I remembered all the different roles she played, displaying a new dimension of her personality every time. She became the first resident of Shantidham, the cemetery in Anandwan. Her life's struggle had ended finally, and no sound could now disturb her soul in its eternal peace. Verses from the Geetai were recited in the midst of tears which refused to stop. She was no more. I felt like an orphan despite being the mother of two children myself.

An early morning walk has been our habit ever since we made our home at Warora fifty years ago. Baba would never miss it even in my absence. Once, when I was away at Hemalkasa, Baba met with an accident. A serious one indeed! A truck had hit him when he had gone for his morning walk. He lay in a pool of blood by the side of the road, completely unconscious. It was his good luck that Mr Shirpurkar, a lawyer from Warora, and his friends saw him. They too had gone for a walk. They immediately got in touch with Vikas at Anandwan and Baba was carried home in a van. He was seriously injured; his clothes were drenched in blood. It was a long time before he came back to consciousness. I returned to Anandwan the same day, and regretted that I wasn't present when this happened. And it was on the same morning, that S. M. Joshi had arrived at Anandwan. He too was shocked when he heard of the accident. My time for daily worship was fixed; I never compromised with the eight o'clock prayers. On the day Baba met with the accident, I did not want to miss it at any cost. You may also wonder at my uncompromising nature on such issues. Being what I am, a devout worshipper and a faithful believer in my god, I refused to go against my grain. Moreover, in times of difficulties I would never miss it, and in fact, I derived strength from it. Vikas became desperate at my insistence but no one could have stopped me from it. My faith in god and daily worship, rather elaborate, as well as my fasts, have invited the displeasure of many close ones, relatives and friends. But I cannot help it.

Baba was admitted at the medical college hospital. His condition was miserable; continual vomiting and the tubes in his mouth and the nose, along with the saline, put me on tenterhooks. Even the smell of food would make him sick. I would sit in a corner and finish my lunch. Twelve days and nights stretched before me like an age. After about a fortnight, we returned home.

On the Republic Day of 1983, the first get-together of the parents of the tribal children was arranged at Hemalkasa. They responded in large numbers. Baba too was ready to leave for Hemalkasa, when he had a mild heart attack. We took him to Nagpur immediately. A message had to be sent to Prakash. Ultimately, through the wireless system of the police department, we managed to convey the message. Disappointment and anxiety clouded their joy. Prakash and Vilas rushed to Nagpur by jeep. Gopal and Dada took charge of the function, but all the children who waited eagerly for Baba were distressed at his absence. There was distress on our side too. Baba's regret on his inability to attend this function was no less.

On recovering from this attack, Baba started eating raw garlic petals regularly. This gave his body an odour, but he was determined. After one and half months rest, he went to Hemalkasa.

Another get-together was held at Anandwan in 1986. The tribals from all over Maharastra thronged here. Almost all the tribes were represented—there were the Madias, Gonds, Pardhans, Vatankars, Korkus, Katkaris, Bhillas, Varlis and Mahadeo Kolis. The cultural programme they put up was a feast of folk arts. Though most of them live very primordial lives, I have often wondered at their urge and capacity for art and some of their customs too. You will be surprised at the equality between men and women among the Madias, and an equality that exists without any fuss or fight. Looking after children and cooking are not essentially feminine duties here. Men do it willingly while the women are away at work. Equally shocking is their commitment to honesty. They would rather starve to death than steal something. It was extremely enriching to have met these people living in remote corners and below subsistence level. If you have an open mind stripped of pride or prejudice, profit will always be yours.

Baba's wish to open a school in the hills of Vinaguntha remains unfulfilled even today. It was his fascination for Abujmad, a part of Baster, that made him dream this but the borders of Baster set limits to his wish. Another wish which could not see the light of the day, is his desire to spend the last years of his life at Nelgunda, by the side of the river Indravati. Here, the call of the Narmada put a bridle over it.

Around this time, Mr And Mrs Bartholomy, a couple from France, paid many visits to Hemalkasa. They had earlier worked with Dr Albert Schweitzer in Africa. They compared the work at Hemalkasa with that of Dr Schweitzer's. There could not have been greater appreciation than this. For the Bartholomys, it was a journey into their past. A small country like Monaco had once honoured Schweitzer by releasing a postal stamp in his name. After years, the same honour was conferred on Prakash and Manda by Monaco. It was through the Bartholomy couple that they came to know about the work being done by Prakash and Manda.

A strange thing happened during this French couple's stay at Anandwan. Sometimes, gaps between cultures lead to unnecessary misunderstandings. I was born and brought up in an orthodox family. The customs and practices, if observed for a long time, become your second nature. The religious practices in my mother's house were strict. Even after marriage, I continued with some of them, though most of them disappeared soon in Baba's company. Of the few which lasted was the habit of closing the door when I prayed. That day, by sheer coincidence, Mrs Greet Bartholomy arrived just at the moment when I half closed the door. She felt offended and could not hide her displeasure. For the next two days, she did not talk to me and kept aloof. I could not explain to her our norms of sanctity and purity in the puja-ghar. After a few days, I invited both of them into this room and gave them a shawl as a gift, telling them that this was their second wedding in the presence of god as a witness. They were pleased and the mist of misunderstanding was cleared in minutes.

I think, I am reasonably tolerant and flexible. I do not know what others would call it; perhaps they would see the typical Indian wife in me, but let me tell you that it all came naturally to me. I did not have to acquire these as desirable virtues for a woman. I did not have to surrender my natural self for that. And perhaps, that was the binding force between Baba and me. Both of us have been as true to ourselves as we were to each other. Neither of us would have liked the sacrifice of the self for the other. There were occasions when I stubbornly held on to my views. We have fought over many issues and never made a secret of it. In matters of worship, for instance, I am extremely uncompromising, to the extent of being a fanatic. For others, it may be a trifling thing. Let them have their pleasure of laughing at me. I enjoy the freedom of ignoring them. My faith has never wavered, in life's little things or in the face of big problems, with the thought of what others would say. If I had cared for the view of the world, I would have never married Baba. Baba was no less stubborn. We were very much made for each other indeed! When Baba opened his arms to those for whom every other door was shut, hostile forces surrounded him from every side. But, he never allowed the world to interfere in matters of his conviction nor did he bother to react to its criticism. My faith in god remains unflinching and I have never compromised with the rituals performed to fulfil my vows. Once, in the month of shravan, I vowed to offer 1,08,000 bel leaves to Lord Shankara.

That meant making a thousand sheaves of 108 leaves each. It took us twelve hours to complete the task.

Often, happy couples are compared with the divine couple of Vitthal and Rakhumai, but people often compared us with Shankar and Parvati. I think they are right in this. Baba's fury and his refusal to control it, bear close resemblance to these same qualities in Lord Shankara. My stubbornness, too in such matters remains incurable. My spiritual weak point (others may call it a weakness) – an attraction for the sacred flame of the oil-lamp lit in front of god's idol – led to many spontaneous rituals and practices. I remember bringing a small pitcher filled with the water of the Narmada in Madhya Pradesh to pour into the well at Anandwan. I admitted to myself at times that this was irrational. But, I could not help it. Every bit of air I breathed in my mother's house smacked of such things. Almost a writ that none could erase. And there was no particular reason. Moreover, I derived peace from such simple things; even in giving away brooms to married women on the sacred day of Makar Sankranti, or giving earthen lamps as sacred gifts. People must have laughed at this madness. I never cared, for it was an expression of my faith and a sincere longing of my soul. My inner instincts spoke louder than the need for social conformity. It is not necessary to have public approval for things that come from genuine, devout faith. We have no right to disrespect one's faith, even though we may have reasons to disagree with one's practices.

Walking down memory lane uncovers many treasured moments as well as the scars of time. How can I forget our meeting with Lata Mangeshkar, the nightingale of India, the queen of the music world? Her contribution to Anandwan is certainly commendable. She raised funds for us through her charity show. The few moments we spent with her in her house over a cup of tea revealed her inherent courtesy and righteousness. Who does not know her? The spell of her voice, experienced by the whole world, is irresistible; however her courtesy is sweeter. I can never forget it.

The year 1984 saw the arrival of a swarm of workers in Anandwan. Among them were Dilip Herlekar, Philip George, Dr Pol, Retired Colonel Rege and Mr Ketkar. With all these men around, the change was noticeable. Being intellectuals, and highly educated, a new chapter was opened in Anandwan's history. Dilip, a textile engineer from Mumbai did some pioneering work in starting the power-loom in Anandwan. Sandhi Niketan, our small-scale industrial unit, set up to rehabilitate the physically challenged or the people who were cured of leprosy, received a boost under his guidance. However, after his father's death, his family responsibilities took him away from us. Since then, Mr Tanjane, despite being handicapped, has been successfully looking after this unit. His perseverance and efficiency have infused a new life into the workshop, where deformed fingers are free to choose what they want to work on; wood, paper, tin, bamboo, leather or even a printing machine.

We had our share of failures too, though we were not to blame always; the reasons lay somewhere else. Once Pratima Joshi brought eighteen children (of the sex workers) from Mumbai to stay at Anandwan. They were all between five and ten years of age. Muktabai and Sarvagaud maushi from Uttarayan, used to teach them. Within a short time, their faces beamed with delight. Mind you, they had never seen a kitchen in their life, footpath dwellers as they were. They thrived on the leftovers from the hotels in Mumbai. In Anandwan, very soon, they felt free as if they were at home. They played about and bounded with joy. When they first came, they looked much older than their age. Those signs were disappearing fast. Their faces reflected the change. The colour returned. They found friends in the deaf, dumb and blind children. It was as though they had lived all their lives in Anandwan and would breathe their last here too. But this was not to be. Fate had something else in store for them. Their mothers, dissuaded by rumours about leprosy, feared that their children would catch this deadly disease and came to take them away. The children wept and sobbed. They could not understand why their mothers did not want them to live in such a beautiful place.

Muktabai found the pang of separation unbearable. She had dreamt of their bright future here. To think of their re-entry into the hell of the abused lanes of Mumbai was a nightmare. We were aggrieved that this project could not materialise; that the buds would never bloom now. To have seen the world from the wrong side, and that too so early in childhood was their fate and we wanted to remove those 'pain-stains' before they could be transformed into permanent scars. How we wished that they be saved from the consequent bitterness! Such violent jolts are not for children of such tender age. It awakens the beast in them in no time. They are born again as criminals.

Among the many friends of Anandwan is Dr Shirole from Pune, a renowned paediatrician. He hails from a noble family. Despite the wealth he was born into and brought up in, his humility is exemplary. He is courtesy incarnate. His gift of oration and his capacity for public relations have won many friends for Anandwan. He has penned a beautiful imaginary dialogue between Baba and the sacred river Narmada. He is a living encyclopaedia.

Dr Abhay Bang and his wife Dr Rani Bang work for the tribals in Gadchiroli. They have set up an institution called Search, which caters to the needs of the underprivileged. Along with medical services, the centre works to effect prohibition and women's liberation. Their team of Abhay, Rani, Mohan and Satish is doing an excellent job in the neighbouring villages—they are very committed social workers.

They once invited me to address a women's meeting. I do not think I have any talent for public speaking but it was impossible to say no to them. Moreover, I thought I had no right to speak on women's liberation; I wasn't even a member of any such organisation. My life and work is confined to a small world of our own. More than forty years of my experience of working with the diseased and the physically challenged left me no time to think of such issues as women's social status or their liberation. Besides, my daily contact with women who were different from the others, posed a different set of problems altogether. Their physical deformities deprived them of many things. Most of them preferred to work only with their husbands. A lot has been said and done for women's liberation in urban areas, and especially for educated women. But there is a lot to be done for the cause of working-class women too. I accepted the invitation, and seized the opportunity to voice my own feelings.

Life has many unexpected things to offer, which often test our strength. A single moment of heart wrenching agony may turn everything upside down. Especially between spouses. What they need is mutual love and understanding. Nothing else really matters. Every act has to be an act of love. You do not have to fight for rights or worry about duties then. Within the magnetic field of love, everything melts or is transformed—the ego, the selfhood. There is a willing submission and sacrifice in love. It does not impoverish one. On the contrary, it is enriching. Do I sound old-fashioned? I am not saying it out of respect for tradition. My words are steeped in my experience. In many homes today, values – borrowed from western cultures under the name of modernity – have commercialised human relationships; between husband and wife, and between parents and children. Children suffer the most in such circumstances. It is no wonder that they turn their back on their parents later. It is dangerous to make sweeping generalisations like this; you may dismiss them as being stray instances. You are at liberty to do so. But I would rather stick to them, not because this is my philosophy but because in doing so, I am only following my instincts. There is no sense of burden.

Women's liberation and their awakening from the fetters of slavery imposed either by social custom or the paternal system are oft-discussed issues. Many great men and women have contributed to this cause. However, this has not been my sphere of activity. It seems to be the privilege of men to use 'high' words such as service, pity, faith, mercy, inspiration, and agony. But, to be frank, these words have something feminine about them, I think. They are a woman's other names. I am aware that today's young women would not like this kind of language; it sounds like the tongue of a traditionalist. Nevertheless, I will stand by my words because they are soaked deep in my experiences. I often wonder why women have to stand in conflict with men to establish their identity. There are many ways of relating to this world, more meaningfully, in fact. I am certainly not excluding men from the qualities mentioned above. What is good for one is good for the other too. More importantly, what I am suggesting is that women should extend these qualities beyond their family to the society. A greater affiliation with pain is what is required and is capable of transforming this world. We need no other religion. A woman need not confine herself to her home alone. On the contrary, she can utilise her capacity and compassion for the world beyond.

On this occasion, I shared my personal experiences with the women at the centre. I did not forget to tell them that when some work begins, there are many to give free advice. When it begins to take shape, you have to work very hard and put up with a lot of inconvenience, and many sympathise with you. Then there are admirers when the hour of fulfilment arrives. Finally, even after you make the impossible possible, critics are ready to pounce on you. We have gone through all these stages. We have been tested again and again—by destiny, society, critics, and calamities. And we have also tasted the warmth of selfless love.

I have sweet memories of blind Paru who had a special claim on my love. She used to come running to me and ask me to close my eyes and open my mouth; and would thrust a laddoo in it. My heart fills up with gratitude at the thought of the tenderest emotions these blind children evoked in us. Baba made a special arrangement with P. L. Deshpande to plant thornless roses for the blind children.

Like some other honourable visitors to Anandwan, the late Mrs Indira Gandhi has left a permanent imprint on our minds. For days after she left, we thought of her eternal freshness, a legacy from her father perhaps, framed by the iron curtain of her inner strength. She came here amidst high security arrangements. However, as she spoke, she allowed her mask of a politician to drop completely, and we discovered another Indira that day. We witnessed the other side of her face, a woman's face every line of which spoke of her essentially feminine tenderness. For hours she sat on the cot by Baba's side, freely exchanging thoughts and expressing her deep concern for Baba's work and health.

TEN

1984 turned out to be a year of countrywide social and political unrest. Baba's anxiety over this would not allow him to sit quietly. His inner voice urged him to do something to restore peace. He was also convinced that only the common man could do what was needed at that hour. Baba is no politician. He decided to unite the country with young boys and girls who belonged to no political party. The Knit India Movement (Bharat Jodo) owes it's birth to Baba's growing anxiety over the political unrest at the time. He planned to travel from the south to the north of the country with the youth who gave an overwhelming response. During the entire campaign, the common man in India welcomed his efforts towards the restoration of peace. Some close friends and a few workers from our institution too joined Baba.

I could not take part in this campaign. I had to stay back at Anandwan to look after the routine matters. As secretary of the institution, I had to shoulder many responsibilities such as signing cheques and important documents, taking decisions and hundreds of other things. Baba's journey began from Kanyakumari. I went there to see him off. I insisted on his visiting the famous temple there before he set out for his destination. I knew that he would never agree and hence I had to conspire with Mr Vajram, our friend from Pune, to make Baba do this, and we succeeded. Early at dawn, the three of us went for a walk on the seashore. While returning, Vajram casually asked Baba to visit the temple as it happened to be on the way. Vajram had taken an extra shawl with him. I knew that in this temple, they do not allow people to enter without a shawl. He handed over the shawl to Baba as we had planned and Baba, without any fuss, visited the temple. I was very happy because everything happened as we had planned. The faithful devotee in me was pleased. I have always treasured these moments of simple delight in small things. I returned to Anandwan after flagging him off.

From the very first day, people welcomed the participants who cycled beside Baba's bus. There were 150 cyclists, whose enthusiasm proved to be infectious wherever they went. The media also gave wide coverage to this cycle-march; columns of praise occupied large spaces in the papers.

The visit to Punjab was the most important part of this march. There were no signs of the violence abating in Punjab. Ambala was the last station before they entered Punjab. Baba addressed the participants here to warn them against this violence and the impending danger. Baba was advised to take the help of the commandos, a normal thing for them to have advised, and the refusal to do so was equally normal for Baba. Even the participants were determined to enter without protection, though Baba had given them a choice. Surprisingly enough, the youth in Punjab also welcomed them with great enthusiasm. Baba could not hold a public meeting due to the curfew there. The violence and the unrest in Punjab had created a seething turmoil in Baba's mind and no balm could have removed the scars. Prakash and I joined Baba in Punjab. We visited the holy Golden Temple.

Where was the real Punjabi? Baba desperately looked for the typical, courteous and generous, cheerful and hospitable, fearless and forever-ready-for-sacrifice kind but he regretted their disappearance. Instead, there was this angry, suspicious, unbelieving and reckless youth now. The killing of one man by another was beyond Baba's reason. The Punjab that was rich in natural wealth, was reduced to a terrorist camp. Baba thought about returning to Punjab after completing the Bharat Jodo march.

During the first Bharat Jodo march Baba had thought of a concrete follow-up plan according to which he wanted to set up a countrywide network of Yuvagram. This was an experiment, for which, he needed committed young men and women, willing to live in remote villages and work toward national integration with the help of the local populace. Vidyavrat Nair and his wife, Nafisa, participants in Bharat Jodo, volunteered for the first Yuvagram. They started their work at Zabua, in Madhya Pradesh. Jacob and Himanshu assisted them. However, this experiment did not succeed. Vidyavrat died in a street accident and within a short time, Jacob and Himanshu also left. Difficult though it was for Nafisa to overcome the grief, she carried on, single-handedly, for a few years and finally, she also left.

In 1986, Baba paid three visits to Punjab. During these visits, he spent time with the families of the victims of terrorist attacks; talking to them and trying to help them maintain the spirit of communal harmony, despite the continual eruption of violence. What else could he do? The gloom that pervaded Punjab, the broken hearts of the victims, the faces darkened with fear—everything was depressing for us. It was, as if the sky had fallen on them and Baba was making futile efforts to pick it up and put it together. He knew his limitations, but he could not escape the agony that the sight of all this bred. We are familiar with feuds between nations, communities, the rich and the poor. But, the violence here had a sharper edge and a darker side to it. To see people of the same community fighting amongst themselves was heart rending. What pleasure did they seek by producing pain for others, was the dilemma we faced.

In 1988, Baba set out for the second Bharat Jodo march. This time he travelled from the East to the West, from Arunachal to Okha. The institutional responsibilities prevented me from joining Baba this time too. Nevertheless, I went to Calcutta with him. I did not forget to pray to the local deity Kalimata before I left. I felt worried about Baba's health. The enthusiasm of the first march was missing. We had our lesson; people do not like repetition. There were some new issues at stake this time. The validity and the utility of mega projects such as the Sardar Sarovar and the Narmada Sagar were being questioned and the workers of the anti-dam movement insisted on Baba's open support and his public appraisal when he passed through Gujarat. Baba refused to do so on principle. The focus of Bharat Jodo was on a national issue and Baba did not want to mix up inter-state issues with national issues. On his return from the second Bharat Jodo march, he called for a meeting of all the NGOs that were against big dams, at Hemalkasa. More than 20,000 tribals from various regions and about a hundred workers and environmentalists attended this meeting. On the banks of Indravati, they took an oath to fight with all their might against big dams. They raised their voice against displacement unanimously. Baba extended support to this cause in his address. It was perfectly in keeping with our life's principles: justice for the underprivileged, the handicapped, the socially ostracised, and the poor. Baba could easily identify himself with the commonest of the common. Whenever Baba addresses crowds, he begins his speech with the following words:

I sought my soul, my soul I could not see,
I sought my god, my god deluded me,
I sought my friend, I found all the three.

Imitating Baba's lines, I once composed a triplet of my own:

I sought my lover, my lover I could not see,
I sought my friend, my friend eluded me,
I sought my husband, I found all the three.

Baba spontaneously appreciated my flight of imagination and creativity and always insisted on my saying it at the end of a speech. (He always reserved a seat for me next to his on the stage). After leaving Anandwan for Kasrawad on the banks of Narmada, I added one more sentence to it:

When we left Anandwan and joined Narmada Bacho Andolan
I lost all the three.

Baba is uncompromising when it comes to his principles, whether in public or private life. Nevertheless, he compromised with some of them for my sake. He does not believe in idol worship, but he took me to holy places, visited temples, and worshipped with me. Nothing else but love for me prompted this change in him. It has been his unwritten rule to reserve the seat next to him for me always, and he doesn't allow anyone else to occupy it. Nor did he ever shy away from a public avowal of his love for me. I remember his having said to someone once:

> After I leave for work in the morning, I meet Tai only at night. In case I go away before she gets up, I leave her tooth brush to soak in warm water so that it becomes softer and she will find me by her side in my absence.

When I recall the happenings around the year 1986, a dark cloud crosses my mind's landscape. It was April I think; the beginning of summer. One day, the news came that Dajisaheb (Shivajirao Patwardhan) had stopped eating food. He had decided to leave this mortal world and embark on the journey to the eternal. On reaching his place on the 27th, we were told that he had stopped talking too. It was almost a week since he began the fast. It was difficult for us to bring ourselves to go back without talking to him or at least reaping a glance from him. We requested Anutai to tell him about our arrival and our desire to see him. Anutai complied with our request and whispered into his ear that Baba had come to see him. Suddenly he opened his eyes, and taking my hands into his, put them on his head, and murmured blessings for my children. I was overwhelmed and could only ask for his blessings. The next minute he took Baba's hands and put them on his head and recited a Sanskrit verse. He too was overwhelmed. His voice faltered as he said, 'I was waiting for you only.' Thinking that it would be giving him more pain if we stayed on, we returned with a heavy heart.

The only wealth we possess is love, boundless and unconditional, because we believe that it is the only preservative that saves life from rotting and helps everything last longer and taste better. If only people would extend it beyond their personal life! I feel indebted to people who showered it on us. I am not saying it out of modesty or politeness; in the matters of the heart I am far from being polite. Politeness in such matters is just another name for hypocrisy. Preposterous benevolence is worse than hatred. In 1988, on my way back to Hemalkasa, I met with an accident. My leg was fractured. Eventually, I was confined to bed for quite some time. Baba was away. I missed my daily rounds in Snehsavali, the colony for the old people.

They too yearned to see me. Finally, they wrote a letter to me wishing me a speedy recovery. The letter was steeped in their love and spoke of their feeling of loneliness in my absence.

ELEVEN

In 1990, leaving Anandwan in the hands of Vikas, we made for the quiet village of Kasrawad on the banks of Narmada, ten kilometres off Badwani in Madhya Pradesh. The villagers had built a humble house for Baba on the outskirts of the village. The ground on which the house stood, a small hillock, served as the cemetery for the local people. Close to it was a beautiful, ancient Shiva temple. The river Narmada flowed by the foot of the hill, silently. We had a view of the river from our courtyard. No other location would have been more enchanting for Baba. The hill was bare. There were no trees. The heat of the sun blazed down directly. The workers from Anandwan, mostly lepers, accompanied us by turn. Among them was Lotu. He came and never left. He had a green thumb. He transformed the surroundings within a short time. The brown that dominated the landscape was replaced by green now. The variety of trees that he planted, competed with each other in height and width. The shadows of the trees stretched themselves to protect us from the scorching heat in summers.

The river had its own magic; it opened its arms to me. The gentle caressing touch of the stream beckoned me to her bounty. I had never imagined that I would find myself by her side. How many sages, yogis and ordinary pilgrims must have coursed along the banks of this sacred river over the years? The thought flitted across my mind, filling it with serenity. And yet, the struggle and the plight of the tribals who were perched along the same stream made me cringe in pain. Nevertheless, I had revelations too. The holy pilgrimages along the river Narmada by bare-footed pilgrims who had no provision for food, had more to teach than I thought. I came to know about the unwritten rules of this sacred pilgrimage, when I came to stay here with Baba. Isn't life also like that? Uncertainty is common to both. Baba was in love with it from the beginning. Probably he hated the satiety that comes with fulfilment. It will not be wrong if I say that the thing that unsettles him the most is settling down in one place. He consciously chose to remain a pilgrim who makes for the next destination after a night's stay, making himself comfortable among different people and in strange lands.

Baba made a home for himself here. However, I kept coming and going, as work in Anandwan and some other projects demanded my presence for a month or two. How easy it was for Baba to distance himself from his first creation and roost in a distant soil on the banks of the Narmada, I thought. Being a woman, perhaps, it was difficult for me to sever the ties with the past, with our beginning so easily and entrench myself here. The pang of separation was on the other side too. It was difficult for the people of Anandwan to restrain their tears, when I had to depart, and it was always with a heavy heart that I left. Baba has an inbuilt mechanism not to lose his equanimity on such occasions. Moreover, it does not take time for him to root himself anywhere, especially when there is a challenge. Baba's unparalleled courage, untiring spirit, and his exceptional capacity for pity led him to seek adventures, one after another, tons of them, I must say. An intelligent man like him, who is adventurous at the same time, can never be confined to a single frame for a long time. He would rather break the frame and search for another horizon. His creative impulse would not let him stagnate in one place. The pressure was from within; his work has been only a means to fill up the vacuum he experienced after each fulfilment.

The inconvenience I found most difficult to cope up with at Kasrawad, was the lack of any means of communication. There was no telephone. There was only a rough and narrow road, which made communication with anyone at Badwani difficult. There was initially no means of transport except our own bus. The mails took longer than usual. During one of my visits to Anandwan, I came to know that the respectable Bhalji Pendharkar had remembered us. I felt guilty for not having written to him. Both Baba and I had tremendous respect for this man. Especially, after the publication of Baba's first volume of poems, we became very close friends. We often thought of him and conveyed our regards through somebody, mostly through Dr Bawdekar and his wife Sarojtai. I wrote to him from Anandwan, regretting our inability to contact him. It was a pleasure to share with him all the things that weighed on our mind—our new struggle for the displaced in the Narmada valley, the tensions of different kinds, new problems, new hostilities, my agony over separation from my own people, and no less, Baba's failing health. Baba had to undergo another operation at Indore to reset the pacemaker. As the memories unroll before me in these comparatively passive moments today, I feel happy that there were people like Bhalji, P. L., R. K., Dada Dharmadhikari, and many others, with whom we could share things close to our heart; joy and anxiety, pain and pride, love and insult. Continual action marked the course of our life; emergencies cropped up, or we invited them, you may say. There were moments of dejection when truth was stifled by untruth, and there were epiphanies too, enlightening us in many ways. Among all these things, I valued the blessings of good souls more than anything for enabling us to steer clear of all the mists and snags that seemed to block our way temporarily.

The anti-dam movement in the Narmada valley is synonymous with Medha Patkar; a highly educated and intelligent woman, who, with all the statistics (real ones, obtained through the study of the project) of the project on the tip of her tongue—the area of submergence, the environmental losses, the benefits and the beneficiaries, the threatening number of the displaced, the dearth of available land for rehabilitation—could unnerve even the political leaders, let alone the government officers. Hardly anyone had the courage to face her, when it came to authentic figures and details. She has a rare combination of qualities—the dynamism of an activist and the discipline of an intellectual fused together. Baba and Medha together led the march of the tribals of the valley to Ferkuva. They came in thousands. Chimanbhai Patel was the Chief Minister of Gujarat then. He too had planned a strategy to stop them from entering Gujarat. At the border, he had thousands of supporters of the dam waiting for Baba. As Baba's bus reached the small bridge, they lay down on the road in front of the bus and warned that Baba could proceed only by running the bus over them. Baba stopped. He had tough time explaining to them, that his agitation was not against the people of Gujarat, but in support of the poor tribals, who would be displaced. Moreover, they left nothing undone to intimidate Baba and Medha. The cacophony of the loudspeakers, installed in front of Baba's bus made it impossible for him to sleep. Slogans rained during the day and were replaced by blaring bhajans at night. They excelled in parodies of Gandhiji's favourite song and made it, 'Raghupati Raghav Raja Ram, Baba ko sanmati de Bhagwan'. Baba spent three sleepless nights until the deafening sound made him faint! I saw the news on television at Anandwan and rushed to him the next day with Prabhu. The journey was long. We had to go to Kasrawad and then to Ferkuva.

Baba had recovered after some medical treatment and he was feeling better when I reached there. But, he refused to shift to Indore. Madhubhai Pandit accompanied him throughout on this march. The large number of people in uniform gave the place the look of a police camp. We made the bus our home. I had to bathe on the steps of the bus with temporary makeshift curtains made of bed sheets. There were no signs of the tension subsiding. People on both the sides firmly stuck to their positions. Baba had his fans in Gujarat too. Those who were familiar with his work, came to see him. They had respect for Baba, but, on the issue of the dam, they refused to budge even an inch. As the heat subsided in course of time, the talks began. Harivallabhdas Parikh came to see Baba, and took me to see his project at Rangpur, and also the dam site at Garudeshwar and Manibeli. I stood aloof from this movement. It was because of Baba's involvement in it, that, I came into contact with the voluntary workers of this movement. I have respect for all of them, but I could not become a part of it. We belonged to a different field.

After a week or so, Prabhu returned to Anadwan and Prakash came instead. The activists were on a fast. Medha's condition had deteriorated. On both the sides, it was people, who stood as rivals. In this situation nothing could be done. We decided to come back.

The struggle continued for years. All the means of protest were tried—demonstrations, morchas, fasts, appeals, and the like. In Bhopal, in the hurry and bustle of the police, who arrested the workers on fast, I fell down and escaped the lathi charge but was under medication for a muscle pain for a month.

In Delhi, the situation was worse. During the demonstrations at Rajghat, Baba and I were without food for thirty-six hours. Baba was taken to the government hospital. The hospital staff was indifferent, and had no time to look at us. Finally, when Madhu Dandawate came to see Baba, they were on their toes. Maneka Gandhi, the then Minister for Environment, never came. Perhaps, Prime Minister Vajpayee could not overcome the sense of guilt for this and he regretted it, when years later, Baba went to Delhi to accept the Gandhi Peace Prize.

Kasrawad was our permanent home now and we left it only when the occasion called for our presence elsewhere. After three or four years' stay here, we went to Mumbai during the riots in Gujarat and Mumbai. The monstrous violence caused by casteism and communalism left scars that could not be erased by anything. The sight of the victims who lost everything and were thrown at the mercy of fate, sent chills down our spines. We had no balm that could have healed their wounds except words of love to wipe their tears. We spent one month in Mumbai, visiting the affected families from both the Hindu and Muslim communities in the sensitive areas. We returned to Kasrawad with a fractured mind. For months we carried the burden of that heart-rending misery. I could only pour it out in a letter I wrote to P. L. and Sunitabai.

Anandwan
19/4/1993

Dear Sunitabai and Bhai,

Baba is right in saying that there is no distance in the world of remembrances. How many times I have experienced it! The gap, whether of days or months, is nothing when a momentary thought puts me by your side. It is almost a month since I came away from Kasrawad and am hoping to return on the 23rd. Baba is alone. Except for the cook and the driver, there is no one who can look after his correspondence or at least the acknowledgement of mails. Baba's health is a permanent problem. You know his eternal restlessness. Sparks of religious or communal discord, anywhere in the country, set his heart on fire and the consequent loss of peace of mind is reflected automatically in his body reflexes. I cannot bear all this. To see his impotent suffering thus becomes my ordeal. That is why, disregarding the doctor's advice, I took him to Mumbai. He felt happy to do what he could, though for a little while. We had to get back to Kasrawad from Surat and Ahmedabad, against our wishes within a week, because rumours spread faster, that we had backed out of the anti-dam movement. Baba had high temperature; nevertheless, he tried to meet as many people as possible, people from all stratas of the society. Violence has such an ugly face that the senses become numb. The faces, that we saw, revealed little and concealed a lot perhaps. We were unable to tell the true from the false. The more we thought, the more stunned we became. It was a lifelong experience.

Our life looks like a never-ending pilgrimage. How much to see and feel in one life? It is like living many lives in one. There is not a bit of exaggeration in what I am saying.

No sooner had we returned from Gujarat, than we heard of the deafening sound of bomb explosions in Mumbai. How will Baba endure this deadening series of violence, I do not know. It seems that people have gone mad and anarchy has been let loose. To think of it, is to faint. Baba feels as if he is standing in a blind alley, as helpless as a wingless bird. There is no one here even to write a letter of protest. Baba always said, 'Heart is where the hurt is'. I think he would rewrite it now and say, 'Heart is where hatred is.'

I think I have gone too far in writing to you about all these things. However, it happens with the close ones, doesn't it? I mean the spontaneous emptying of the mind burdened with dark thoughts. The responsibilities are forever increasing.

May I hope for your eternal spring of love and sympathies for us?

Yours,
Sadhana

My stay at Kasrawad brought me many unexpected opportunities too. A daily bath in the sacred river Narmada for a faithful believer like me was a feast. The Shiva temple was close to our house, on a nearby hill. I used to worship there every morning and evening. Baba's involvement in the anti-dam movement invited a lot of trouble from the government officials. They set up a police station on the same hill, a few feet away from the temple. The policemen on duty taunted me on my way to the temple. Passing sarcastic remarks became their favourite pastime. Once, all of them occupied the temple before my arrival and started singing bhajans to tease me. I proceeded for my regular worship, Baba was silently watching all these things. He became furious at their arrogance. However, I stopped him from reacting strongly. I knew that they were trying to provoke us. An idea crossed my mind. I went back and brought half a kilogram sugar, went inside, said my prayers, lighted the lamp and came out. I said to them, 'You are singing nice bhajans. I have brought prashad for you.' It had the desirable effect. They politely agreed to stop their devotional songs for me. The atmosphere changed within minutes. Love is the magic wand, which can work miracles. I have full faith in the power of love. I could not believe that they could be won over so easily. They were supposed to be our rivals but became our friends soon. Since that day, there was a marked change in their behaviour and they became our well-wishers too.

The love of Tulsiram and Ismail made our stay at Kasrawad comfortable during this decade-long isolation from Anandwan. They belonged to this place and actively participated in the anti-dam movement. They never failed in their daily visit and we got so used to it that we missed them if something prevented them from dropping in. The awakening, brought about by the Narmada Bachao Andolan, had put new life into these small dull-looking unknown hamlets on the banks of the Narmada. They did all kinds of odd jobs for us, especially buying things from Badwani or passing on our messages. We eagerly waited for them, and as the tiny speck of their bicycle-wheel appeared from a distance, we were sure that either of them was coming.

Goodness is often reciprocated, I believe. A good deed calls for another from the other side. At least, it becomes a moral obligation to do so. I remember our trip to Vaishnavidevi. The temple is high up in the hills and was a hard climb for me. We hired a palkhi that was to be carried by four people. This was the first time I was sitting in it. I felt guilty at being carried by those men, whose livelihood depended on it. But I had no other alternative. But, whenever they halted to drink a glass of water, I would get off and walk a few yards. Finally, we reached the temple and spent the night there. The next morning, when they came back with the palkhi, they expressed their desire to serve me and despite my refusal to accept any service from them, pressed my feet because they remembered how far I had walked the day before and probably thought that my feet were aching. This was unadulterated love. There were no calculations of profit or loss.

On another occasion, at Haridwar, Suma and I hired an auto from the temple. The driver had a bad cough. Poor fellow! He was not well, but had to work for his daily bread. It is my habit to carry medicine, whenever I go on a tour. I gave him some pills. It was nothing for me, but he was overwhelmed. The feeling that a stranger cared for him must have soothed him first, even before the medicine had its effect. He did not stop at a formal thanks, but invited us to dinner at his house. He would not listen and I could not hurt his feelings, genuine as they were. If only people could understand the benefits of transparent, selfless love – a rare thing in today's world – half of the problems would be solved. I believe in the power of love though people, communities and often nations live by hatred. My experiences have endorsed it again and again. I believe in the essential goodness of man. Sometimes you have to make efforts to stir it, until it surfaces in little acts of kindness. If Baba and I have given a gram of love to people, it has come back to us in tons. Friends of Anandwan, from far and near, have showered it on us. In the last decade, the help that Rameshbhai Kacholia and Narendrabhai Mistri, one of our trustees, have extended, smacked of their love for us and their involvement in our work. To have met Rameshbhai, is a happy coincidence in our lives. It will not be wrong if I say that he not only thinks of Anandwan but breathes Anandwan. Based in Mumbai as a businessman, he has done more work than a public relations officer for us. Through him we could establish relations with many other people whose friendship is valuable to us for more reasons than one. During the financial crunch, he campaigned to maintain the influx of funds. He is always courteous and soft-spoken, and a member of our family.

Ever since Baba posted himself at Kasrawad, I had to look after official matters. I kept travelling between Anandwan and Kasrawad for a few years. Every year, I attended our ten-day camp in summer at Somnath. Over the years, the camps that I attended have taught me a lot. I noticed a change in the ambience of the camp first in 1992. A few traces of a form of antagonism were found taking root for the first time. There were sparks. It was extremely difficult for me to confront it. Nor could I ignore it. I never liked making speeches. But, that year, I finally decided to address the participants. The speech had the desirable effect. Most of them regretted their misbehaviour afterwards and did not hesitate to apologise to me.

The annual camps that were conducted with certain goals and values in mind and which we religiously attended once upon a time, have deteriorated into a festival of fun for many participants. The passion with which the participants worked, is replaced by fashion now, it seems. It pains me to see this moral decay in society. We had great expectations from this annual camp; we hoped that it would be the breeding ground for committed social workers, a laboratory for producing and fashioning dedicated reformers. We had imposed certain restrictions on ourselves for that. What you want others to do, must begin at your home first. The religious fasts had a similar function, I believe; they were intended to teach self-control.

When the common goals and values disappear, factions grow in no time. The contours of individual opinion become harder and eventually clashes spoil the ambience to the extent of converting the site into a battleground; regional feelings become stronger. Unfortunately, I have been witness to such untoward happenings in the camps. This puts more pressure on the organisers, I think. They have to act responsibly, and with a certain amount of objectivity, dispensing justice to everyone. The participants must have confidence in the organisers' sense of justice. To achieve this, the conduct of the organisers has to be above criticism. Only then can they command the respect of others.

We expected the participants to be well behaved and to have an awareness of their social responsibilities. However, they did not always pass this test. The world from which they came, a world that is corrupt and racked by violence, governed by the rule, 'Grab if you can rather than wait', had left indelible marks on them. It would have been insensible to expect them to change overnight. We had to give them lessons in cleanliness; mental, moral, and material, all at the same time. This should be the objective of such camps. Educating the young for life is the purpose behind organising such camps. There is enough hatred and revenge in the world. The camps are intended to purge young minds of these destructive elements. The most difficult task is to bring about this change in human nature. The organisers of such camps have to shoulder greater responsibilities. It is a tightrope walk for them.

The world is full of evil—injustice, corruption, lust, bribery, scams, dirty politics, jingoism, fundamentalism, and what not. We had to take care that these things did not infect our camps at Somnath. After all, the participants come from the same world. We try to provide a different environment for them here. The inmates of our institution are also human beings, however, they are partners in pain and that makes all the difference. We believe that pain has the capacity to transform human beings. The camp can become a site for bringing together the insiders and the outsiders; to bind the two together in pain-friendship. All these years, we worked with this hope and succeeded to an extent. I believe in self-restraint and only the thought of the other can breed it. It is required in all walks of life, all spheres of work, in all relationships. The mind that yearns for construction, knows the value of self-restraint. Another objective in holding such camps was to create awareness among the so-called intellectuals, about the dignity of manual labour. In the beginning of this activity, we used to reserve three hours a day for shramdan, actual labour at the site. Over the years, the time allotted to this activity has been reduced considerably. Lethargy has crept in, though there are more comforts. I wish the young would take cognizance of it.

Baba had decided not to return to Anandwan, and spend the rest of his life on the banks of the Narmada. He would have never gone back on his words, had it not been for the love of P. L. Deshpande. P. L. was suffering from Parkinson's disease. The disability caused by continual muscular tremors in this disease makes the person completely dependent. It was difficult for people to see P. L. in this condition. He was their idol and they worshipped him. The whole of Maharastra venerated him beyond measure. People have enjoyed his writings – essays and plays – immensely. In such a condition, P. L. was reluctant to leave Pune. But, he was ready to come to Anandwan to see Baba. One day he rang Baba and said, 'If I spend two hours in your company, I will get a lease of life for two years more.' The efforts of Raosaheb Shinde and Rajabhau Mangalwedhekar played a significant role in bringing about this meeting. Finally, Baba submitted to the will of his well-wishers and promised to be in Anandwan to receive P. L. in person. P. L. stayed at Anandwan for about a month. Sunitabai left after a week. She left Sudhakar, his assitant, behind, to take care of P. L. Gladly did he do everything for him, leaving nothing undone.

Baba was pleasantly surprised when he saw the transformation of Anandwan during his prolonged absence. Vikas was the architect behind this multidimensional development at Anandwan. It was indeed amazing. He really deserves my praise for it. Between the two brothers, Vikas is more extravagant than Prakash. He wants the best in everything, and for everyone. He always dreamt of providing everything to the inmates of Anandwan and worked in that direction. He shares everything with the patients. When we were at Kasrawad, I used to go to the temple on the hill for my daily worship. It was a dirt road and bumpy too. Vikas brought bamboo from Anandwan and erected a temporary structure round the temple to ensure my safety. I took him to task for providing this luxury but he would not listen. I have often taken him to task for these simple luxuries. I keep telling him, our journey began with 'nothing'; but he is out for 'everything', everything for all.

Prakash is the opposite. He luxuriates in hardships, not for its own sake of course. If he finds someone denied of something,

A daily walk along the banks of Narmada:
During the stay at Kasarawad, Madhya Pradesh, when Baba joined the Narmada Bachao Andolan

Sadhanatai, unbeaten at eighty.

Young Sadhanatai with children.
Front row: Renuka, Tai and Bijali (from the left)
Back row: Prakash, Vikas and Narayan (from the left)

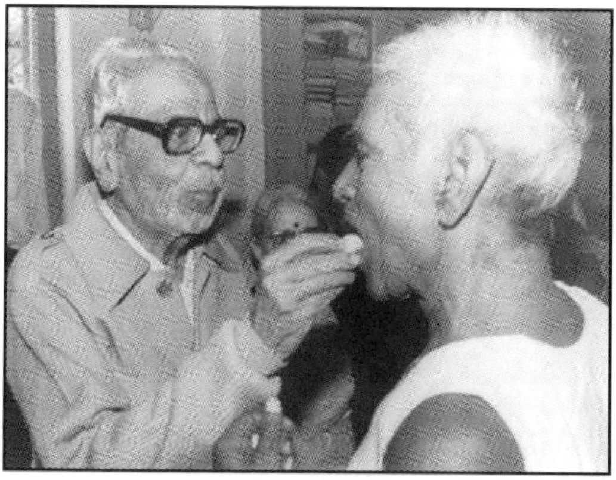

The legendary Marathi writer and a friend of Anandwan, late shri P.L. Deshpande offering sweets on Baba's birthday. This was P.L.'s last visit to Anandwan before he passed away.

Young Dr Prakash Amte treating a tribal patient in the yard at Hemalkasa.

Trying each other's strength? Or love? Dr Prakash Amte with his animal friend.

Team Anandwan: Dr Vikas Amte (at the centre), Dr Pol (Second from the left) Mr Tanjane in the wheel-chair and the dedicated crew at Anandwan.

Sadhanatai serving food to the members of Uttarayan in the community mess at Anandwan.

Team Hemalkasa: Front row- Renuka, Vilas, Dr Prakash and Dr Mandakini.

The only hour of rest is the evening walk to the river. Dr Prakash Amte and Dr Mandakini Amte by the river Indrawati at Hemalkasa.

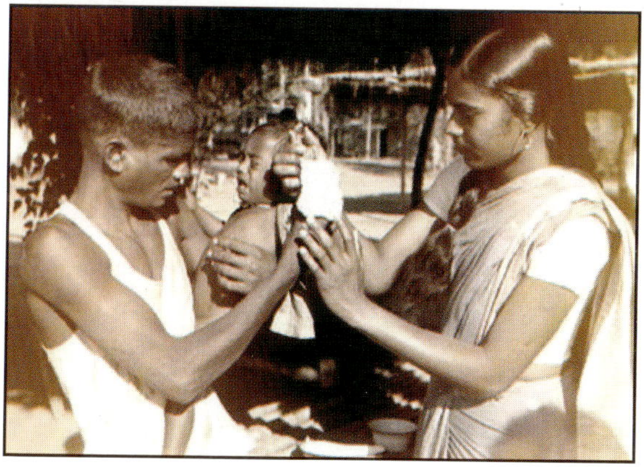

Renuka was the first nurse at Hemalkasa.

Dr Vikas and Dr Bharati Amte have been responsible for the expansion of Anandwan.

Dr Vikas at check-dam with a leprosy worker at Zari, sixty miles from Anandwan. This new project offers out-reach programme, a model of sustainable development. This region known for a record number of farmers' suicide in Vidarbha.

Baba receiving the Maharastra Bhushan Award at Anandwan from the Deputy Chief Minister of Maharastra Mr R.R.Patil in 2004.

Tai, celebrating little Sheetal's birthday with the children of Gokul.

His Holiness, the Dalai Lama had a lot to share with Baba and his greater family, Anandwan, during his three day visit in 1990.

Tai at Somnath, in the district of Chandrapur, where a leprosy rehabilitation centre was set up in 1967.

Tai and Baba on their evening walk (on wheels for Baba now) with the help of dedicated workers of Anandwan.

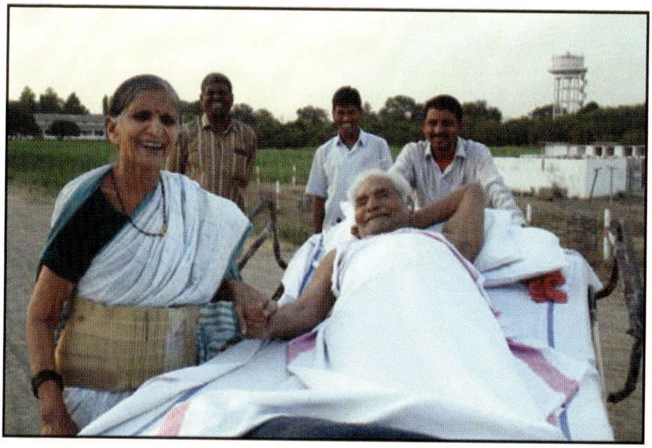

Baba with little Arnav, great grandson, cutting cake on Baba's birthday.

The third generation of Amtes: Kaustubh, Digant, Aniket, Sheetal and Aarti.

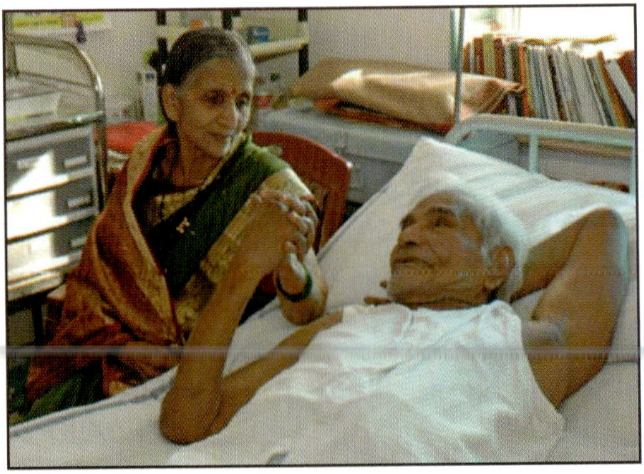

Not out sixty! Baba and Tai celebrating their 60th wedding anniversary.

he would deny it to himself too. His life at Bhamragad, has been a long chain of denials. He lives with the bare minimum and would like other people too to do so, rather than aspire for material comforts. The projects, that Vikas completed, dazzle the eyes of the onlookers, those of Prakash, open their eyes. Vikas complains that he is always criticised for everything he does. That is not true. That Prakash has been admired more, does not mean that Vikas doesn't possess excellence. His strength lies somewhere else. Vikas has a versatile brain, a sharp memory and excellent aesthetic sense. I feel, Prakash and I share several characteristics while Vikas has taken after Baba. Vikas went for large-scale projects. The measures he took to provide water for Anandwan deserve all the praise. Despite being a doctor, he has carried out important engineering jobs in the institution. There could not have been better town planning than what he has done. The network of roads made it easier to contact anyone anywhere, almost immediately. Above all, he can raise a battalion of efficient workers, ever ready to do anything, even at midnight.

No doubt, that the face and ambience of Anandwan has changed considerably after thirty years, since Vikas took charge. The number of lepers has reduced. Those who have been rehabilitated have been given the right to have only one child. Each one is given a separate house. The pressure of providing houses to all of them is increasing.

On returning to Anandwan, we could see that more seeds had sprouted than we expected; the blossoms had attracted many a bird and on every branch, they had built a nest for themselves, a cosy home, whether in Yuvagram or Himmatgram. Vikas had infused a new life into many projects such as Salori, Khambada and Ashokwan; and quite a few new ones were undertaken at Masal and Khamancheru. Vikas had his gang of able and dedicated assistants, Mr Rai and Mr Kavishwar and others, equally intelligent and selfless, to make his dreams and schemes, a reality. P. L. openly commended all this work. As Baba's eyes feasted on these sights, he did not forget to warn Vikas about the pitfalls he was likely to encounter in times to come. Baba was not against expansion, but he would never go for it unless he was sure about the availability of dedicated workers, who would shoulder this responsibility. Most of them, who worked with zeal with Vikas, had crossed the fiftieth year of their life. There was a time when we had a handful of them, the frenzied ones, who risked their life for a well-defined cause. Over the years, the deterioration in the moral standards of the society has been so fast that we wonder whether we belong here or not. In this prolonged phase of decadence, how difficult it is to breed honest and sincere workers. Where is the creative frenzy to be found? When the tree branches out, the roots have to go deeper and deeper to support the tree. There is a dearth of such men and women, who can root themselves permanently in one chosen field without thinking about another sky. The world has become more practical today and it was not without reason that Baba felt worried about the expansion. He has full faith in Vikas, his capacity, his flight of imagination, his organisational skill, and his love of labour. What is lacking prominently, he thinks, is the swarm of ambitious eagles with mighty wings to span the new horizons. They are a rare species.

Vikas personally showed all these projects to P. L. This constant flow of energy in Anandwan had the desirable effect on his health. His walks became longer. Once we took him to the forest of Ramdegi, for a picnic. But nature had conspired against us. A storm rose unexpectedly. The water in the stream started rising very fast. Baba and P. L. had to be lifted along with their cots, to cross the stream. We had to pack up and return to Anandwan. P. L. said that it was a memorable experience for him.

Despite his failing health, P. L.'s sense of humour was as fresh as ever. He talked much less then, but a pun or a quibble was released occasionally. He still played those good shots which had always drenched the public in pure laughter and delight once. In fact, we were the real beneficiaries of his stay in Anandwan. Every moment we spent with him will go on record as one of the most treasured moments in our life. This was to be our last meeting. When the news of his death came after a few months, a feeling that we had lost a vital part of our being, gnawed at our mind for long.

Baba's return to Anandwan after nine years of absence, was greeted by the people with joy. Every year Baba spent one month with them and went back to Kasrawad. When the Hemalkasa project celebrated its silver jubilee, we went there. Thousands of tribals, and friends of our institution attended the humble celebrations. In their presence, Digant, the elder son of Prakash, who had just finished studying medicine, publicly declared his commitment to follow his father's footsteps. His batch-mate, Pandurang Pongati, also announced his desire to join him. This was an overwhelming moment for both of us, a moment of fruitful fulfilment. The third generation of the Amtes had decided to take the same road, had chosen the same destination. I could not put my heart into my mouth at that time. On my return, I allowed the locked up emotions to flow freely in a letter. I wrote to him:

Dear Digant,

My blessings to you.

I wanted to talk to you on that day but, both of us were lost in the crowd and even if I had found time, I wonder whether I would have been able to express my feeling. I was overwhelmed. That day, words kept mum at the sight of tears peeping from behind the eyelids. However, the joy cannot be contained in the heart for long; it is knocking at the gates with the speed of light. Words have taken wings. I am just trying to tell you how happy I am.

Your announcement on the stage to dedicate your life to the service of the tribals, was the happiest moment of my life. There could not have been a better reward for our efforts of the last fifty years. What a splendid moment of fulfilment indeed! How I wished I could gather you in my arms! I was reminded of Prakash entering into the same forest twenty-five years ago. The course of events of the last twenty-five years unreeled before me in a minute. Poverty, when chosen willingly, gives a righteous pleasure. May god bless you with all the joy that such work brings.

You must have thought long and deep before taking such a major decision in life. I have always known you as a thoughtful and passionate person. I know, you would never make a compromise with your freedom of thinking. You won't accept anything unless your reason gives the signal. You have been free from prejudice and very assertive when it comes to express your thoughts in your own style. But let me tell you one thing—the youth of today has little patience and a craze for speed. Never forget that the people you are to lead are the lepers, the destitute, and physically handicapped. In social service, you have to accommodate all and justly too.

Collective effort is the key to success and there can't be collective work without a meeting of the minds. Only love can bind the minds in harmony. Baba and I were alone when our journey began; there was no one to fall back upon in crisis; each one, a support to the other; witness to each other's joys and sorrows. But they came. One by one we took their sufferings and gave them joy in turn. Hands multiplied, like mushrooms. Ten, hundred, thousand; today there are five thousand. Joy also multiplied, by leaps, and bounds. Work expanded, vertically and horizontally. The map of the projects kept on changing. What, do you think, made it possible? Pain was added to pain and we transformed it into power, collective power born out of mighty pain! Our only capital was love. Only love can breed real equality. You must have faith in your work.

Service is a deceptive word. No one serves another. You serve only yourself. By serving others, you win lots of joy for yourself. Now that you have decided to work for the tribals of Bhamragad, never pose yourself as a teacher, an advisor. Keep an open mind and be ready to learn from them. Never forget that the common man is capable of uncommon thought. We were surrounded by the illiterate in the beginning, but, they enriched us by their wisdom. Always have respect for honest labour.

You are lucky to have been the son of Prakash and Manda.You have been groomed by everything they had and also by what they did not have. Light and shadow always follow each other; let neither of them ride over you for a long time. The evening is come for us.

My blessings are always with you.

Baba is calling me. Probably it is time for our evening walk. He too wants to talk to me, but the crowd of visitors has stolen our time. I am sure, he wants to talk about you and your decision only.

Aaji

As I wrote the letter, the image of Prakash setting out for Bhamragad, two decades ago, stood before my mind's eye; how, with a smiling face, he entered the dense forest along with Manda, a true consort in everything, everywhere. They command our respect for the work they have done in the last twenty-five years or so, and the odds they fought against. The ease with which they accomplished it, is admirable. They talk very little and never about their work. But, their work speaks for itself. Their's was a twenty-four hours' service, and they never complained. The tribals' love for them holds a mirror to their dedication. Destiny devised different tests for them, and everytime, they passed with flying colours. Their lives, like pure gold, shone brightly and in full splendour.

Baba's work was widely acknowledged by the world. The list of the awards and prizes he won, is pretty long. Some of them gave us special pleasure. Among these, the Babasaheb Ambedkar Dalit Mitra Puraskar, the Gandhi Peace Prize, the Father Damion Dattan Award, and the Bhai Kanhayalal Puraskar, matched perfectly with Baba's ideological commitment to Gandhian thought and his active subscription to Babasaheb Ambedkar's fight against casteism. These two great souls have guided him in life.

I was honoured with a few awards, such as the one from the G. D. Madgulkar Pratisthan. It gave me an opportunity to interact with the people in Pune and feel grateful for the love they showered on me. My real pleasure comes from the work I do.

It was our luck that stalwarts in different fields such as literature, sports, arts, cinema, social service and even politics were drawn to our work. It is our pleasure to have met them. We embraced everyone, even those who criticised us. Fifty years have elapsed since we set foot in the forest of Warora. Thousands of hands joined in transforming this wilderness and the waste land around, into earthly paradise. All our fellow beings, the lepers, the handicapped, the disabled, the destitute have all contributed their best to this mammoth task. They gave away freely what they received from god.

There was a time when people were scared even of breathing in Anandwan. Under the auspices of the Gandhi Memorial Fund, Dr Subba Naidu came and stayed here for two years. He was extremely cautious. Every day, on returning from the college, he used to wash his bicycle with soda water. There was no electricity; he never forgot to clean his lantern with soap. Sometimes people came in cars, but refused to get down. They did not dare to drink water here. If a few coins were exchanged, they used to wash them in lysol. Now, when I look back, and muse over these dark hours of social ostracism, I am amused, but at that time, it tried our strength. The picture has changed drastically over the years. Today, people come in thousands, from all over the world. How did this miracle come about? Without advertisement or publicity of any kind? We feel happy that we could educate people this much; nothing can stand between us and them, not even leprosy. Our college was inaugurated by a first year student. No ministers were invited nor did we ask anyone for funds. We did not know that the tiny seeds we sowed would reap such a mighty harvest. God's grace! What else?

One among those who showered selfless love on Baba is Raosaheb Shinde from Shrirampur. He would make us halt at his place, while on our way to Kasrawad. People thronged to see Baba there. Once, during our stay there, an acquaintance of Mrs Shinde came from Shirdi. He distributed prashad to all of us. I could not resist the temptation of visiting the holy place and Mrs Shinde made all the arrangements promptly. After the darshan, we came out of the temple. In the corridor, we saw a sadhu who had taken a vow of maun. He looked at me and made some signs with his hands. On my failing to decipher this, he wrote something on a slate and held it before me. It read, 'You are the mother of all.' The blessings from saintly people and sadhus have always given me joy and peace. Baba does not have faith in such things but I have derived strength from them, whether it was from Nanamaharaj Taranekar or the men of god from Shegaon and Karanja.

Thoughts of Medha haunt my memory. Not a single day passed without her occupying a few lines' space in the papers. She could stir my motherly instincts whenever around. I was more involved with Medha than with the movement she led. I experienced a pang at her ceaseless toil and felt worried. I often felt like prescribing compulsory rest to her, just as the mother forces the child who tires herself in play to sleep. She would come with a bundle of unwashed clothes, just a pair of them; go down the hill to rinse them in the Narmada and leave them for drying in the open space in front of our house. Then she would spend hours talking to Baba, till late at night and get going at the first crow of the cock at dawn. The rigour with which she worked for the displaced in the Narmada valley, the battle she fought with those in power for justice to the powerless, the awareness she created among the humble folk, as she went on combing the valley is awe inspiring. This didi of the tribals, has the swiftness and energy of lightning.

Parting with Narmada was an impossibility. We would have never dreamt of it. But, Baba changed his decision and that too for my sake. It was an ordeal for Baba. There is not a single entry in his life's account, of ever having changed his decision. My failing health was the reason he decided to go back to Anandwan. He would have happily breathed his last in the lap of river Narmada. However, as my health deteriorated, his anxiety grew. My daily cycle of sleep was adversely affected. I would fall asleep at any hour of the day, sometimes, immediately after performing the puja. I became hypersensitive. I could not endure pain at all. The sight of anybody's plight made me weep. Sometimes tears rushed on their own, without any apparent cause. I could not tell what had happened to me. Perhaps I longed to be back to our beginning, to the soil where I belonged. Was it the frailty that came with age, and made worse by failing health? Initially, I tried to hide it from Baba. During this turbulent time, how many times I prayed to Mata Narmada to settle the dam issue instantaneously, so that I could go back to Anandwan. Baba was intelligent enough to read my mind, and was convinced about the urgency of the matter. He took the decision to return to Anandwan. He did not need any justification for it. All his life, he was answerable only to himself. Never in my life had I made fuss about my health or stood in his way. It had happened for the first time. I would have never pardoned myself if he had been prevented from doing his work because of me. In a Hindu wedding, the bride walks seven steps with the groom round the holy fire. I think, in the first six I followed him; in the last one he came after me. The decision to go back cost him his selfhood, yet he never complained. To call it sacrifice on his part, would be questioning his love. I will never commit that sin. It was just his way of expressing his love for me. Everything between us has been an affair of love.

It was time to say goodbye to the Narmada; a trial for both of us! As the time drew nearer, a strange silence prevailed everywhere. It was a question of no less than a decade's intimate associations with the people and the place. This relationship was endorsed that day by tears. From Ismailbhai to Dr Yadav, everyone spoke the language of tears. Below the hill, the Narmada flowed quietly. Words had frozen until little Mohit cried out, 'Look, the Narmada is also crying, aaji'. Tears rose from a trickle to a spate to swell the river. Lighting the lamp in the Shiva temple for the last time, I took a quick look at her silent stream and we got into the bus with a heavy heart. My eyes lingered on, until the hands, that waved, faded into the distant dust clouds as the bus nosed forward.

TWELVE

The evening came stealthily. We had decided to rest on the banks of the Narmada after joining hands with Medha. My journey with Baba began at the marriage altar and would have ended here. Not that we had planned it. Throughout our life, we were guided by our instincts more than by anything else. It was mostly a spontaneous response to the occasion. Only our life's work was planned. Life unrolled before me, like the changing patterns in a kaleidoscope, with the same amount of uncertainty, but not without its exciting colours and delicate rhythms, powerful enough to sustain me throughout. Like objects that speed past as the train moves forward, Baba's passions sped past, putting me always on the alert for a new venture, and inviting me to partake in their pleasing, soothing aura. Nevertheless, coping with Baba's passions, has been a rewarding experience. As I look back, I feel, we have been blessed in everything we did together. We used the dark hours for weaving new dreams, and thereby earned some light. Today, I feel heartened to see quite a few footsteps of the young following the same path we treaded once. I am grateful to all those who gave us the best of themselves, along with their love.

There never was anything extraordinary about us, we are as common as any one else, vulnerable to human passions and subject to the weaknesses and follies, except for our unflinching faith in our work. We are the children of the soil. Our bond with the soil was sealed long back, and remains so even today. The more we gave to the world, the more we received from the people we met. We had our sermons in the disfigured faces of the lepers, and hope in the innocent smile of a destitute child. Little Mohit is Baba's treasure trove today; Baba's guru, you may say. How time passes when he is around, neither of us knows.

In our account, there are no regrets. I am not saying, that we did not make mistakes. Unknowingly we might have hurt somebody too. We are far from being perfect. To be frank, perfection is divine. I am an ordinary woman and tried to give the best of myself. Mine is a very humble contribution to Baba's mammoth task, nothing more than love's labour. He is a living storm, a storm come to roost in my arms. I tried to tame it, and became a part of the storm myself. Years passed by. I thought I was fagged out, like a burnt out candle, but Sitakant Prabhu coaxed me into talking and promised to put down the words, and he worked hard. It is only ashes, gathered round the cinders, he said. He fanned them and everything became visible. I was on my toes again, to have another round of our life. I am only seventy six, I told myself; and a voice was heard, 'I can still look into the eye of the storm.'

I do not believe in rebirth. However, if there is any, I would like to be born again to redeem myself from the debt of love, that people heaped on us. And I would like to be Baba's wife again; life would be very dull without him. Once more, I would nestle the eagle, and he would teach me to fly. He would split the rock again, and there would be another saxifrage for me to water. All that, an affair of love! What else? But mind you, there will be no more telling of the tale. Once is enough.

GLOSSARY

Bailpola	A festival of bulls celebrated especially in rural areas towards the end of rainy season. On this day, all the farmers give them a ritual bath, decorate them with garlands and take them round the village in a procession accompanied by local bands. The bulls are given complete rest from work and sweets are offered to them. This is the way the farmers express their gratitude to the animal on whom they depend for work related to agriculture.
bhajans	Devotional songs in praise of God
Dada	honorific term used after male proper nouns, also for elder brothers or used for addressing elderly strangers.
dalia	sweet dish made of wheat, milk and sugar
dulai and rajai.	A woollen blanket made of soft material.
Hartalika	A vrata observed by virgins and married women alike. Virgins pray to the divine couple Shiv-Parvati to bless them with a good husband. Married women pray to be blessed with the same husband in the next birth
Hemadpanthi	this is an ancient style of architecture used for temples in olden times in India
Kokam sharabat	a lemonade made from kokam, a fruit red in colour and sour in taste, especially found in Konkan region of Maharastra. It is good for health in summer.
mahars	a lower caste, its members were treated as the untouchables
mahatma	a great man who is benevolent and possesses many qualities which make him a good soul.
Narmada parikrama	a holy pilgrimage on foot along the banks of the sacred river Narmada by a circular route.

Navaratri	It is a vrata observed both by the individual for personal gain and collectively by Hindu communities in certain states of India. It is a ritual worship of the goddess with eight hands. An altar is made in the house or a temple for the specially made idol of the goddess. By her side, they put an earthen pot and worship it too. Everyday the pot is adorned with one garland. A lamp is kept burning for twenty four hours throughout the period of nine days. Women fast for nine days. In ancient times, people observed it to gain victory in war, prosperity, or kingdom.
Pakodas	A favourite recipe in Maharastra as well as in the north, fried tasty snack, made of thick chana flour paste (just like potato vadas), generally served hot. This is an important item of a traditional special dinner on any occasion in all strata of the society in Maharastra.
puranpoli	a sweet stuffed chapatti, favourite sweet dish in Maharastra, specially prepared on festival days and for guests
tiffin	lunch/ lunchbox
Tulsi vivaha	A custom to celebrate the wedding of Lord Vishnu, one of the Hindu Trinity, and Tulsi after the Dewali festival. Myth has it that Lord Vishnu awakens from four months sleep. All the vratas observed in Chaturmasa are completed with this wedding.
Vatsavitri	A vrata (for married women) seeking the blessings and the long life of the husband.The myth tells that Savitri, a woman chaste and pure, brought her dead husband back to life, by worshipping under a Banyan tree. On this day, a full moon day in the month of Jestha, married women worship the banyan tree and pray for the long life of their husbands.

Other Titles in Literature in Translation

Mirage by Kokilam Subbiah
Translated from the Tamil by the author

Moon Mountain by Bibhutibhushan Bandopadhyay
Translated from Bangla by Pradeep Kumar Sinha

The Grip of Change by P. Sivakami
Translated from the Tamil by the author

Mole! by Ashokamitran
Translated from the Tamil by N. Kalyan Raman

The First Promise by Ashapurna Debi
Translated from Bangla by Indira Chowdhury

Kuttiedathi and Other Stories by M. T. Vasudevan Nair
Translated from the Malayalam by V Abdulla

Pratdwandi by Sunil Gangopadhyay
Translated from Bangla by Enakshi Chatterjee

Sand and Other Stories by Ashokamitran
Translated from the Tamil by N. Kalyan Raman and Gomathi Narayanan

Son of the Moment by Nazir Ahmad
Translated from the Urdu by Mohammed Zakir

